PRAISE FOR STEPHEN CAVE AND

"Cave has produced a strikingly original and compelling exploration of the age-old conundrum: Can we live forever, and do we really want to?"

—John Horgan, science journalist and author of *The End of War*

"*Immortality* is a fascinating history of man's greatest obsession and poses a stunning theory of society."

—*The Daily Beast*

"In *Immortality* Stephen Cave tells wonderful stories about one of humanity's oldest desires and comes to a wise conclusion."

— Stefan Klein, author of *The Science of Happiness* and *The Secret Pulse of Time*

"A beautifully clear and entertaining look at life after death. Cave does not shrink from the hard questions. Bold and thought-provoking."

—Eric Olson, author of *The Human Animal* and *What Are We?*

"A must-read exploration of what spurs human ingenuity. Every once in a while a book comes along that catches me by surprise and provides me with an entirely new lens through which to view the world. . . . Such is the case with Stephen Cave's book *Immortality*. . . . Cave presents an extremely compelling case—one that has changed my view of the driving force of civilization as much as Jared Diamond did years ago with his brilliant book *Guns, Germs, and Steel*."

—S. Jay Olshanksy, *New Scientist* magazine

"An epic inquiry into the human desire to defy death—and how to overcome it. Cave traces the histories of each of his four immortality narratives through the world's great religions, heroes, leaders, thinkers and stories. It's an epic tale of human folly, featuring a cast of characters including Gilgamesh, Dante, Frankenstein, the King of Qin, Alexander the Great and the Dalai Lama. Cave, a Berlin-based writer and former diplomat, is an admirably clear elucidator, stripping down arguments to their essences and recounting them without any unnecessary jargon."

—*Financial Times*

"Informed and metaphysically nuanced . . . Cave presents his arguments in a brisk, engaging style and draws effectively upon a wide-ranging stock of religious, philosophical, and scientific sources, both ancient and contemporary."

—*Weekly Standard*

"In his survey of the subject, Stephen Cave, a British philosopher, argues that man's various tales of immortality can be boiled down into four basic "narratives" . . . If anything, readers might want more of Mr. Cave's crisp conversational prose."

—*Economist*

IMMORTALITY

THE QUEST TO

LIVE FOREVER

AND

HOW IT DRIVES

CIVILIZATION

IMMORTALITY

STEPHEN CAVE

FOREWORD BY
MICHAEL SHERMER

Skyhorse Publishing

For Friederike

CONTENTS

Foreword/ xi
Preface / xv

1

A BEAUTIFUL WOMAN HAS COME / 1
THE FOUR PATHS TO IMMORTALITY

PART I: STAYING ALIVE

2

MAGIC BARRIERS / 31
CIVILIZATION AND THE ELIXIR OF LIFE

3

THE VITAMIN CURE / 55
SCIENCE VERSUS THE REAPER

PART II: RESURRECTION

4

ST. PAUL AND THE CANNIBALS / 85
THE RISE OF RESURRECTION

5

FRANKENSTEIN REDUX / 113
THE MODERN REANIMATORS

PART III: SOUL

6

BEATRICE'S SMILE / 141
WHAT HAPPENS IN PARADISE

7

THE LOST SOUL / 169
REINCARNATION AND THE EVIDENCE OF SCIENCE

PART IV: LEGACY

8

LOOK ON MY WORKS, YE MIGHTY / 201
EVERLASTING FAME

9

THE IMMORTAL SEED / 227
GENES, GAIA AND THE THINGS IN BETWEEN

CONCLUSION

10

HE WHO SAW THE DEEP / 253
WISDOM AND MORTALITY

Acknowledgments / **287**
Notes and Further Reading / **289**
Index / **311**

FOREWORD

BY MICHAEL SHERMER

O N Friday, April 13, 2012 in the chapel of the New Orleans Baptist Seminary, I debated a Liberty University philosopher and theologian named Gary Habermas on the question: "Is There Life After Death?" I went first. I began with this thought experiment:

> Imagine yourself dead. What picture comes to mind? Your funeral with a casket surrounded by family and friends? Complete darkness and void? In either case you are still conscious and observing the scene.

I then outlined the problem we all have in thinking about life after death: we cannot envision what it is like to be dead any more than we can visualize ourselves before we were born, and yet everyone who ever lived has died so death is inevitable. This leads to either depression or humor. I prefer the latter. As Steven Wright said: "I intend to live forever—so far, so good." Or Woody Allen said: "It's not that I'm afraid to die. I just don't want to be there when it happens." Of course, you won't be there when it happens because to experience anything you must be conscious, and you are not conscious when you are dead.

I was well prepared for this debate as I had just read a book by the British philosopher Stephen Cave, titled *Immortality: The Quest to Live Forever and How It Drives Civilization*. It is a work of monumental importance, and his outline of the four narratives about immortality that have been generated by people over the ages is a useful heuristic that I put to good use in my debate. It is a book that you can put to good use in your life if you have ever thought about death and how that thought can change your life. The four narratives are:

1. *Staying Alive.* One way to achieve immortality is to not die. In my debate, I reviewed the various problems involved, such as the one hundred billion people who lived before us who have died, and the various problems associated with radical life extension efforts, such as caloric restriction, genetic engineering to change the telomeres involved in aging, and cryogenically freezing yourself to come back later.

2. *Resurrection.* I began here with the problem of identity and Theseus's Ship: Poseidon's son Theseus sailed to Crete to slay the monster, Minotaur, and so his ship was preserved for posterity but rotted over time and every board was replaced with new wood—is that still Theseus's ship? I then segued into discussing the transformation problem—how could you be reassembled just as you were and yet this time be invulnerable to disease and death? And then there's the problem of what age you would be resurrected? Fifteen, thirty, eight-five? And how would duplicates be any different from twins?

3. *Soul.* I explained to these young seminarians that there isn't a shred of evidence for anything like a "soul" that survives death; no new physical system that scientists have dis-

covered to allow soul stuff to survive. I noted that although we do not yet fully understand how thoughts are transduced into physical movements, adding a soul only doubles the mystery, as believers would then have to explain how the soul affects the mind or the brain. In reality, I continued, there is no soul or mind. Just brain. I then asked, rhetorically, "Under anesthesia, where's your soul? Why is it knocked out? And, if the soul can see, why can't the souls of blind people see when they are alive?"

4. *Legacy*: Glory, reputation, historical impact, or children. But as Woody Allen said: "I don't want to live on in the hearts and minds of my countrymen. I want to live on in my apartment." Clearly this is not what most people desire for life after death.

Then, there is the matter of which religion's afterlife story is the right one? I reminded my debate opponent and the audience of the fact that Egyptian, Greek, Roman, Jewish, Christian, Muslim, Mormon, Buddhist, and Hindu religions all have different ideas about the afterlife and heaven. Which one is right? I noted the fact that afterlife myths all follow the same pattern as all religious myths: where you happened to have been born and at what time in history determines which myth you believe.

I then challenged these seminarians to tell us where heaven is. Ever since Copernicus and the rise of modern astronomy, there is no place for heaven "above." This has led some to speculate that perhaps it is in another dimension. But those dimensions are physical systems subject to the laws of entropy, so that doesn't help. I then mentioned a few other "theories" of the afterlife:

Egyptians: A physical place far above the Earth in a "dark area" of space where there were no stars, basically beyond the Universe.

Vikings: Valhalla—a big hall to drink beer and get ready to fight again.

Muslims: A "Garden" with rivers, fountains, shady valleys, trees, milk, honey, and wine—all the things Arabian desert people would crave, plus seventy-two virgins for the men. (No one seems to have asked what the women would want.)

Christians: An eternity with angels at the throne of God.

I added the observations of the ethnologist Élie Reclus, who described Christian missionaries attempting to convert Inuits with the promise of a God-centered heaven.

Inuit: "And the seals? You say nothing about the seals. Have you no seals in your heaven?"

Missionaries: "Seals? Certainly not. We have angels and archangels . . . the twelve apostles and twenty-four elders, we have . . ."

Inuit: "That's enough. Your heaven has no seals, and a heaven without seals is not for us!"

I ended my opening statement on immortality with these beautiful and poignant lines from Matthew Arnold's poem *Empedocles on Etna*:

Is it so small a thing,
To have enjoyed the sun,
To have lived light in the Spring,
To have loved, to have thought, to have done;
To have advanced true friends, and beat down baffling foes—
That we must feign a bliss Of doubtful future date,
And while we dream on this, Lose all our present state,
And relegate to worlds . . . yet distant our repose?

THIS is a book about life, death and civilization.

    I aim to show how we, like all living things, are driven to pursue life without end; but also how we, alone of living things, have in the process created spectacular civilizations, with stunning artworks, rich religious traditions and the material and intellectual achievements of science.

All of this, I argue, we have done through following four paths that promise immortality. The final aim of this book is to ask if any of these paths can deliver on that promise and what the answer means for how we should live.

"History is Philosophy teaching by examples," wrote Thucydides. I am a philosopher by training, but I have also drawn widely on the examples of history, as well as on insights from many other disciplines, from anthropology to zoology and most in between—universities might divide up neatly into subjects and faculties, but life does not. When making such excursions into other fields, I have attempted broadly to follow consensus opinion—though I have also not shied from taking a stand when necessary for my own argument.

I am aware of the immodesty of making sweeping claims about such grand matters. Experts will shudder at my simplifications of complex debates, some of enormous antiquity. But it was always my intention to keep the book short and succinct, and I hope that some readers at least will be stimulated to go farther down alleyways of knowledge to which I could only briefly point.

IMMORTALITY

IMMORTALITY

1

A BEAUTIFUL WOMAN
HAS COME

The Four Paths to Immortality

THEY tried to destroy her. Hammers swung to smash the elegant nose and break her long and graceful neck. All across the kingdom, the statues and busts of the great queen were pounded to dust. Her name was chiseled from the monuments, its utterance banned. This embodiment of regal womanhood was never to be seen or spoken of again.

It was a sentence made to last for eternity: no cult would tend her tomb, keeping alive her soul with incense and offerings; she would not be preserved in dignity so that she might reign in the Otherworld. Her brief dynasty was extinguished. By systematically erasing her from history, the new pharaoh was not only purging Egypt of her ideas and influence—he was knowingly consigning her to cold, endless oblivion. Or so he thought.

Three thousand two hundred and thirty years later, Ludwig Borchardt, Egyptological attaché of the German Reich, hurried across a dusty, pockmarked plain. His young assistant was waiting impatiently at the entrance to one of the many excavation pits; he explained that they had found the remains of a buried house—though it was once grand, it had seemed that thieves and the passage of time had left little of value. Then a local workman, clearing away thousands of years of muck and rubble, had found a section of wall that seemed bricked up in haste. The age-old blocks had given way at the touch of his chisel, falling into blackness on the other side.

Borchardt climbed into the ditch and made his way hastily through the dust and shadows to this secret chamber. Reaching the opening cleared by the workmen, he stepped carefully over the broken bricks. Pushing his torch ahead of him, he peered into the small room—and froze. Rows of stone heads gazed out at him like ghosts, lines of shimmering faces, each one unique, each perfectly rendered with the kinks and scars of life—a furrowed brow, a wrinkled smile. It was as if an assembly of these ancient people had gathered to pass on a message from the other side.

Then he saw her: on the floor, half hidden by a fallen ledge. With his bare hands, Borchardt thrust aside the debris to pull her out. When he held her up to the torchlight, he became the first man in over three thousand years to look upon the full beauty of Nefertiti.

Back in his office that night, December 6, 1912, Borchardt scribbled in his diary, "absolutely outstanding; describing is useless, must be seen." Then he began plotting how he could bring the great queen back to his kaiser.

THE FOUR PATHS

ALL living things seek to perpetuate themselves into the future, but humans seek to perpetuate themselves forever. This seeking—this will to immortality—is the foundation of human achievement; it is the wellspring of religion, the muse of philosophy, the architect of our cities and the impulse behind the arts. It is embedded in our very nature, and its result is what we know as civilization.

Although magnificent in the scale and sophistication of its expression, ancient Egypt's obsession with eternal life was otherwise no different from that of every society, ancient or modern, Eastern or Western. The dream of some kind of life without end is a universal feature of human experience, common to all cultures across time and place—and still today driving us on toward new achievements that surpass even the pyramids.

This book will do three things: First, it will show that beneath the apparent diversity of stories about how immortality is to be attained there are just *four* basic forms—what I will call the four *immortality narratives*. All attempts at everlasting life that have ever been made—and ever will be—follow one or another of these four. From Egypt to China, New York to New Delhi, people today are following these narratives in the belief that they will deliver them from death, just as people always have. We can imagine them as four paths leading toward the mythical Mount of the Immortals.

These narratives are responses to fundamental constants in the human condition. Yet different cultures at different times have shown enormous ingenuity in elaborating these basic frameworks; they are a continuous source of inspiration, innovation and creativity. They are the ways in which we channel our most simple urge—to live on—yet they have led to our most sophisticated intellectual, religious and artistic achievements. The second aim of this book is to show how our efforts to clear these four paths and prepare for the ascent up the Mount of the Immortals have thrown up what we know as civilization—the institutions, rituals and beliefs that make human existence what it is.

But although the summit of everlasting life is where these four paths are pointed, whether they get there is an altogether different question. The peak remains above the clouds; those who reach it do not return to tell the story. Today we are in a far better position than any of our ancestors to map out this terrain and assess whether any of these paths reach their destination. Modern science is giving us fresh insights into the origins of life and the end of the universe; we can peer into brains in search of the soul, and we are developing new technologies that promise to defeat aging. Therefore the third thing this book will do is draw on these new insights to examine which of these four narratives have a real prospect of taking us to where we might live forever.

ALTHOUGH these four paths explain many mysteries of human behavior, they are also intuitive and straightforward. The first springs most directly from our instincts: like all living systems, we strive to avoid death. The dream of doing so forever—physically, in this world—is the most basic of immortality narratives. I will call this first path simply *Staying Alive*. It sounds unpromising, absurd even, in the face of the basic fact of death and decay. But it is hugely pervasive: almost all cultures contain legends of sages, golden-age heroes or remote peasants who discovered the secret to defeating aging and death.

This narrative is really nothing more than the continuation of our attempts to stay young and healthy, to live that little bit longer—an extra year or two or ten. Those aspects of civilization that provide for our bodily needs—the food supplies and city walls—are the first steps along this route, medicine and hygiene the next. But most civilizations promise much more than merely safe passage to old age: they hold out the hope of an elixir that will defeat disease and debility for good. This promise has sustained whole religions, such as Taoism, and esoteric cults, such as that of the Holy Grail, but it has never been more widespread than today. The very idea of scientific progress is predicated on its delivering ever-extending lifespans, and a host of well-credentialed scientists and technologists believe that longevity liftoff is imminent.

But betting everything on the Staying Alive Narrative is a risky strategy: success rates to date are not reassuring. The second path therefore offers a backup plan: it claims that even if death finds us, we can have a second bite at life's cherry. This is the *Resurrection Narrative*, the belief that, although we must physically die, nonetheless we can physically rise again with the bodies we knew in life.

Though not as basic as the attempt to simply stay alive, the hope of resurrection is also rooted in nature: we are used to seeing the natural world die back in winter, only to return with new vigor the following year. Billions of people around the world celebrate this triumph of life over death in spring festivals such as Easter, with its explicit association with the promise of human resurrection. Unbeknownst to many of their followers, the three great monotheistic religions of Judaism, Christianity and Islam all also believe in literal, physical resurrection as a central doctrine——a belief that was crucial to these religions' early success.

But as well as these ancient traditions, versions of resurrection are also gaining popularity among those who would rather put their faith in technology than in gods. Cryonics, for example, in which people pay to be frozen on death in the hope of one day being repaired and revived, is one new track on this route. As technology rapidly develops, even more high-tech versions are being proposed, such as the possibility that we will upload ourselves onto computers and then reload ourselves into new bodies or digital avatars.

Some, however, are not keen to reinherit their old bodies in the next life, even in digital form; the material world they believe to be too unreliable to guarantee eternity. They therefore dream of surviving as some kind of spiritual entity——or *Soul*, which is the third path. The majority of people on earth currently believe they have one, including two-thirds of people in the United Kingdom and even more in the United States. It has come to be the dominant belief in Christianity and is central to Hinduism, Buddhism and many other religions.

Unlike followers of the Resurrection Narrative, believers in the Soul Narrative have mostly given up on this earthly frame and believe in a future consisting of some more spiritual stuff. Though less rooted in nature, this belief also arises intuitively: in dreams and mystical experiences, humans have long had the feeling of leaving their bodies behind. To many, soul or mind has seemed separable from the flesh in which it resides—and therefore able to survive without it.

Although the idea of the soul has flourished in both East and West, it too has its doubters, particularly among the materially minded. But even they can find solace in what is perhaps the most widespread narrative of all: the fourth path, *Legacy*. This requires neither the survival of the physical body nor an immaterial soul, but is concerned instead with more indirect ways of extending ourselves into the future.

The association of fame and immortality was widespread in the ancient world, and many people since have followed the example set by the Greek hero Achilles on the battlefield of Troy in choosing eternal glory over a long life. The Greeks believed that culture had a permanence and solidity that biology lacked; eternal life therefore belonged to the hero who could stake a place for himself in the cultural realm. Today we seem to be as desperate for celebrity as Achilles was for glory; the competition for cultural space is as hot as ever.

Some of us also leave a more tangible legacy than our reputations alone: children. Our genes have been called immortal because they stretch back millions of years in a traceable line to the very beginnings of life, and if we are lucky will also continue into the distant future. Or perhaps, as some claim, our legacy is to have been part of life on earth—part of Gaia, the superorganism that will remain long after we individually are gone, or even part of the unfolding cosmos itself.

THESE narratives are manifested in many different forms, from ancient myths to political manifestos, but at least one is present in every culture, providing the milestones and signposts on life's road. Some civilizations have followed a single path for thousands of years. Others have shifted from pursuing one path to the next.

But no civilization has survived unsupported by one of the four: all have immortality narratives, and all immortality narratives fall into one of these four kinds.

Today in the developed world, all four narratives are as present as ever—though not interwoven into a single story. Rather, they are competing views in a marketplace of beliefs. Some of us shop around, reflecting deeply before taking our pick; others follow the latest fads; while most of us simply do whatever our parents did. But whether we know it or not, the vast majority of us have bought into one or another of the immortality creeds.

SUNSET OF THE ATEN

IN the course of this book we will see many examples of the four narratives in action, but there is no better starting place than the banks of the Nile, where the pursuit of immortality achieved an unrivaled sophistication and splendor. The civilization of ancient Egypt survived almost unchanged for some three thousand years. Even after it was conquered—first by the Persians, then the armies of Alexander the Great, then, following Cleopatra's famous suicide, by Rome—it continued to have immense cultural and religious influence. Among the Greeks and Romans, Egypt stood for ancient wisdom; there was a powerful feeling that the Egyptians had found some truth that other cultures struggled to capture.

The Egyptians' pantheon was only finally suppressed when their Roman conquerors converted en masse in 380 ce to a potent new immortality system: Christianity (only for it to be replaced a few hundred years later by its close cousin Islam). What made the Egyptian worldview so enduring and attractive was its rich and satisfying immortality narrative. And part of what made this particular narrative so impressive is that it interwove *all four* basic forms into a single whole within its vibrant mythology. As we mentioned, all four narratives are also present today—but as alternatives, not as an integrated story. In other cultures too, all four have been present—but with only one or two in the foreground. Ancient Egypt is unique in weaving all four narratives into a single beguiling thread. It is a spectacular example of the human religious imagination and of bet-hedging on the way to eternity.

This is why the pharaoh who set out to destroy Nefertiti—Horemheb, a former general—had his work cut out for him: ancient Egyptians might hope to use any of the four paths to live beyond their natural span. First, although they are most famous for their careful preservation of corpses, the Egyptians were also very keen on pursuing the most basic path, Staying Alive. They had a highly sophisticated system of medicine-cum-magic to ward off aging and illness. Herbs, spells and amulets aimed to keep their recipients alive for as long as possible, and preferably forever—numerous surviving papyruses focus on the prolongation of life and reversing aging. For all their colorful accounts of how to make the best of being dead, Staying Alive was very much Plan A.

Nonetheless, these tactics were clearly limited, so they also set their hopes on the Resurrection Narrative. Mummies are perhaps the strongest symbol of the idea that our physical remains can be made to breathe once more. Egyptians went to enormous lengths to ensure that a body was properly preserved in the belief it could be magically revived. This was a massive industry, entrusted to the priests who would drain the corpse's fluids, remove and separately preserve the soft organs and then apply natron, a naturally occurring salt, to suck out moisture. They then stuffed the body with cloth or sawdust and wrapped it in hundreds of feet of linen, sometimes treated with resin or bitumen as waterproofing (giving rise to the word "mummy," which comes from the Persian word for bitumen, *mum*).

Conditions for mummification were far from sterile—maggots, beetles and even mice have been found caught in the linen wrappings—and the priests were far from always trustworthy: the Greek historian Herodotus reported that the bodies of young women were not handed over until they had decomposed a little, to discourage frisky embalmers from abusing their privileges. The whole process took seventy days and climaxed with the "Opening of the Mouth" ceremony, in which the deceased would be magically reanimated (though their realm of action was confined, of course, only to the Otherworld). The pyramids—which were only built for a relatively brief period early in Egypt's history, as they proved too attractive to tomb robbers—were constructed in alignment with where the Egyptians believed this Otherworld to be, so helping the inhabitant to launch into the next phase of life.

But the Egyptians did not put their faith in body alone: they also had a version of the third narrative, Soul. Like many ancient peoples, they believed in multiple souls, most important of which was the *ka*, or life force. Breathed by the gods into each person at the instant of birth, the *ka* was what enabled a person to produce a child—something like sexual potency, or what blues singers call "mojo." After death, it was thought to continue to live in the mummy and required a steady supply of sustenance. It was therefore crucial that friends and relatives of the deceased brought food to the grave upon which the *ka* could feast—consuming of course only the spiritual life force of the offerings, not the physical stuff, which would be conveniently left for the priests.

We have seen that the final punishment meted out to Nefertiti was the attempt to wipe her from history—what the Romans called *damnatio memoriae*. This is because the Egyptians also regarded the fourth narrative, Legacy, as crucial to their survival. They believed that a person's name and reputation were fundamental parts of them; for a person to live fully in the next world, these had to be preserved too. They therefore took great care to keep their names alive, inscribing them, like modern-day graffiti taggers, on almost anything they could find, from tomb walls to pots and combs. But most important, their friends and family were expected to continue to remember them, chanting their names when bringing food for their *ka*. If your name was spoken and your monuments still stood, they thought, then at least a part of you still lived.

If all these components came together, then the ancient Egyptian expected a glorious and eternal second life. But if they were all destroyed, neglected or forgotten, then the deceased would be condemned to utter, final extinction——the "second death" that all Egyptians dreaded. This was the sentence that Horemheb imposed on Nefertiti and her husband, the pharaoh Akhenaten. Their crime? To hijack Egypt's ancient immortality system for themselves.

WHEN the archaeologist Ludwig Borchardt found Nefertiti beneath the desert it was in the form of a full-color life-sized bust of the great queen in her prime. Her neck rises long and slender from an elaborate necklace sculpted in exquisite detail; her lips are full, and her eyes are large and seductively lidded. Her face is framed by a unique blue crown that continues the lines of her cheeks and jaw. She radiates authority and ease; she appears both resolved and inscrutable. It is an image of power and beauty as potent now as when it was cast over three thousand years ago.

That was around 1340 bce, and she enjoyed a status and influence unprecedented in Egypt's long history. Nefertiti, whose name means "a beautiful woman has come," was not only the pharaoh's great queen, his foremost consort and mother of six daughters by him——she was his equal, portrayed smiting enemies, riding chariots and worshipping alongside him.

The pharaoh, Akhenaten, on the other hand, was a freakish figure, spindly limbed and potbellied, far from the Egyptian ideal of the broad-shouldered warrior. As head of state and religion—— the two were inseparable——he played a crucial role in the immortality narrative: he was expected to lead the rituals and ceremonies that kept the cosmos in balance, ensuring for his people safe passage through this world and into the next. But he and his bold and beautiful wife had other ideas.

At first they merely neglected the other gods, building instead vast temples to the previously obscure deity Aten, associated with the sun disc. After five years on the throne, they broke with the old ways completely and abandoned the historic seat of Thebes for a new capital, which they called Akhetaten—"horizon of the Aten." Rising from a dusty plain in a just a few years, this sparkling city was filled with images of Akhenaten and Nefertiti bathing in the light of the sun, their god, its rays reaching out to offer them an ankh, the cross-shaped symbol of eternal life; underneath, inscribed in hieroglyphs: "may they live forever." But even this was not enough, and once established in their new palace they announced that the old religion was dead—that there was no god but Aten and they were his prophets. They had launched the first recorded monotheism in history, with themselves as its sole ambassadors on earth.

This shook Egypt to its core. All good Egyptians were raised to respect the many deities that governed every aspect of life on the Nile. They turned to the goddess Isis when sick and thanked falcon-headed Horus for keeping Egypt's borders strong; they prayed to the mummy-god Osiris to ensure safe passage for their loved ones in the life to come. For Egypt's already ancient and conservative society this was a revolution far more dramatic than Christianity's Reformation—more akin to the Pope today declaring himself the incarnation of Horus and swapping the Vatican for a pyramid. Not only must this blasphemy have filled ordinary folk with dread of divine retribution, but they would have believed, with the temples closed and the ancient rites banned, that their route to the next world was barred.

BUT such a powerful narrative as that of the old gods, so deeply embedded in the institutions and habits of Egyptian civilization, could not be so easily overturned. After fourteen years in power, one by one, the living embodiments of the Aten began to disappear. First, three of their daughters fell to a plague. Then, quite suddenly, Nefertiti herself vanished from the records. Two years later, Akhenaten also simply disappeared.

Their dynasty was not quite over: one of their daughters was married to her half brother, the nine-year-old Tutankhamun, Akhenaten's son by a secondary wife. Together these children were permitted to rule while the old guard—the priests and generals—slowly dismantled everything their parents had done: the capital was moved back to Thebes, the temples reopened, Aten marginalized. When this young pharaoh died he was briefly succeeded by an aging adviser, before Horemheb, who had been commander in chief of the army, seized power and set about destroying all trace of the heretic and his dynasty. Ironic, then, that thanks to the discovery of his intact tomb, Tutankhamun is better known now than he was in life.

Scholars speculate about what happened to Nefertiti and Akhenaten, but the destruction wrought by Horemheb left little firm evidence. One theory is that Nefertiti changed her name in order to first become full coregent with her husband, then (briefly) to succeed him and rule alone. As to Akhenaten himself, some scholars have speculated that he was driven out of his own land and continued in exile to preach his monotheistic creed. It is indeed striking, as Sigmund Freud pointed out, that the Bible records a tale of an Egyptian prince—Moses, which in Egyptian mean "child of"—who around this time led believers in the one true god out of Egypt to a promised land.

We do not know how the Aten's reign was brought to an end, whether a full-blooded rebellion, an assassin's poison, or some more subtle pressure. But brought to an end it was. Osiris was put back on his throne in the Otherworld, and the mummifiers were put back in business. The city of the Aten, with its palaces and temples, was abandoned and left to sink back into the desert sands, ready to be discovered by intrepid archaeologists millennia later. Branded as "heretics" and "enemies," Akhenaten, Nefertiti and their children were expunged from the records, their hiero-

glyphs excised from the monuments and their images everywhere
erased. They were to be cut off from the land of the living; their
spirits were not to be fed, and their names were not to be
chanted.

They had usurped the immortality system that gave order,
meaning and hope to their people, and that system had its revenge.
With remarkable speed, Egypt's ancient society healed its wounds
and resumed the business of preparing for the next life—but the
great queen and her heretic husband were to be forever excluded
from it. Those who followed did their work so thoroughly that, for
millennia, no one knew that this royal couple had ever existed. The
vengeful priests must have believed Nefertiti had been destroyed
for good. But they were wrong, for beneath the shifting sands of
her ruined city, she was waiting.

THE WILL TO LIVE (FOREVER)

"**G**ROUPS are always collectively seeking modes or combina-
tions of modes of immortality and will celebrate them endlessly, fight and die in order to affirm them or put down rivals who
threaten their immortality system," wrote the psychiatrist and historian Robert Jay Lifton. So it was with Akhenaten and Nefertiti,
who, despite having all the power and wealth of the royal house,
were swept away by the currents of Egypt's ancient immortality
system.

But what is it that drives us first to create such systems and then
to fight and even die to defend them? The sheer universality of immortality narratives, the fact that they seem to be central to every
culture, suggests that the root is in human nature itself. Indeed, it
is deep in the nature that we share with all living things: the urge
simply to live on. But we alone of animals—at least, as far as we
know—have developed religions, artistic traditions and honor systems that give expression to this urge and transform it into sophisti-

cated narratives. These are the result of the very particular way
that we, with our outsized minds, regard life and death—a way
that is deeply paradoxical.

SOME are skeptical when they first hear the claim that a will
to immortality is the underlying driver of civilization; it sounds
too metaphysical to be the instinct behind our everyday actions,
too mystical to explain the behavior of a creature evolved from
the apes. But the origin of our eternal longings is neither mystical
nor metaphysical—on the contrary, nothing could be more natural. That we strive to project ourselves into the future is a direct
consequence of our long evolutionary legacy.

   This determination to survive and reproduce—to extend into
the future—is the one thing that all life forms have in common. The
mightiest mountain passively allows its own erosion, no different
from the grain of sand washed over by the sea. But the tiniest organism will fight with all it has against the assaults of elements and
predators—against the descent into disorder that otherwise charac-
terizes the universe. Living things are by their very nature dynamic
systems for sustaining themselves against the odds. Whether dogs,
worms or amoebas, they continually struggle with what seems to be
a single purpose: to just keep going. This striving to perpetuate is
the essence of life. As the evolutionary biologist Richard Dawkins
put it, "We are survival machines, but 'we' does not mean just people. It embraces all animals, plants, bacteria, and viruses."

   This has become a truism in modern biology—the preservation
and reproduction of self in some form belongs to all definitions of
what life is. The process of evolution by natural selection tells us just
why this should be so: in a varied population, those creatures best
able to survive and reproduce are those that will pass on their genes
to the next generation. Every cat, tree and dung beetle that we see
around us exists only because its ancestors were the best at preserving themselves and their offspring. Successfully projecting them-

selves into the future, through surviving and reproducing, is therefore exactly what distinguishes evolutionary winners from losers.

To make this clearer, just imagine for a moment the opposite: a life form indifferent to its own future prospects. The apathetic mouse that makes no effort to hide from snakes and owls would quickly be gobbled up, and its lugubrious germ line would die with it. We would never meet such indifferent creatures because their genes would never have survived. Its striving cousins, on the other hand, who do everything to live on and fill the world with their offspring, would pass on their striving genes. Soon enough, the world would be full of only those mice with fighting spirit. Natural selection produces self-perpetuators.

As a consequence, as the sociologist Raymond D. Gastil wrote, "all forms of life behave as if persistence into the future— immortality—were the basic goal of their existence." Everything that living things do is directed toward this goal. The leading neuroscientist Antonio Damasio has shown that gut feelings, complex emotions and our sophisticated reasoning processes all exist to contribute, directly or indirectly, to the aim of survival. The biological anthropologist James Chisholm deduced further that all values—all ideas of good and bad, right and wrong—arise from this single goal, as he put it, "the complex action for the sake of which bodies exist: indefinite continuance."

The German philosopher Arthur Schopenhauer called this primal urge simply "the will to live." Given, however, that it is not limited in time—that, as Chisholm said, the continuance we desire is "indefinite"—we should instead call it the will to live *forever*, or the will to immortality.

This drive can explain a great deal of what we do, including much of civilization. The first of the four basic immortality narratives—Staying Alive—is simply the will to live forever in its basic form, and staying alive is something we humans have become very good at, spreading across the globe to countless different climates and habitats, where we enjoy, by mammalian standards, exceptionally long lifespans. But the other three forms of immortality narrative go far beyond the animal urges to flee from fire or store food for the winter—and, indeed, sometimes run contrary to them. Although motivated by the will to immortality, these narratives are the products not only of what we have in common with other living things but also of what sets us apart.

THE MORTALITY PARADOX

WHAT sets us apart is, of course, our massive, highly connected brains. These too have evolved to help us perpetuate ourselves indefinitely, and they are enormously useful in the struggle to survive. Our awareness of ourselves, of the future and of alternative possibilities enables us to adapt and make sophisticated plans. But it also gives us a perspective on ourselves that is at the same time terrifying and baffling. On the one hand, our powerful intellects come inexorably to the conclusion that we, like all other living things around us, must one day die. Yet on the other, the one thing that these minds cannot imagine is that very state of nonexistence; it is literally inconceivable. Death therefore presents itself as both inevitable and impossible. This I will call the *Mortality Paradox*, and its resolution is what gives shape to the immortality narratives, and therefore to civilization.

Both halves of this paradox arise from the same set of impressive cognitive faculties. Since the advent some two and a half million years ago of the genus *Homo*, the immediate ancestors of modern humans, our brain size has tripled. This has come with a series of crucial conceptual innovations: First, we are aware of ourselves as distinct individuals, a trait limited to only a handful of large-brained species and considered to be essential for sophisticated social interaction. Second, we have an intricate idea of the future, allowing us to premeditate and vary our plans—also an ability unseen in the vast majority of other species (one of the rare exceptions being the case of the chimpanzee in Furuvik, Sweden, who collected stones by night to throw at zoo visitors by day). And third, we can imagine different scenarios, playing with possibilities and generalizing from what we have seen, enabling us to learn, reason and extrapolate.

The survival benefits of these faculties are obvious: from mammoth traps to supermarket supply chains, we can plan, coordinate and cooperate to ensure our needs are met. But these powers come at a cost. If you have an idea of yourself and of the future and can extrapolate and generalize from what you see around you, then if you see your comrade killed by a lion, you realize that you too could be killed by a lion. This is useful if it causes you to sharpen your spear in readiness, but it also brings anxiety—it summons the future possibility of death in the present. The next day you might see a different comrade killed by a snake, another by disease and yet another by fire. You see that there are *countless* ways in which you could be killed, and they could strike at any time: prepare as you will, death's onslaught is relentless.

And so we realize, as we see the other living things around us fall one by one, that no one is spared. We recognize that death is the real enemy; with our powerful minds we can stave him off for a while with sharp spears or strong gates, full larders and hospitals, but at the same time, we see that it is all ultimately fruitless, that one day we not only can but surely will die. This is what the twentieth-century German philosopher Martin Heidegger famously described as "being-toward-death," which he considered to define the human condition.

We are therefore blessed with powerful minds yet at the same time cursed, not only to die, but to know that we must. "Man has created death," wrote the poet W. B. Yeats. Other creatures blindly struggle on, knowing only life until their moment comes. "Except for man, all creatures are immortal, for they are ignorant of death," wrote the Argentinean author Jorge Luis Borges. But we bring death into life: we see it coming for us in every storm or forest fire, snake or spider, illness or ill omen.

This is a central theme of philosophy, poetry and myth; it is what defines us as mortals. It is represented in that most ancient and influential of stories, the book of Genesis: if they eat the fruit of the Tree of Knowledge of Good and Evil, Adam and Eve are told, they will die—mortality is the price of knowledge. Since we attained self-awareness, as Michel de Montaigne wrote, "death has us by the scruff of the neck at every moment." No matter what we do, no matter how hard we strive, we know that the Reaper will one day take us. Life is a constant war we are doomed to lose.

BUT the second idea—and the other half of the Mortality Paradox—tells us quite the opposite: that our own obliteration is impossible. The fact is, whenever we try to imagine the *reality* of our own deaths we stumble. We simply cannot envision actually not existing. Try it: you might get as far as an image of your own funeral, or perhaps a dark and empty void, but you are still there— the observer, the envisioning eye. The very act of imagining summons you, like a genie, into virtual being.

We therefore cannot make death real to ourselves as thinking subjects. Our powerful imaginative faculties malfunction: it is not possible for the one doing the imagining to actively imagine the absence of the one doing the imagining. "It is indeed impossible to imagine our own death; and whenever we attempt to do so we can perceive that we are in fact still present as spectators," wrote Sigmund Freud in 1915. He concluded from this that "at bottom no one believes in his own death . . . [for] in the unconscious every one of us is convinced of his own immortality." Or as the English Romantic poet Edward Young put it: "All men think all men mortal, but themselves."

This applies no matter how far into the future we attempt to look: whether one or one thousand years from now, we cannot help but be present in what we see. There is no limit to just how far into the future we can project; it is not as if our imagination stops at a million years, or a billion. And so, to quote the Bible's book of Ecclesiastes, God—or nature—"has set eternity in the hearts of men." In our own minds, we are part of the very fabric of the universe, ineradicable, here forever. The great German writer Goethe is reported to have concluded that "in this sense everyone carries the proof of his own immortality within himself." We cannot conceive of our own nonexistence, he reasoned, and therefore our nonexistence is impossible.

Modern cognitive psychology gives a scientific account of this ancient intuition. Our acceptance of new facts or possibilities depends upon our ability to imagine them—we accept, for example, that playing with matches could cause our house to burn down because this is something we can easily picture. But when our minds come across an obstacle to imagining a certain scenario, then we find it much more difficult to accept. Our own death is just such a scenario, as it involves the end of consciousness, and we cannot consciously simulate what it is like to not be conscious.

Research by the psychologist Jesse Bering has shown that even young children who have not yet been socialized into any particular religion or worldview believe that the mind survives bodily death. He and his colleagues argue that this is because the alternative—that the mind is extinguished—cannot be grasped. He concludes that we have "an innate sense of immortality" that stems from this cognitive quirk—that is, the seeming impossibility of our annihilation is hardwired into our brains.

AND thus we have a paradox: when we peer into the future we find our wish to live forever fulfilled, as it seems inconceivable that we might one day cease to be. Thus we believe in our own immortality. Yet at the same time we are painfully aware of the countless possible threats to our being, from poisonous snakes to avalanches, and we see all around how other living things inevitably meet a sticky end. And thus we believe in our own mortality. Our very same overblown intellectual faculties seem to be telling us both that we are eternal and that we are not, both that death is a fact and that it is impossible. In Zygmunt Bauman's words, "the thought of death is—and is bound to remain—*a contradiction in terms*." Both our immortality and our mortality present themselves to our minds with equal force.

Both these ideas, as we have seen, have found their champions among the poets, thinkers and myth makers: half suggest that we must live with the awareness of inevitable extinction, while the other half argue that we can never doubt that life is eternal. A few, of course, have also recognized the underlying paradox that both these ideas seem true. The Spanish-American philosopher and writer George Santayana, for example, captured it perfectly when he wrote of our clumsy struggle to reconcile "the observed fact of mortality and the native inconceivability of death."

The paradox stems from two different ways of viewing ourselves—on the one hand, objectively, or from the outside, as it were, and on the other hand, subjectively, or from the inside. When we deploy reason to view ourselves as we do other living things around us, then we realize that we, like them, will fail, die and rot. From this outside, objective perspective, we are mortals. But when we switch to our own perspective and try to make sense of what this means subjectively, then we encounter the imaginative obstacle—the inability to accept the prospect of annihilation. Our introspection tells us we are as imperishable as the angels, indivisible and everlasting; yet when we look in the mirror we see ourselves as others see us, with sagging flesh and the first signs of decay—an imperfect and impermanent creature fated to a brief existence and a miserable end.

The difference between these two perspectives, the objective and the subjective, explains how the Mortality Paradox arises—

but it is one thing to explain it, another to resolve it. The paradox is composed of two contrary yet powerful intuitions about our ultimate fate; we cannot—and do not—live with such a tension. Such a state would be a continuous, paralyzing struggle between dread and hope. But that is not how most of us live; we are not, as a rule, paralyzed by the contradiction at the heart of the human condition. This is because we have developed stories that help us make sense of this existential impasse—and these are, of course, the immortality narratives.

THE ENGINE OF CIVILIZATION

IN the 1990s, a group of American psychologists found that briefly reminding people of their own mortality had remarkable effects on their political and religious views. For example, they asked a group of Christian students to give their impressions of the personalities of two people. In all relevant respects, these two people were very similar—except one was a fellow Christian and the other Jewish. Under normal circumstances, participants rated them fairly equally. But if the students were first reminded of their mortality (e.g., by being asked to fill in a personality test that included questions about their attitude to their own death), then they were much more positive about their fellow Christian and more negative about the Jew.

These psychologists were testing the hypothesis that we have developed our cultural worldviews in order to protect ourselves from the fear of death. They reasoned that if this was true, then when reminded of their own mortality, people would cling more fiercely to the core beliefs of their worldview and would be more negative about those who threatened those beliefs. And this is exactly what their experiments found.

In another study, American students were asked to assess how "likeable and knowledgeable" they found the authors of two essays, one of which was positive about the U.S. political system and the

other critical. The students were invariably more positive about the
pro-American writer and more negative about the critic—but this
effect was hugely exaggerated after they had been reminded of their
mortality. According to the authors of the study, this shows that it
is not only religion to which we cling all the more tightly in the face
of death—even the sense of belonging to a nation can provide us
with existential comfort.

These researchers, now professors—Sheldon Solomon, Jeff
Greenberg, and Tom Pyszczynski—were inspired as graduate
students by reading Sigmund Freud and an American anthropologist called Ernest Becker. They were convinced by the idea that
civilization provided psychological protection against the fear of
oblivion and have since conducted more than four hundred
experiments like those described above in order to test it. Their
conclusion is that cultural worldviews, including our religions,
national myths and values, "are humanly created beliefs about
the nature of reality shared by groups of people that serve (at
least in part) to manage the terror engendered by the uniquely
human awareness of death."

What they call Terror Management Theory of the development
of human culture now has a wide and increasing following. It concerns our response to the realization that we must die—in our
terms, the first part of the Mortality Paradox. Its supporters believe that this realization is potentially devastating: we must live in
the knowledge that the worst thing that can possibly happen to us
one day surely will. Extinction—the ultimate trauma, a personal
apocalypse, the end of our individual universe—seems inevitable. If people were fully mindful of this inescapable catastrophe,
then, according to the proponents of Terror Management Theory,
they would be "twitching blobs of biological protoplasm completely
perfused with anxiety and unable to effectively respond to the demands of their immediate surroundings."

They therefore hypothesized that we have created cultural in-

stitutions, philosophies and religions that protect us from this terror by denying or at least distracting us from the finality of
death—and this is just what their experiments have borne out.
These death-denying institutions and religions vary enormously
across time and space, from the polytheism of ancient Babylon to
the consumerism of the contemporary West. But they all provide
some account of why it is that we don't really need to worry about
dying, from the claim that we are really spirits who will live on in
another realm to the belief that with enough vitamins and jogging
we can outrun the Reaper.

TERROR MANAGEMENT THEORY is therefore a modern scientific account of how the first part of the Mortality Paradox, the
awareness of our own mortality, motivates the development of immortality narratives. But we have also seen that the second part of
the Mortality Paradox, that we cannot imagine our own nonexistence, already predisposes us to believe that we cannot die. That,
after all, is why we have a paradox. This second intuition—that we
cannot ever truly be annihilated—is very useful for someone
seeking to develop a death-defying story. It provides a kind of conceptual peg on which narratives can be hung that explain how it is
that we do not really die.

The belief in an immortal soul, for example, admits that our
bodies will expire—in line with the first part of the Mortality
Paradox—but then runs with the second part of the paradox, that
we cannot completely cease to exist, in order to make the claim
that we survive bodily death and live on in spirit form. *Both* parts of
the paradox are therefore accepted and made part of a story that
removes their apparent contradiction. Our fear of death is assuaged, and the story has an intuitive plausibility because it is based
on ideas we are predisposed to believe.

Thus are immortality narratives created. Each one finds some
way of resolving the Mortality Paradox, some way of convincing

us that, contrary to appearances, we really will live on, that bodily death is either not inevitable or not what it seems, that we are *right* to believe in the impossibility of our extinction.

In the competitive environment of academic psychology, experts ferociously debate which of these two sides of the Mortality Paradox is primary in explaining human culture. Social psychologists, such as the supporters of Terror Management Theory, passionately advocate the primacy of death denial in shaping our worldviews. Whereas cognitive psychologists such as the aforementioned Jesse Bering emphasize that our inability to imagine our nonexistence suffices to explain the kind of religious beliefs we see all around us. But we can see that the effects of these two halves of the paradox are complementary: the fear of death provides a strong motivation to develop worldviews that promise immortality, and the sense of our own psychological permanence provides the peg on which such views can be hung.

Some aspects of our culture are straightforwardly products of our insatiable will to live. Agriculture, defense, housing, et cetera, all help us simply to survive. But religion, for example, or poetry is not the best way of putting food on the table or keeping enemies at bay. From the perspective of straightforward survival, self-flagellating monks or starving would-be artists are hard to explain, let alone dying for glory or sacrificing it all for posthumous fame. These distinctive features of human society can only be understood as attempts to resolve our paradoxical perspective on mortality. The writer Bryan Appleyard summed it up: "Everybody dies, therefore I must die. This being inconceivable, we invent immortality and these inventions are civilisation."

Progress itself is a product of our lust for indefinite life: not only are individual civilizations shaped by our attempts to live forever but so are their interactions, their rise and fall. "History is what man does with death," observed Hegel, the nineteenth-century German philosopher. The aforementioned psychiatrist

Robert Jay Lifton explained what this means: "Much of history can be understood as the struggle to achieve, maintain, and reaffirm a collective sense of immortality under constantly changing psychic and material conditions." Almost all facets of humanity's development can be understood as expressions of the will to live forever.

I say "almost" all facets can be explained by our will to live forever because there are other prisms through which we must also view human culture. First, each civilization is as much a product of untold historical contingencies as of the core underlying currents. A painter might paint because of prevailing immortality narratives about art as an assertion of the individual's timeless uniqueness, or about the self-transcending power of the creative process, but to understand why she paints that particular painting, we must look through the prism of art history or individual biography.

Second, some thinkers, aware and critical of our instinctive attraction to these immortality stories, have even attempted to develop alternative worldviews——but as these are the exception, they can still best be understood in terms of the rule that they are breaking.

And third, as Freud is rumored to have said, a cigar is just a cigar——a particularly telling example, as smoking is seriously detrimental to our survival prospects (Freud, who smoked cigars daily, died of mouth cancer). But smoking does provide an immediate——and indeed addictive——pleasure. Seeking pleasure and avoiding pain do not need any grand scheme or deep psychology to explain them: such actions speak for themselves. It is entirely possible that we might plant a rose bush neither to serve as a memorial to our spirit once we're gone nor to attract a mate who will help us pass on our genes into the future, but just because we like the smell of roses. It is what goes beyond simple pleasure seeking and pain avoidance that makes human civilization distinctive and that must be understood in terms of the quest for eternal projection. It is not sufficient to understand civilization from the per-

spective of these death-defying narratives—but it is necessary. As
the sociologist Zygmunt Bauman put it, "Without mortality, no
history, no culture—no humanity."

IN the following chapters we will examine each of the four immortality narratives. We will see how each has contributed to making
our civilization what it is, but equally we will ask which of these
four paths might actually deliver on its promise. That they are motivated by deep-seated aspects of the human condition tells us
nothing about whether or not these narratives are true. They could
be genuine discoveries made by humanity at the dawn of history or
elaborate products of wishful thinking; we could have been driven
by the Mortality Paradox to uncover the secrets of immortality or
to invent them. Each path has had millions, if not billions, of followers throughout history—and still does today; each has been defended by thousands of philosophers, theologians or sages. We will
look to see whether one, none or all of them might lead us through
the thick forest, beyond the clouds and up to the sunny peak of the
Mount of the Immortals.

Like other ancient Egyptians, Nefertiti was set on pursuing all
four options for attaining eternity. But the odds cannot be good on
her having escaped the fate of other mortals, especially given the
anger she aroused. So she likely had little success with the first narrative, Staying Alive. Assuming she did succumb to the frailties of
the flesh, she would certainly have been mummified. But given
the thoroughness with which her successors sought to destroy her,
it is unlikely they would have left her remains intact—therefore
ruling out any hopes of the second narrative, Resurrection. And
her *ka*—deprived of the sustenance the Egyptians believed it
needed—would long ago have withered away. So the Soul Narrative could also provide her little solace. The only way left for her to
satisfy her overweening will to immortality was therefore the
fourth: Legacy.

A BEAUTIFUL WOMAN RETURNS

SIX weeks after Ludwig Borchardt first set eyes on Nefertiti, the mood in the German camp was tense. The inspector of antiquities, Gustave Lefebvre, was due the next day, and it was this Frenchman's duty to take half the spoils of the season's excavations for the Egyptian state, in accordance with Egyptian law. He was free to choose which half, and no one in the German team believed he would allow the bust of Nefertiti to go back to Berlin. After sunset that night, the Germans processed by candlelight into the hut that served as her temporary throne room and said their farewells to the lady they called simply "Her Majesty."

The next day, the inspector was greeted by Borchardt and taken into the hut where the artifacts had been gathered. The sun rose high over the plain as the rest of the expedition waited for the decision. Eventually the pair emerged to sign the paperwork; the Frenchman ordered his half packed up and prepared for the return to Cairo. As the boxes were assembled, realization slowly spread through the unbelieving German camp: they were to keep Her Majesty.

No one knows what sorcery Borchardt wove in that hut to prevent Nefertiti from disappearing into the cavernous cellars of the Cairo museums. Wild accusations of duplicity, corruption and incompetence continue to fly. Some say the inspector was shown only a hazy photograph of the bust, or that he was permitted to see her only in a dark box in the darkest corner of the hut, or that Borchardt lied and told him it was a worthless plaster cast—even that he was bought off with a forgery Borchardt had had made in the Cairo underworld.

But Borchardt's—and Nefertiti's—battle was not yet won. Fearing she might still be stolen from him at the heavily controlled Egyptian customs, Borchardt commissioned the German Foreign Service to help him get the bust back to the kaiser, "not only discreetly, but secretly." They succeeded—and the great queen arrived in Germany. When she was put on display in Berlin she caused an instant sensation across Europe—and outrage in Cairo. The Egyptian government immediately called for her return and stopped all further German excavations. To this day the Egyptians continue to demand that Berlin restore this *Mona Lisa* of the ancient world to her homeland.

Borchardt took his secrets with him to his grave. All we know for sure is that Nefertiti's striking beauty seduced him as completely as it once seduced the young pharaoh Akhenaten. Now she resides on Museum Island in Berlin, where more than half a million visitors per year come to pay tribute. Her name is once again spoken; her image can be seen all across Egypt, just as it could during the reign of the Aten. With her serene and confident smile she says simply: I am returned; I am immortal.

PART I

STAYING ALIVE

2

MAGIC BARRIERS

Civilization and the Elixir of Life

THE king of Qin was right to be paranoid: they really were out to get him. His predecessor, who may or may not have been his real father, had lasted only three years on the throne, and the king before that a mere twelve months. His court was built on a legacy of conspiracies, plots and coups. Even his own mother had conspired against him, planning to put her younger sons on the throne. The poor king of Qin could trust no one. But then, he did have a particular knack for making enemies.

This was China in the period known as the Warring States Era, a little over a thousand years after Nefertiti's fall. It was a blood-soaked time, as competing warlords allied, intrigued and fought for survival. In one action alone——the infamous Battle of Changping——the armies of the king of Qin's great-grandfather had killed some four hundred thousand men from the neighboring state of Zhao. Our hero was eagerly following this family tradition: his reputation was one of arrogance and cruelty, a barbarian in borrowed finery.

He, however, considered himself simply misunderstood. For in truth, the king of Qin was a man of vision——and his vision was of a unified China, its many peoples living in harmony with each other and with heaven. And this was why his black-clad armies had been steadily encroaching on his neighbors' territory, pushing eastward from his northwesterly mountain stronghold. His soldiers—who were promoted according to the number of severed heads they gathered—were ruthlessly effective. Soon Qin had swallowed two of the other warring states whole and was turning its attention to the small easterly state of Yan.

To the king's satisfaction, in 227 bce Yan sent two emissaries offering submission to the overlordship of Qin. As signs of their goodwill, they brought with them gifts: a detailed map of Yan's most fertile regions . . . and a severed head.

The head was that of a senior Qin general who had fallen out of favor with the king and fled to Yan. Most pleased at news of the traitor's decapitation, the king, who had already killed the general's entire extended family, prepared to receive his two visitors in grand style. What the king did not know was that the general had willingly given his head—assisting Yan's emissaries by cutting his own throat—in the hope that it would bring about the king of Qin's downfall.

The envoys were granted an audience. One climbed the steps to the throne and presented the gifts. The king put the casket with the head to one side and slowly unrolled the map. Just as he reached the end, he saw a glint of metal—but too late. Concealed in the map was a poisoned dagger. The envoy grabbed the weapon with one hand and the sleeve of the king's robes with the other, and stabbed.

But the king was too fast and had already reared backward, the sleeve of his robes tearing off. He reached for the mighty ceremonial sword that hung at his side, but it was too long to shift from its scabbard, and the assassin was coming at him again. The king fled behind a pillar while his courtiers, all ironically unarmed to prevent their making an assassination attempt, scattered in terror.

The guards who stood outside the throne room were allowed in only on the king's express order—and he was too busy fighting for his life.

As the assassin made another lunge, the king's old physician blocked the weapon with his medicine bag, giving his master time to swing the scabbard behind him and free the blade. Suddenly the assassin was confronted by an angry king with a very large sword. He threw the dagger at him but missed. The king hacked him down; it took eight blows until he was dead.

The next day, the king sent the armies of Qin to attack Yan. Within a year they had taken its capital, and within five years, they had wiped it from the map. One year after that, his armies had conquered the known world—"all under heaven." And the king declared himself the first emperor of China.

IT is little wonder that the First Emperor, as he is usually known today, was acutely aware of his own mortality. Many people would have liked to have thrust a dagger between his ribs, and a good few tried. In another legendary assassination attempt, a blind lute player lured the emperor into his proximity, then attacked him with his specially lead-weighted lute. Being blind, the lute player missed and was summarily executed. In another attempt, a hired strongman dropped a 220-pound metal cone from a mountainside onto the emperor's carriage as it was passing below, destroying it utterly. The emperor, however, was traveling in another carriage in anticipation of just such an ambush. Lest he be tempted to forget his mortal frailty for a moment, the world conspired to remind him.

The first part of the Mortality Paradox tells us that we must live in the consciousness of our own frailty; we are all aware that everything born must die. But for most of us the trappings of culture exist to keep this fact from our minds. Except when death suddenly claims a friend or relative, we are happy to be distracted from our inevitable end. Those who live in the shadow of the assassin, however—the pharaohs, dictators and kings—are continually reminded of the precariousness of their lot. It is a nice irony that this consciousness of vulnerability clings to those in positions of greatest power—as Shakespeare's Henry IV put it, uneasy lies the head that wears a crown.

It is therefore in these rulers that we see the full effects of this awareness of inexorable extinction. The First Emperor prohibited—on pain of capital punishment—all mention of death in his presence. Instead, his courtiers were to compose odes on the theme of immortality to be sung wherever he went. On once hearing that graffiti suggesting he would soon die had been found in a distant part of the empire, the emperor sent officials to find the culprit; when they failed, he had all the people living in the district put to death. He was not a man to take intimations of mortality lightly.

But rulers do not just have an exaggerated awareness of the Mortality Paradox; they also have the means to do something about it. By unifying China and declaring himself emperor, the king of Qin had become the most powerful man in the world. If anyone could summon the means to defy death, it was him.

BUILDING WALLS AND BURNING BOOKS

STAYING Alive is the first and most straightforward of the immortality narratives. It is a dream that can be found in the earliest recorded cultures and still thrives today. Indeed many believe that we are now on the verge of the scientific breakthroughs that will finally make this dream a reality. We will examine these claims in the next chapter, when we assess our prospects of following this path to the summit of the Mount of Immortals by banishing disease, aging and death for good. First, we will see how the promise that we can stay alive indefinitely is at the very foundation of civilization.

The psychologists behind Terror Management Theory, discussed in chapter 1, argued that if we confronted the inevitability of death without any protective narrative, we would become "twitching blobs of biological protoplasm completely perfused with anxiety." The First Emperor certainly appears to have been perfused with anxiety, but he was otherwise successfully able to direct his energies with enormous productivity—because of his belief in an immortality narrative. He believed that it was possible to become invulnerable to death and so stay alive forever. In his attempt to do so, he created China.

Staying alive indefinitely is a continuation of staying alive here and now; it is our day-to-day struggle for survival extended without end. It therefore begins with the basics, the things that all humans need to keep going: food and drink, shelter and defenses. As societies develop, they refine the provision of these essentials, through collaborative efforts, specialization of labor and passing on of skills. At its core, a civilization is a collection of life-extension technologies: agriculture to ensure food in steady supply, clothing to stave off cold, architecture to provide shelter and safety, better weapons for hunting and defense, medicine to combat injury and disease.

But whereas most people are satisfied with applying these technologies to themselves, their families or their villages, the First Emperor had a much grander vision. He ruled an empire, and his intention was to make it everlasting, with himself forever at its head. To achieve this, he began to separate his dominions from all that was unpredictable and dangerous—all that could bring death. And he went about this literally, in the form of a wall that would stretch for over six hundred miles along his northern border. People of many cultures had long been in the habit of building barricades around houses, villages and even cities—but never before an entire empire. This was the beginning of the Great Wall, built on the blood and sweat of conscripted labor and in whose construction hundreds of thousands of people are thought to have died.

Within these bounds he instituted unprecedented reforms to

improve the economy: weights, measures and currency were unified; the written language was consolidated; government and administration were rationalized. From the many warring states, a single nation was created—one that is still widely known as China after the First Emperor's home kingdom of Qin (pronounced "chin").

Then infamously, in 213 bce he declared that all books from schools of thought that opposed his new system were to be burned. Chronicles of past times were destroyed; history was to begin afresh. Only documents thought to assist in prolonging life were spared—those on agriculture, divination and medicine. The rest were banned and their possession deemed a capital offense.

The Argentinean writer Jorge Luis Borges recognized both the Great Wall and the book burning in the context of the emperor's quest to live forever: "The data suggest that the wall in space and the fire in time were magic barriers intended to halt the advance of death," he wrote. The First Emperor was attempting to establish a new order that could perpetuate life—his life—indefinitely. This is what the distinction between civilization and barbarism represents: in Borges's words, the magic barrier between life-sustaining order on one side and chaos, disease and disintegration on the other.

But as he grew into middle age, it became clear to the king-cum-emperor that high walls, productive fields and even new history books would not suffice to keep off aging and disease. So he surrounded himself with the very best doctors, sorcerers, alchemists and sages. Their mission was not only to cure the emperor of common ailments but to hold back the decline that comes with age—and so stave off its end result: death. This task did not strike anyone at the time as impossible; on the contrary, for a civilization that had brought peace to the land, could create architectural marvels and already had a rich tradition of medicine, it seemed only one more step down the same golden road.

So just as he believed in the possibility of orderly government and well-regulated commerce, the First Emperor believed too in the elixir of life. Legends abounded of those who had found such a thing and been transformed into immortal beings, immune to the ravages of time. It existed, he was sure, and it had to be found: it would be the crowning glory of the civilization he had created. And so he traveled the length and breadth of his empire, performing sacrifices at the sacred mountains, consulting the shamans and scholars he met on his way and avidly consuming the cocktail of potions, pills and putative elixirs that they prescribed. Then one day he met a wise man called Xu Fu, who claimed to know where the immortals kept their secrets.

Xu Fu lived on one of the islands off northeast China that had long been associated with the elixir. He told the emperor that there were three mountains in the Yellow Sea. Though they were not far from the coast, they were protected by magical winds that blew any boats off course that tried to reach their shores. But those lucky few sailors who managed to land had found a country where the animals and plants were all of the purest white and the palaces were made of silver and gold. Those who dwelled on these islands were the immortals, for they had discovered the true elixir of life.

In great excitement, the First Emperor commissioned Xu Fu to lead an expedition to find this elixir. The magician set off with three thousand virgin boys and girls—only the innocent, he claimed, would be granted the magic formula. They would sail to these islands and beg the immortals to share their secrets.

Several years later, the emperor's travels once again took him to the northerly coast of his vast dominions. There he sought out Xu Fu to hear his progress in securing the true elixir—much to Xu Fu's surprise. The magician had nothing to show for himself except an enormous bill of expenses and fewer virgins in his party. When he heard this, the emperor was furious; he had killed many a man for less.

The quick-thinking wizard reassured his ruler that he was more certain than ever that the elixir was to be found on the spirit islands. During their many difficult and dangerous attempts, he claimed, they had even come close to mastering the terrible winds that surrounded the isles. But whenever they were within reach of their pure white shores, huge sea beasts blocked the way and chased them back to the mainland. If only they had a squad of crossbowmen, they would surely be able to defeat these beasts and secure the elixir.

Desperation had made the First Emperor credulous: his desire to find the cure for mortality was such that he gave Xu Fu the troops he asked for. That night, inspired by Xu Fu's story, the emperor dreamed he was fighting a mighty sea spirit armed only with a crossbow. Convinced that this was an omen that an evil sea demon was blocking his route to immortality, he ordered the local sailors to catch the monster. Then he himself stood on a nearby beach and waited, crossbow in hand, for them to bring him the beast.

Xu Fu, meanwhile, set sail with his treasure, virgins and bowmen—and was never seen in China again.

WHEN Xu Fu left for the second time with his extraordinary entourage, he sailed off into the realm of legend. According to one tradition he landed in Japan and founded a new society, proclaiming himself king. Known there by the name of Jofuku, he has the status of a saint, even a god, in Japanese mythology. He is credited with bringing agriculture, medicine, metallurgy and silk to the previously primitive people of those islands, transforming their culture.

Remarkably, archaeological evidence suggests there was indeed a major and sudden leap forward in Japanese culture in the third century bce, exactly the time Xu Fu was said to have departed on his voyage: hunting and gathering were replaced by rice farming, stone tools by metal, furs by woven clothes, cave dwelling by freestanding houses. The town of Shingu on the southeastern coast of Japan's Honshu island still celebrates its claim to be the place where Xu Fu landed with his army of virgins and set about civilizing the land.

So as with many myths, it may well be that the tale of Xu Fu's disappearance from China and discovery of Japan contains more than a kernel of truth. But the legend does not end there: having founded his new society, Xu Fu is said to have continued the quest for the elixir of life, traveling to the hermits who lived on Mount Fuji. There he finally found the secret he had been looking for throughout his long voyage. The reclusive sages made him their chief, and there, according to legend, Xu Fu still lives his ethereal and saintly existence, high on the cloud-topped peak.

THE FOUNDING MYTHS OF THE CIVILIZED WORLD

THE bringer of civilization is the bringer of better, longer life. And his reward—and the promise he holds out for his followers—is life without end. This is the message in the Japanese version of the Xu Fu story, and it is exactly the model that the First Emperor was following when he created his own empire, for it is identical to the legend on which Chinese society was based. Indeed, it is a motif we see again and again in the founding myths of cultures around the world: civilization is built on the promise of immortality.

The battery of technologies that Xu Fu is credited with introducing to a still stone-age Japan genuinely would have contributed to increased lifespans for the island's inhabitants. That, indeed, is their point, which is why it is entirely natural that the legend then seamlessly goes on to tell how Xu Fu's genius culminated with his finding the elixir of life. The writer and futurist Arthur C. Clarke wrote that "any sufficiently advanced technology is indistinguishable from magic." For a person wondering at the magical-seeming achievements of civilization, from the plow to heart bypass surgery, an elixir of life can seem an entirely plausible next step. This is as true now as it was in ancient Japan.

Just as it was also already true in ancient China when the First Emperor came to power. The title he took for himself when he ceased to be the humble king of Qin was modeled on a legendary forebear, Huang Di, the Yellow Emperor. In taking on his new title, the king was attempting to take on some of this mythical figure's enormous prestige. And he was also hoping to copy his career: for Huang Di was also a civilization builder who was said to have triumphed over death. It was Huang Di who had introduced the essentials of early Chinese culture—he was to the people of China what Xu Fu was to the Japanese—and his reward was immortality. When the First Emperor attempted to start a new state, founding China anew, he was consciously emulating this predecessor and hoping for the same reward.

According to legend, Huang Di ruled for a hundred years from 2697 bce. His reign ushered in a period of peace, unity and progress in which, according to tradition, all the fundamentals of civilization were invented: plows, animal husbandry, music, the calendar, martial arts, medicine, silk weaving and even writing. Having thus brought order and prosperity to his kingdom, Huang Di was able to dedicate himself to his true goal: the pursuit of eternal life. According to legend, he enjoyed the assistance of a goddess, who sent three handmaidens to instruct him personally in the arts of longevity; one of them even taught him how to channel sexual energy in his quest, an association of sex, semen and lifespan that survived well into modern times. Huang Di's diligence and virtue were eventually rewarded with the elixir of life; on partaking of his discovery he was instantly transformed, becoming immune to aging and disease—whereupon a kindly dragon arrived to take him to live in the far-flung Kunlun Mountains of northern Tibet to dwell for eternity.

As in the Xu Fu story, the elixir features as the pinnacle of civilization's achievements. After a long life spent innovating, developing and ordering, the final defeat of death was achieved. This is the real promise of civilized life: why should we give up the freedom of the nomadic hunter in order to till the soil, obey the laws, and pay the taxes that society requires of us? Because if we do, we will live longer—and perhaps indefinitely longer. Even those who do not wear the crown—the simple citizens, the little guy—could hope to benefit from the order and safety of life within civilization's walls. What keeps us diligently working at the drudgery of desks and production lines is that we too believe in the magic barrier.

The founding myth of ancient Egyptian civilization provided exactly the same answer to the people of the Nile, albeit in a slightly more fanciful manner. It revolves around Osiris, the god of the next world mentioned in chapter 1. One of the oldest deities known to humanity, like Huang Di he was considered originally a real ruler who introduced both material and symbolic aspects of civilization—including agriculture and a code of law—to his people. When Osiris was murdered and dismembered by his jealous brother, his wife, Isis, managed to mummify and resurrect him. The first mummy, he then took his place as lord of the next world. Through emulating him in leading a good life and following the ancient rites, other Egyptians could hope to join him for eternity. Once again, the founder of civilization, with all its rules and rituals, is explicitly associated with the promise of immortality.

We will see that this pattern of the founding myths of civilization repeats itself in many other cultures—including the modern and scientific just as much as the ancient and mythical. They are therefore quite different from *creation* myths, which concern the origins of the world—and very often explain instead mortality and the fact of death. In such creation myths, humans are not made immortal—this would make an elixir and indeed civilization obsolete; in Chinese mythology, for example, humans are made rather unlovingly from sprinkled blobs of clay. A transformation is required to make such beings fit for eternity—the transformation achieved by Huang Di and sought by the First Emperor.

Such myths demonstrate the extent to which the very idea of civilization is bound up with our hopes of living forever. We are created mortal, but civilization can redeem us. Many in the developed world today might take its benefits for granted, but the people of these early civilizations knew very well how valuable was this magic barrier between them and barbarism. For these peoples, it was a simple continuum from the manifestly life-extending technologies of agriculture and medicine to an elixir of immortality.

The elixir was understood to be something real and material, yet its role was also symbolic. It represented the highest aim of civilization—the completion of the conquest of death that began when the first seeds were sown and bricks laid. Some of the most ancient documents in existence attest to its pursuit, and the search continues today.

THE ELIXIR

THE world's oldest surviving epic tale, that of the Sumerian king Gilgamesh, has the hero seek a plant of rejuvenation he calls "Old Man Grown Young." We saw too in chapter 1 that the ancient Egyptians believed in an elixir of youth—one recipe dates back to 1600 bce. In the thousands of years since these texts were written, there has never been a time when the quest for such a substance has not continued. Now, at the beginning of a new millennium, the elixir industry is as busy as ever: in the decade up to 2010 the respectable science magazine *New Scientist* reported on no fewer than twelve new "elixirs" that promised to halt aging.

Lest we are tempted to think that the ancient legends were all mythical mumbo-jumbo in contrast to today's laboratory-tested wonder drugs, it is worth noting that one of the twelve cures for aging among the dozen mooted by the *New Scientist* is extracted from the root of the astragalus, an herb of the legume family. This plant is one of the "fifty fundamental herbs" of traditional Chinese medicine and very likely was among the prescriptions given to the First Emperor. There is no stark dividing line between sorcery and science: our methods have become more rigorous, efficient and productive over the centuries, but we are otherwise still pursuing the Staying Alive Narrative just as humans always have, since history began.

"This quest was never merely the province of cranks or quacks," wrote the historian of medicine Gerald Gruman. On the contrary, entire religions, famous philosophers and important scientists have dedicated themselves to finding the key to unlimited lifespan. Every generation has its technology of hope: at the beginning of the last century, it was the Steinach operation, named after the Austrian physiologist Eugen Steinach. This operation promised, in the words of one of Steinach's colleagues, "indefinite prolongation of life," and Steinach himself was nominated six times for the Nobel Prize (though he never won it). Many leading scientists and intellectuals and thousands of others underwent the procedure in the hope of rejuvenation, including Sigmund Freud and W. B. Yeats. Today, however, this operation is known simply as a vasectomy, and its rejuvenating powers have proved to be all in the mind.

The hope, however, of defeating death remains. It is fueled by the tales of super-long-lived persons who populate almost every culture. Alongside Huang Di, the First Emperor could look to plenty of other long-lived sages for inspiration, such as Peng Zu, said to have lived to eight hundred. The Roman historian Pliny also recorded cases of eight-hundred-year-olds (though noted that at this age they were so tired of life they would jump into the sea). Those in the Jewish and Christian traditions could look to the Old Testament for even longer-lived forefathers—Noah was said to have made it to 950 and Methuselah to 969. Although in our own time, better record keeping and higher standards of evidence make such tales rare, nonetheless they still circulate, such as, for example, the popular story of very long-lived Georgians in the Caucasus Mountains—a myth that inspired millions to buy yogurt after a hugely successful set of 1970s television commercials assured viewers that this was their secret elixir.

• • •

As natural as it might be to dream of staying alive, the nature of our bodies is working against us. Unaided or unrefined, they will ail, age, die and rot. Something must be done; in order to withstand the trials of time we must somehow transcend the ordinary limits of biology. We must somehow be *transformed* to be made fit for eternity. The idea of an elixir of life embodies this desire for transformation: it is the legendary substance that, when consumed, will halt the usual processes of decline and decay, elevating the imbibers above the fate of mortals, making them what the Chinese call *hsien*—transcendent, celestial, immortal.

Although we might now imagine the elixir of life to be a bubbling potion or a neat pill, the First Emperor would have had no such preconceptions: he would have been equally unsurprised to discover it was a single plant, or a set of exercises, or some arcane combination of powders and spells. Tales of life-giving objects of one kind or another were remarkably diverse and widespread: magic cups, cauldrons, fountains, springs, rivers, trees, mushrooms, fruits, vegetables, horns, hairs, animals, spirits, witches, monsters, spells, curses, rings—all have at one time or another been ascribed death-defying properties.

When aspiring to live forever, it was therefore best to keep an open mind about the means. The elixir was whatever helped to stave off aging and death for a little bit longer, and its pursuit encompassed what we would now consider to be very disparate traditions, from medicine to magic and science to religion. But despite these many strands, the quest for the elixir has come to be known by one name: alchemy.

The oldest mention of alchemy in history is in the records of the first-century bce Chinese historian Sima Qian, who also recorded most of what we know of the First Emperor. He describes how the court alchemist sought to transform cinnabar, a bright red mercury ore, into gold—and that if this was then used for eating and drinking it would ensure "you will never die." Thus from its earliest days, alchemy has been associated with the pursuit of two goals united by the idea of transformation: the transformation of base metals into gold and of base humans into immortals.

Although now more associated with the first of these, most alchemists would have considered at the very least that they were inextricably linked, and very often, as in Sima Qian's description, that the production of gold was merely a means to the end of indefinite life. This was equally true of Western alchemy, as the Oxford scholar Roger Bacon, an early advocate of scientific experimentation, put it in 1267: "That medicine which would remove all impurities and corruptions of a baser metal so that it should become silver and purest gold, is thought by scientists to be able to remove the corruptions of the human body to such an extent that it would prolong life for many ages."

The name "alchemy" itself reflects the art's mysterious origins. We have inherited the word from the Arabic *al-kimia*, as it was the Islamic world that did most to keep its practice alive during the early Middle Ages. But the Arabs took the word from the Greek word *chemeia* when they occupied Alexandria in the seventh century. And *chemeia*, which is also the origin of the word "chemistry," meant "those who have knowledge of the Egyptian arts." As usual with the quest for immortality, all roads lead back to the Nile.

In China at the time of the First Emperor, alchemy was a vital part of the prevalent religious-philosophical system: Taoism. Its practitioners developed life-extension techniques that are now, over two thousand years later, continuing to prosper: meditation, breathing exercises, the gentle gymnastics of tai chi and qigong, and the consumption of tea, ginseng and many other herbs and minerals. One of its core texts, known as *The Yellow Emperor's Inner Canon*, remains the central source for Chinese traditional medicine.

Until well into the Renaissance in Europe, there was no

distinction between chemistry and alchemy or scientist and wizard. What we now see as the rigors of the scientific method, the antithesis of all superstition, emerged only slowly from the alchemical quest for immortality. Many of the great figures at the dawn of the scientific age, such as Robert Boyle and even Sir Isaac Newton, were steeped in alchemical teachings—Newton himself saw his contributions to alchemy as more important than his discoveries in physics.

As the successes of the new evidence-based methods rapidly grew, faith in ancient wisdom and the occult eventually declined. If nature's secrets were to be unlocked, it was through testing new theories against methodically acquired experimental data—not through deciphering old hieroglyphs. But although methods and cultures have evolved, the idea of an elixir survives, keeping countless researchers busy, and is being used to sell us everything from margarine to face cream.

But the modern, scientific versions of this quest, in abandoning their mythic past, have also lost a crucial aspect of the elixir legend: that it is not intended for everyone. Rather, like the Holy Grail, which was also credited with powers of healing and resurrection, it was available only to the wise and virtuous. Everlasting life had to be earned through hard work and good behavior: that was the deal, as it was these qualities that prevented civilization from collapsing into barbarism. In the very same legends that put immortality at the heart of advanced society, there are therefore also warnings that it is not for the foolish or fainthearted.

WHO WANTS TO LIVE FOREVER?

THE Japanese tale of Xu Fu does not end with his ascension to the peaks of Mount Fuji; as guardian of the elixir, he could hardly expect to enjoy his peace undisturbed.

One day, a rich, idle young man called Sentaro decided to seek the elixir for himself, so he sought out a shrine to Xu Fu and prayed.

At midnight on the seventh day, Xu Fu appeared to the young man. He judged him a selfish fool and so decided to set a test. He presented Sentaro with a tiny crane made of paper and announced that it would bring him to the land of perpetual life. When Sentaro mounted the crane it expanded to an enormous size, flapped its wings and lifted him into the air. They flew out to sea for thousands of miles before eventually landing on a remote island. The crane then folded itself up until it was once again tiny and flew into Sentaro's pocket.

To the young man's astonishment, the inhabitants of this island told him that no one ever died there and sickness was unknown. How blessed they must be, he thought. But to his greater surprise, the islanders begged Sentaro for some clue as to how they might find death. They were tired of their long, long lives. They had tried all the known poisons, but to no avail—the very deadliest of them had become wildly popular on the island simply because it turned their hair slightly gray and caused mild bellyache. Death, however, eluded them.

Sentaro could not begin to understand these people's unhappiness. He started a little business and settled down to live forever on this magical island. But after three hundred years, he too was growing weary of life's monotonies—the frustrations of work, the arguments with the neighbors. It all seemed dull and pointless. Finally, having once prayed to Xu Fu to make him immortal, he prayed to him once again to bring him back to the land of mortality. Instantly the paper crane flew out of his pocket and unfolded to its giant size. Sentaro climbed onto its back, and they took off.

But on the way a terrible storm struck: the paper crane crumpled and fell into the sea. As Sentaro struggled to stay afloat, he saw a great shark coming toward him, its terrible jaws open—he screamed for Xu Fu to return and rescue him.

And then he woke up—in the little shrine where Xu Fu had first appeared to him. The whole adventure had been a dream to expose to Sentaro his foolishness: he had wished for eternal life but found it dull, yet wishing to return to the land of the mortals, still he was afraid of death. Xu Fu told him to go back to his people and learn to live a virtuous and useful life.

XU FU's message is that immortality is not for the weak and foolish. Most of us want to live on, to be free from the fear of death, yet such a wish alone does not prepare us for its consequence: being alive *forever*. It is doubtful we can even grasp what that really means. Forever is not just a long time—it is much, much more than that. A million years is a long time. A million million even longer. But if I filled this book with a million zeroes, then wrote a million more books just like it, that number would not be halfway to the length of eternity. Or even a millionth of the way there. For no matter how long you lived, how many millions or trillions of years, that would still be a tiny fraction of the infinite life still ahead of you. An infinitely tiny fraction. That is an awesome prospect.

We are all, like the First Emperor or poor Sentaro, driven to seek immortality, to somehow overcome the frailties of the flesh and just live on. This drive arises from our capacious imaginations projecting the instinctive will to survive into the unending future. But are our unique imaginations powerful enough to tell us what forever would really be *like*? As no mind can encompass the infinite, every attempt falls short. In pursuing immortality, it is as if we were compelled to journey to a promised land to which we have never been and from which no one has ever returned.

The Xu Fu story does not say living forever is bad; the sorcerer himself enjoys the immortality of the sages and shows no sign of regretting his achievements. Rather, it problematizes immortality; it says eternal life may not be for everyone, and not all immortalities are equal. The sage finds enlightenment and eternal peace; the fool is driven to distraction by the cycles of his petty life. When seeking the elixir, we must think not only of what we want to *have* but also of who we want to become. As the novelist Susan Ertz put it,

"Millions long for immortality who don't know what to do with themselves on a rainy Sunday afternoon."

This is an important corrective after the unquestioned pursuit of the elixir that set Xu Fu on his quest. Many stories and legends assume that more life is an unadulterated good; yet in most cultures, as in most people, there is also a small voice saying: But what immortality? Where? With whom? When being offered the elixir, we ought to ask these questions *before* we take a sip.

It is clear what we could have to gain from taking such a potion: first and foremost, freedom from our mortal fear, the dread of death in all its guises. Seekers of the elixir believe that this removal of angst alone would be enough to transform the human condition, rewriting the play of our lives from tragedy to comedy. For them, living with the certainty of death is like trying to enjoy a car ride knowing the road heads straight off a cliff, whereas to drink the elixir would be to find the turning that leads instead to endless gently rolling hills.

If we value life, it is natural to think that more of it must be good. Life is the prerequisite for everything else; only with life can we have any kind of happiness. And as immortals, we would have all the time in the world—to develop new skills, to explore every culture and corner of the earth, to become everything we can be and have ever dreamed of being. We could find ourselves spiritually, develop new ways to worship our god or become like gods ourselves. We could explore new galaxies or simply enjoy the companionship of our loved ones without the anxiety that they might be taken from us or we from them.

In theory, at least. This all depends, however, on who we are and the circumstances of our exemption from death. Sentaro grew bored after a few hundred years, but his life was that of a staid shopkeeper on a small island. In our modern culture, convinced of inevitable progress, we expect that extended life will bring the thrill of the new; we expect to live through exciting and dramatic change. With the ever-accelerating pace of technological development, who knows where civilization will be in a hundred, a thousand or a hundred thousand years? And who would not want to be around to see it?

Sentaro was also far removed from his family and friends. To outlive everyone one knows and loves—even one's own children—could easily be seen as a curse. This is the situation of the heroine in Karel Čapek's 1922 play *The Makropulos Affair*: she alone has the secret to the elixir of life. Like Sentaro, after three hundred years, she has had enough: nothing interests her, she has lost all passion; the men she once loved have grown old and died, and their young replacements seem absurd; she is beyond even boredom. In visions like Čapek's, the immortal is an outcast, envied and loathed and misunderstood by mortals.

But we need not imagine such a lonely existence; many of those hoping or expecting to live forever are banking on there being enough elixir for everyone—or at least everyone they like. A society of immortals would of course need to be very different from this one: relationships—especially marriage—would have to adapt; study, work and retirement would take on different meanings. But humans are adaptable: we already take current life expectancy, historically exceptionally long, entirely for granted, and within a generation we have become so used to the revolutionary technologies of the Internet and mobile communications that we can barely imagine life without them. Those who seek a modern elixir—and we will see in the next chapter that they are many—are therefore optimistic that we will take immortality in our stride.

When we dream of the elixir, we are dreaming of the familiar fairy-tale ending: "and they lived happily ever after." But the Sentaro story tells us that we cannot take this for granted; there is much to be gained by death's infinite postponement, but we need to look carefully at the price tag. We are driven to pursue unending life but not to ask where this drive is taking us. In the chapters to come, we will examine these costs and benefits in the context of the four immortality narratives and ask whether they would deliver the kind of eternity that we might want.

THE QUICKSILVER SEA

THE First Emperor was untroubled by doubts about immortality's desirability: ruling all under heaven seemed an occupation with which he could happily continue for a long time to come. When we left him, he was standing on a beach, crossbow in hand, waiting to kill the sea demon that stood between him and eternal life. But all he managed was a few potshots at some sharks hauled in by his sailors—the demon, it seems, eluded him. As he returned inland toward his capital in 210 bce, aged only forty-nine, he fell seriously ill and died.

But while quaffing unsavory tonics and sending off expeditions in the search for the true elixir, the First Emperor had also been busy constructing a Plan B. For years, a staggering seven hundred thousand laborers, mostly convicts fallen foul of his draconian legal system, had been working on the complex that was to be the emperor's tomb. Contemporary sources say that a replica of the entire empire was created underground in bronze, with China's great rivers reproduced in flowing mercury that ran perpetually into a quicksilver sea, ever renewed by magical mechanisms. Above, the heavenly constellations were reproduced, representing the emperor's status as ruler of the cosmos. The whole was guarded by automatic crossbows that would shoot dead anyone who approached.

The First Emperor's successor—a younger son whose reign was to prove brief—ordered that all his father's concubines who had not borne a male child should be killed and buried with their master. They were soon followed by the craftsmen who had built the tomb's defenses and therefore knew the whereabouts of its treasures. "Those who died were extremely numerous," say the records. They were all buried with their king, then the tomb was sealed, covered with earth and planted with trees to disguise it as an ordinary hill.

The emperor was following tradition in building his own tomb, though the scale was unprecedented. It is difficult to know if he believed he could live on in his replica empire——his words and deeds show clearly that he first and foremost strove to avoid physical death, in keeping with Taoist practice. But for anyone following the Staying Alive path, a Plan B is only prudent, and as we saw with ancient Egypt, it is by no means unknown for cultures to have multiple coexisting immortality narratives. According to Chinese traditions, what happened to spirits of the deceased depended much on proper burial and ritual. The First Emperor, if he was to go into the void, had every intention of going in the style to which he was accustomed.

For centuries the extravagant accounts of this giant tomb were considered apocryphal. The mound beneath which the tomb was hidden was well-known to locals, but superstition and the legend of the deadly traps kept them away. Then in 1974 a few peasants began to dig a well about one mile from the mound itself. To their surprise, they broke through into an underground chamber. Staring back at them was a Qin soldier.

This soldier was made of terra-cotta, and so far a further eight thousand of his comrades have been found. All are life-sized, intricately molded and as individual as their models in life. The terra-cotta army, as it is now known, is one of the most sensational finds of the last century and is widely recognized as on a par with the wonders of the ancient world. But what is perhaps more wondrous is that this great army represents only a tiny fraction of the enormous burial complex——a fraction that contemporary records did not even deem fit to mention when compared to the other treasures.

The complex covers an extraordinary fourteen thousand acres and includes pits with terra-cotta administrators, acrobats, chariots and even a menagerie. The army guards the entrance to the tomb's outer wall, which is nearly four miles long. The ongoing excavations are likely to continue to uncover treasures for decades to come; the main tomb itself has not yet been opened for fear that its contents cannot yet be properly preserved—and perhaps for fear of the automatic crossbows. But preliminary scans of the soil have revealed unusually high levels of mercury, suggesting the ancient account of a quicksilver sea is true.

But how did the First Emperor, who had the finest physicians of the day at his disposal and who followed a strict regimen designed to promote longevity, come to die at such a relatively tender age? The court sorcerers and doctors blamed his punishing work schedule—even while traveling, he would not rest until he had worked through some sixty-six pounds of state documents per day. This control-freakery, they thought, was blocking the beneficial effects of their medicines.

With the benefit of hindsight, however, we can take a different view. From near-contemporary sources we know many of the ingredients that were used by the physicians and sorcerers to make their elixirs. For those who could afford them, the core ingredients were such incorruptible elements as gold, mercury and jade. Other common components included sulfur, lead and orpiment, a compound of arsenic with a striking golden color. The First Emperor's daily dose of vitamins and minerals would therefore have induced any of mercury, lead or arsenic poisoning, and possibly all three. Symptoms would have ranged from headaches, bellyaches, sweating and seizures to insomnia, irritability and paranoia—traits he seems to have demonstrated in abundance. It seems the only time his doctor successfully managed to extend the First Emperor's life was when he blocked the Yan assassin's knife with his medicine bag. Contrary to their promise, his potions had proven to be elixirs of mortality; it was the emperor's quest to stay alive forever that killed him.

• • •

IT was to be another two thousand years before the search for the elixir of life was put on a firm scientific footing: many believe that now, for the first time in history, we stand before the prospect of defeating aging and disease. Our chances of staying alive indefinitely have never looked better. The man responsible sacrificed his double Nobel Prize–crowned career in the process yet profoundly shaped our health-obsessed age. It is to him we now turn.

3

THE VITAMIN CURE

Science Versus the Reaper

THE doctors said she was dying. The cancer was eating Ava Helen from the inside out; the hemorrhages were becoming more frequent. But Linus Pauling believed he could save her. He was after all the inventor of molecular biology, the winner of two Nobel Prizes and author of the book *Cancer and Vitamin C,* arguing that megadoses of vitamins could slow, halt or even cure the Western world's most dreaded disease. And Ava Helen was his wife. Now she had been diagnosed with stomach cancer; fate was daring him to test his theories.

Ava Helen refused chemotherapy and, on her husband's advice, increased her intake of vitamin C. Pauling's views had been lambasted in both the scientific journals and the press. He had once been the star of American science, but as his claims for the benefits of vitamins grew ever wilder—that they could ward off cancer and help us live to 150—he found himself increasingly isolated. His scientific papers on the subject were rejected by the journals; his laboratory space was taken away; he was lampooned in the media as a senile old has-been.

Pauling added raw fruits and vegetables to his wife's diet; he made fresh juice for her from tomatoes and carrots. Her hemorrhages were growing worse and she needed ever more blood transfusions, but he was convinced that the enormous doses of vitamins would work a miracle. They had to: his personal and professional lives—his whole world—were at stake.

THROUGH his enormous energy and intellect, Linus Pauling helped shape the century that his life spanned. From quantum mechanics to nuclear disarmament, from genetics to dieting, he was at the forefront of the developments that define the world we now live in. Yet his life was one of constant controversy and ended with very public accusations that he was nothing but a crank.

As a young boy in Portland, Oregon, he watched his father at work in the back room of his drugstore. Herman Pauling made extravagant claims for his tinctures and ointments—that they could cure almost any ailment and even halt aging. But in 1910 medicine was far from an exact science, and the druggist was unable to heal himself: one day, Linus Pauling's father collapsed in his store in agony, and within hours was dead of a perforated stomach ulcer.

But Herman Pauling had lived long enough to pass on his faith in the healing power of science. By the time he was twenty-nine, Linus Pauling was a full professor at the newly established California Institute of Technology (Caltech). He had an extraordinary scientific instinct that he was able to apply to one field after another, each time bringing revolutionary insights that kept him at the forefront of research. This talent first brought him a Nobel Prize in Chemistry, before he turned his attention to the less orderly realm of biology. He passionately believed that the same underlying laws applied to both disciplines—and proved this when he discovered that the fatal sickle-cell disease was caused by a tiny abnormality in a single crucial protein, a discovery that helped launch the now-booming field of molecular biology.

Then in 1966, at the height of his reputation and when most people would have been looking forward to a comfortable retirement, Pauling experienced a revelation. While giving a speech in New York City, he mentioned that he hoped to live for another fifteen or twenty years in order to witness the further developments in science and society. A few days later, he received a letter from a fellow biochemist, Irwin Stone, who had been in the audience. Stone promised Pauling that he could indeed live this long—if he would take massive doses of vitamin C. Pauling consulted the scientific literature and quickly concluded that vitamins were the compounds he—and his father before him—had been seeking, the magic molecules that could help the body ward off disease and even halt aging: the real elixirs of life.

He launched a crusade advocating megadoses of vitamins that dominated the next twenty-five years of his long life and reshaped our understanding of medicine and nutrition. He saw it as the climax of his life's work—applying the discoveries of science to bring health and longevity to the human race. But the rest of the scientific establishment did not share his enthusiasm for what they saw as a hippie-ish fad. In 1976, the editor of a respected medical journal wrote that the public was losing faith in scientists because they could no longer be relied on to present the evidence plainly, and "the most tragic example" was Linus Pauling. So when his wife was diagnosed with terminal stomach cancer, it was his chance to prove his critics wrong.

ENGINEERING IMMORTALITY

THE first of our paths to immortality—Staying Alive—is as widely pursued now as in the day of the First Emperor: the prospect of the elixir of life continues to intoxicate us. Indeed, it is at the foundation of contemporary Western society, with its faith in science and progress. In this chapter we will ask whether this powerful immortality narrative can deliver on its extravagant promise.

We have seen that civilizations have always held out the hope of thwarting death. Indeed, the innovations that define advanced societies really do bring improvements to the human condition, which really do enable many people to live much longer, if not yet forever. But broadly speaking, early civilizations aspired mostly to maintain the gains they had made—to defend themselves against the onslaught of the barbarians and prevent a collapse into chaos. This is reflected in the form of their immortality narratives: they looked backward to their founding fathers, such as Xu Fu or Huang Di, the Yellow Emperor, who were thought already to have found the elixir. Their ambition was to maintain or rediscover past glories, not to move toward something new.

But the Enlightenment of eighteenth-century Europe, with its newfound faith in reason, changed all that. This was when the modern scientific method emerged, promising previously undreamed-of knowledge. Its followers began to hope that they might surpass the achievements of the past, that the real utopia lay not in a long-gone golden age, but in the future. The scientific version of the Staying Alive Narrative therefore looks forward for inspiration, believing it is there that the Mount of the Immortals is to be found—and that the route to it is called "progress."

The success of civilization comes from breaking down the problems that humans face and solving them one by one, using specialized tools and learned skills—so, for example, agriculture solves the problem of hunger, medicine of disease. We can see *progress* in these terms: as the breaking down of civilization's problems into ever-smaller parts so as to provide ever-better and more specialized solutions. Once we lived in huts, but now we (in the developed world) have houses with air-conditioning and central heating; separate rooms for washing and cooking; and correspondingly complex property laws, building regulations and the like. Whereas in simpler societies, the problem of shelter was solved with a basic roof over one's head, in developed countries houses address countless specific needs and eventualities.

In the past few centuries this form of progress has reached new heights through the effects of science and engineering. Science advances by systematically dividing and subdividing the world in the hope of achieving the fullest possible account of nature's laws; engineering, broadly conceived, puts this newly won knowledge to work in solving our problems. The result is new forms of travel and communication, new drugs and prostheses—all the luxuries and benefits of the modern world. Material progress consists of exactly these engineering solutions, ever more specialized, solving ever-more-specific problems.

But one way or another, lurking behind all the problems we attempt to solve—disease, hunger, cold—is death. The possibility that they may kill us is what makes all these problems so problematic. Progress, therefore, means that we are better at diagnosing death's many modes of attack and developing sophisticated defenses to fend them off. The most comprehensive of the surviving ancient Egyptian medical papyruses, for example, contains an impressive seven hundred afflictions and remedies, but the World Health Organization today recognizes over twelve thousand diseases—and counting. Ever-finer distinctions help us to make ever-finer treatments.

The scientific approach to the problem of death is therefore to break it down into increasingly specific elements and tackle them one by one. This piecemeal problem-solving strategy defines the modern narrative of how we might succeed in staying alive. I will call it the *Engineering Approach* to immortality. It provides both a story we can tell ourselves to assuage the fear of dying and also a genuine source of innovation that really is increasing life expectancy.

THE Engineering Approach begins with an insight neatly summarized by Linus Pauling—that "life is a relationship between molecules." Pauling firmly believed that humans and other living things are made of the very same stuff as stones, sea and sand, and obey the same laws. This is now the accepted view in the scientific com-

munity, but it was only a few centuries old—and still controversial—
when Pauling expressed it in 1962.

The great majority of traditional belief systems and religions have
assumed that life requires some kind of vital spark to ignite it. Usually this magic stuff is a gift from God or gods; it might be equated
with the soul or spirit, like the Egyptian *ka*; and it separates absolutely the living from the nonliving—men from mud, birds from
rocks. But the pioneering philosophers and early scientists of the
Enlightenment challenged this view, arguing that living things were
natural phenomena, obeying the same rules that governed all matter.
By careful study, they argued, we could understand those rules.

To the founders of the scientific method, from René Descartes to
Nicolas de Condorcet, man was a machine. Therefore just as a good
watchmaker could ensure that a watch continues to run perfectly,
so the physicians would one day be able to keep humans in perfect
working order indefinitely. By the time Condorcet was writing in the
late eighteenth century, this link between science, progress and indefinitely extended lifespans was well established. If we employ the
tools of reason, he argued, then "we are bound to believe that the average duration of human life will forever increase."

If Condorcet, who died in the upheavals of the French Revolution, had lived longer, he would have witnessed something like the
progress he described. Life expectancy in the France of his day, as
in most of the rest of the world, was around thirty years. These
people—your great-great-great-great-great-grandparents—lived
in a world of grand cities and gunpowder, yet still their life expectancy was little better than that of cavemen. By the end of the nineteenth century, life expectancy had made the significant leap to
over forty, as the scientific method began to be applied to questions
of public hygiene and the practice of medicine. But then came the
real breakthrough: if we fast-forward just a few more generations,
children born at the end of the twentieth century in France, as in
most of the Western world, could expect to live to over eighty

years of age. That is, in one century, life expectancy *doubled*. This is one of the most extraordinary achievements in history—without which there is a high chance that neither I nor you, dear reader, would be here.

A host of discoveries came together to make this leap possible. One of the most important was that deadly infectious diseases were caused by microbes—tiny organisms that could be spread through contaminated water or bodily fluids. This led to the development of the first vaccines, as well as huge programs of sanitation to clean up the stinking cities of the newly industrialized world. Combined with the discovery in 1928 of the antibiotic penicillin, this sent infectious diseases into rapid retreat: whooping cough, measles, diphtheria and scarlet fever, for example, together accounted for thirty-four thousand deaths in England in 1901, and exactly none in 2001.

Which means we who are alive today are very lucky indeed. Those born in a developed country in the second half of the twentieth century have a very high chance of living well into retirement age, a situation previously entirely unknown in the long history of our species. This was the first longevity revolution—the first real revolution in humanity's attempt to transcend its natural limits and stay alive for longer. After countless thousands of years of trying in vain, in the last few generations humanity has finally managed to make measurable progress toward taming mortality.

No wonder, then, that the narrative that promises we can engineer our way to immortality is so prevalent: it has already produced very real results. The belief that death is an insurmountable problem is paralyzing: if death is certain and could come at any time, then what is the point in struggle or innovation? The belief that death is a set of solvable problems, on the other hand, is a great motivator: it encourages exactly the kind of research and development that brings progress and drives our civilization forward. Now every week come new breakthroughs in our understanding of cancer, heart disease and countless other ailments. This progress is real and is lengthening lives, and every time we read about it, the promise that we can one day altogether eliminate aging and disease is renewed and made more credible. The Engineering Approach appears to be working.

BEYOND HUMAN

THE modern version of the Staying Alive Narrative is working because it focuses on the details, taking problems apart and analyzing them. But this approach has another benefit in addition to actually solving some of these problems: it also distracts us wonderfully from the first part of the Mortality Paradox—the awareness that we will die. By breaking mortality down into innumerable bite-sized problems, we all end up with a lengthy to-do list of tasks to keep ourselves busy, and so we go jogging, do yoga, watch our weight, read food labels for the right kind of fat, drink coffee or avoid coffee, drink wine or avoid wine, and so forth. Newspapers are daily full of such prescriptions. They give the illusion that mortality is something we can do something about—that it is in our hands.

The Austrian philosopher Ivan Illich called this the "medicalization of daily life." The sociologist Zygmunt Bauman has subsequently described it as the primary strategy of modern times for suppressing the fear of death. Following the Engineering Approach, we break death down into its individual manifestations—from salmonella to car accidents—and persuade ourselves that they are individually avoidable if we take the right precautions. "Keeping fit, taking exercise, 'balancing the diet,' eating fibres and not eating fat, avoiding smokers or fighting the pollution of drinking water are all feasible tasks," wrote Bauman, "tasks that can be performed and that redefine the unmanageable problem . . . of death . . . as a series of utterly manageable problems." And through pursuing those precautions, by avoiding smokers or keeping fit, we can avoid facing up to what Bauman calls "the great metaphysical futility of it all."

For the most part, the ultimate goal of this strategy goes unstated; the promise of immortality is implicit in the illusion of control and the downgrading of death, fed by the continual stream of new cures and other innovations announced by the press. Our ever-expanding death-avoidance to-do lists successfully distract us from dwelling too long on the real prospects of the Engineering Approach. Only occasionally does the underlying promise come to the surface when the media declares once again that science is on the verge of finding an elixir of life.

But all such movements need their prophets and rabble-rousers to restore flagging faith and inspire the masses, and this version of the Staying Alive Narrative has a growing band. The most ardent of them claim not only that "medical immortality"—that is, immunity to aging and disease—is theoretically possible, but that it is attainable by those alive today, such as you and me. One prominent group of such believers goes by the name of "transhumanists," so called because they believe we are entering a transitional stage in our development, evolving from mere humans into something far superior—posthuman immortals.

The transhumanists are an odd mix of engineers and ethicists, entrepreneurs and otherwise ordinary people. They are conducting experiments, writing pamphlets and lobbying governments in order to make their vision a reality. For the real advocates of the Engineering Approach believe that radically extending life is not only possible; it is our moral obligation.

They point out that around 150,000 people die worldwide each day—and of those, 100,000 die from age-related diseases. That is a body count the equivalent of the 2004 Indian Ocean tsunami or the 2010 Haiti earthquake every two days. When such tragedies occur the world pools its resources to ensure such massive loss of life never happens again. Yet we accept those hundreds of thousands who fade away because of aging. This must change, the transhumanists argue. If we believe it is right to save lives, then we should do everything we can to save the lives of those being taken by infirmity and old age.

The transhumanists are aware, however, that the task is immense. No one even yet fully understands what causes aging. Indeed, it seems most likely that it is not one single process but a whole host of malfunctions and accumulated damage. This complexity means we will not in the near future invent a simple pill that stops aging in its tracks. Yet many of those who dream of conquering death are already feeling the first effects of time's passing—they know that they cannot wait forever for the cure to come.

Fortunately, they believe they won't need to. This is the beauty of the Engineering Approach: we do not have to win the war against aging all at once. The twentieth century already saw an additional forty years added to life expectancy in developed countries; perhaps, they argue, the next wave of breakthroughs will give us another forty. And in this time, we could be developing the technology that could buy us yet more decades; and in those decades, we could then achieve the breakthroughs that would give us another century—and so on, until the discovery is made that can grant us medical immortality. This is what the optimistic transhumanists describe as achieving "longevity escape velocity," or living long enough to live forever.

THE transhumanists have various strategies for breaking down the problems of mortality into manageable chunks. One prominent advocate, the gerontologist Aubrey de Grey, has suggested that there are exactly seven problems that must—and can—be solved for humans to achieve indefinite youth. They are summed up in his "Strategies for Engineered Negligible Senescence" ("senescence" being a term for the deterioration caused by aging), a paradigmatic example of the Engineering Approach to immortality.

Like most people in his field, de Grey relies on technologies that are now in their infancy but whose promise seems immense—in particular genetics, stem cells and nanomedicine. Genetic engineering should enable us to rewrite our bodies' instruction books, ensuring many diseases that are now fatal never arise. Stem cells, which have the ability to develop into any kind of tissue, from skin to neurons, hold out the promise of growing healthy tissue to replace that which is diseased or worn out—even whole organs. And nanotechnology (engineering on the scale of atoms or molecules) gives hope of the ability to repair our bodies from the inside out using billions of tiny, targeted machines.

These technologies—especially genetics—are already starting to produce real results. As they steadily advance, they demonstrate the huge creative power of the Engineering Approach to the Staying Alive Narrative. Like a self-fulfilling prophecy, the belief that the problems of mortality can be solved is helping to make it so, as thousands of researchers dedicate themselves to finding new cures. As a consequence, life expectancy continues to rise, further confirming faith in the underlying narrative of progress.

The most ardent transhumanists paint a picture of a world in which humans are fully transformed, like the Taoist sages after drinking the elixir. They argue that there is no real difference between preventing disease and enhancing our bodies to become stronger and cleverer. The same technologies that might enable us to triumph over decay will be exactly those technologies that offer superhuman powers: the interventions that, for example, could save our fading senses could also give us X-ray vision; the therapies that allow us to cure muscle wasting would allow each of us to become as strong as Hercules.

Even more revolutionary will be our ability to remodel our gray matter. Researchers believe we will soon be able to control our attention, emotions and appetites. Some transhumanists argue that nanobots be used not only to heal disease and halt aging but to literally expand our minds: within a couple of decades we might be able to supplement the hundred trillion or so existing neuronal connections in our brains with vast armies of nanobots, exponentially increasing our powers to remember, reason and create. Such implants could also be wirelessly connected to each other and to the outside world: we would control computers simply by thinking about it—which, given that all complex objects will soon be computer driven, will mean everything from flicking TV channels to driving the car. We would be effectively telepathic—communicating with each other over vast distances by thought alone and surfing the Internet in our heads.

This, dream the futurists, is the point at which humans and their technology will become effectively indistinguishable. At this point our ability to take hold of our biological destinies will, they believe, take off exponentially. As we use enhancements to become cleverer, new discoveries will become easier and we will be able to design computers and machines that are ever more powerful, which in turn will lead to further enhancements. Before too long we will reach an apotheosis they call *superintelligence*—the point at which some person or device or combination thereof becomes so phenomenally clever that its understanding of the physical universe is effectively total. At that point, everything would become possible: it is the last thing we would ever need to invent; after that, it (or he or she) would be able to do all the work for us, not least answer the little question of how to live forever.

THE TITHONUS PROBLEM

SUCH fantasies of cyborgs and supermen are hugely prevalent in popular culture, reflecting the widespread narrative that we are on the verge of transcending these mortal frames. Of course, not everyone is comfortable with this idea, and it has many outright critics. Many of these subscribe to alternative immortality narratives that could be threatened by the Engineering Approach, such as religions that teach that bodily death is decreed by God for a reason. But when it comes to assessing the plausibility of the Staying

Alive Narrative, it is the attacks from within science itself that are the most damaging.

The transhumanists believe that science is on their side—that it has shown that we are reparable machines and already granted us decades of extra life. But science has other lessons to teach us, not all so optimistic. The progress of the Engineering Approach to immortality has not been as smooth as some would like to think—indeed, it keeps running into one very determined foe. His name is Tithonus.

According to ancient Greek legend, Tithonus was a youth so handsome that he was kidnapped by Eos, goddess of the dawn, to be her lover. Terrified at the prospect of his one day dying, Eos begged Zeus to make Tithonus immortal like her. This the god did; but Eos had forgotten to ask that her lover also be granted eternal youth. As he aged, Tithonus lost all his strength, becoming weak and demented. When all he could do was babble, Eos in desperation turned him into a cicada, forever alive but calling for death.

The Tithonus problem is that we are succeeding in postponing death but are still being struck down by debilitating illnesses. By allowing people to live into very old age, we are unleashing a host of diseases that were once rare, such as dementia, and by relying on technology that can postpone death, we are able to keep people alive who are suffering from terrible sickness and senescence. The result is not a utopia of strong-bodied demigods but a plethora of care homes and hospitals filled with the depressed, the diseased and the incontinent old.

THE transhumanists believe that if we have doubled life expectancy once we can do it again—and again. But this is not as straightforward as it sounds. The breakthroughs behind the first longevity revolution mostly prevent people from dying when young. Just a few generations ago, one in five babies died in their first twelve months—in western Europe that number is now fewer than one in two hundred. This has an enormous impact on life expectancy figures, which are based on calculations of average lifespans—dying young really brings down the averages. It is (relatively) easy to add eighty years to the life of a baby; once you have fended off infections, nature is on your side. A second longevity revolution, however, would require adding eighty years to the life of an eighty-year-old. And that comes at a much higher price.

In recent times, life expectancy in the developed world has continued to increase at the rate of about two years every decade—- i.e., those born in 1990 could expect to live two years longer than those born in 1980. But only *one-quarter* of this additional time is spent *healthy*. In other words, of those additional two years, eighteen months are spent in ill health or disability. We are living longer, but we can all expect to spend many of those extra years unable to wash or dress ourselves, unable to recognize loved ones, our senses fading and our strength gone.

The brutal fact is that increasing survival rates from the deadly infections of the past means keeping people alive long enough to develop the much more lingering diseases of modernity. In the developed world, one-third of people will develop cancer in their lifetimes, while a third can also expect to suffer from some form of serious dementia such as Alzheimer's before they die. This is not what the gung-ho transhumanists dream of when they claim science can defeat death—but it is the nightmare reality. It is not so much living longer as just dying slower.

Some researchers believe that these debilitating diseases like cancer and dementia cannot be separated from aging itself—that they are really just symptoms of the deep underlying degeneration. One demographer calculated that curing all forms of cancer would only add around three years to life expectancy, as by the time we reach the age at which cancer usually strikes, our bodies are already failing in myriad other ways. And even if we found cures for cancer, heart disease and stroke—currently the three biggest killers in developed countries—life expectancy would only push up to just over ninety years. We tell ourselves that we get these diseases only because we do not eat enough fruit and vegetables or do enough exercise. But the reality is we get them because, unlike most of our forebears, we live long enough to suffer the full effects of our bodily systems collapsing. Therefore even if we find cures for these killers, our bodies are already going into shutdown.

WHY is it that science seems unable to bring health and happiness to those whose lives it has rescued? The answer most likely has much to do with the nature of aging itself. Traits that manifest themselves in an organism only after it has reproduced will not be weeded out by natural selection. So, for example, a mouse might have genes that make it particularly strong and frisky but highly susceptible to colon cancer in old age. Being strong and frisky, the mouse is likely to successfully pass on its genes in abundance. If it makes it to old age, it will however die of colon cancer. But by the time it dies, there will already be lots of little mice running around carrying its genes. So, even though those genes carry a cancerous death sentence, they will not be weeded out by natural selection. This applies not only to genes that promote cancer but to any genes that have negative effects only after a creature has reproduced.

Therefore, over millions of years, a veritable genetic junkyard has arisen, full of unsorted, useless and downright dangerous genes that nature has allowed to stay in place. As we pass our reproductive age, these genes kick in, undermining our defenses and bringing disease—in other words, we begin to crumble. To try to keep us indefinitely healthy is like trying to hold together a statue that is turning to dust.

Making the repair job even more difficult is the fact that some genes seem to have a positive effect when an organism is young but a negative one when it is old. For example, our genes allow us to make essential vitamin D by exposing our skin to sunlight, but over time the exposure to the sun's UV rays causes skin cancer.

More worrying still, some researchers believe that we have genes that are essential for energy production and that at some point in our evolutionary history made us significantly stronger and faster—but only by producing toxins (free radicals) that slowly accumulate in the body until in old age they become fatal. If the accumulation of damage to our various bodily systems is an inevitable by-product of their normal functioning, then aging will have no easy fix—there will be no molecular switch that can be flicked without turning ourselves off altogether.

As our understanding of our bodies grows, the immortality engineers' to-do list is therefore getting longer rather than shorter. The prescription for their elixir of life becomes ever more complex: cut back on fats, except omega-3; on alcohol, but not red wine; on bad cholesterol, but not good. One leading transhumanist, the respected inventor Ray Kurzweil, describes taking 250 supplements per day, a diet that would have made even the elixir-obsessed First Emperor balk. All of this might succeed in distracting us from the brute fact of our mortality, but it will not cure us of it.

For centuries, many talented researchers have pursued the secret of aging—and believed they had found it. When Linus Pauling was a boy, sex hormones were considered the thing: one Paris-based medical professor had claimed to have turned back his biological clock by injecting himself with crushed dogs' testicles; another became rich and famous by grafting slices of monkeys' balls onto the private parts of aging millionaires with the claim it would make them twenty years younger. None of these methods have stood the test of time and rigorous trials. Although we might hope for the contrary, we should not be surprised if currently fashionable cure-alls prove to be just as disappointing.

Science holds out the abstract promise that we are molecular machines that can be kept on the road indefinitely. But this is as unlikely to become reality as all other utopian dreams. The odds are stacked high against unlimited lifespans. This is not to say that we should not keep trying: life is precious——we should support the research that buys us a few more years. But life lived in good health is even more precious, so we should be wary of technology that promises to make a Tithonus of each of us——prolonging death but at the price of misery and decrepitude——and we should support the policies and research that make our last years more likely to be happy ones.

There will surely be significant further advances in medicine, and perhaps one day we will all expect to live as long as the Frenchwoman Jeanne Calment, the longest-lived person whose dates have been verified. But even 122 years and 164 days is still a long way from infinity.

ATOMIC HAVOC

L INUS Pauling was a pioneer of the Engineering Approach to immortality, a bold thinker who saw the enormous potential of the new sciences to bring health and longevity to the human race. But Pauling's vision did not only cover the benefits of science——he was also very much aware of the terrible risks posed by the headlong advance in mankind's ability to reshape the world. Indeed, this is what motivated his first sortie out of the laboratory and into the world of politics——one that made him just as many enemies as his later conversion to vitamin C.

Having labored diligently for the war effort, Pauling was horrified on the morning of August 7, 1945, when he picked up the daily paper to read "Tokyo Admits Atomic Havoc" and the details of a single bomb that had obliterated an entire city. He was deeply affected by the scale of the destruction——not least because he had been asked to lead the chemistry division of the project to develop the atomic bomb, turning it down only because of his many other commitments. When he was invited the following year by Albert Einstein to form the Emergency Committee of Atomic Scientists, an elite group who would alert the public to the dangers of nuclear technology, he immediately accepted and began speaking out against atomic weapons testing.

But this was the era of Senator Joseph McCarthy, who was convinced that Soviet sympathizers were working to undermine America; as a prominent scientist speaking out against nuclear weapons, Pauling could not hope to escape his attentions. Just ten days before Pauling was due to attend a symposium in his honor organized by London's prestigious Royal Society in 1952, he was told by the U.S. State Department that he would not be granted a passport: the House Un-American Activities Committee had declared him a supporter of the "Communist peace effort."

It is a nice irony that if Pauling had been allowed to travel to England in 1952 he would most likely have visited the laboratory of a certain young researcher, Rosalind Franklin, at King's College, London, who was producing detailed images of DNA crystals. Pauling was at the time attempting to deduce the structure of DNA—a fact that, when they heard it, almost made the Cambridge University team including Francis Crick and James Watson give up immediately. But, unlike Pauling, Crick and Watson had seen Franklin's crucial images and so were able to work out the now-famous double helix structure—a huge leap forward and triumph of the Engineering Approach. It is likely that if Pauling had been allowed to travel, he would have beaten them to it: by denying him a passport, the U.S. government ironically prevented one of the great achievements of twentieth-century science from being claimed by America.

In November 1954, it was announced that Linus Pauling was to receive the Nobel Prize in Chemistry. Previously, only Nazi Germany had ever prevented Nobel Prize winners from traveling to accept their prizes, and two weeks before the award ceremony the U.S. government finally relented and gave Pauling an unrestricted passport. He continued to campaign against the dark sides of our new technologies and was a crucial member of the campaign that resulted in the banning of atmospheric testing of nuclear weapons, a milestone in the efforts to defuse the Cold War. On the day the agreement went into force in 1963, the Nobel Prize Committee announced Pauling's second award—the Peace Prize, making him the only person to have received awards in two entirely unrelated fields and the only person to have won two Nobel Prizes entirely alone.

By this time the political climate had already changed. In April 1962, Pauling and his wife, Ava Helen, along with various other great minds, had been invited into that most glamorous center of power—the Kennedy White House—to discuss the pressing issues of the day over dinner with the president. But Pauling was by then a veteran campaigner: to the delight of journalists, he spent the day of the dinner picketing the presidential residence in the anti-atomic cause, before going to his hotel to change into evening attire and return as the president's guest. His hosts, however, took Pauling's protest in good grace: Jackie Kennedy, the First Lady, told him that their daughter, Caroline, had seen him outside protesting and asked, "Mommy, what's Daddy done wrong now?"

As Pauling continued to campaign he became increasingly disturbed by the conservatism of the scientific and political elite. Few of his fellows were willing to stand up as he had done to warn of the risks posed by the huge power of the new sciences and to advocate restrictions in the name of peace and justice. Pauling passionately believed both in the power of science and technology to solve the problems of the human condition and in their power to destroy us. In the two decades since his death, the rate of advance in scientific knowledge has accelerated even beyond Pauling's prodigious imagination. He warned that our obsessive quest for greater power over ourselves and our environment could bring about the end of both; it is a warning more relevant now than ever.

DOOMSDAY

THE Engineering Approach is about breaking down problems into solvable chunks. But despite the results it has produced, this strategy is far from perfect. One risk is that the immortality engineers, in focusing on one narrow problem, fail to notice the new problems that their solution is causing. Or they might simply become blinkered in their obsessive quest and fail to notice the oncoming bus. In making a final assessment of whether this route to immortality has a chance of reaching its destination, we must join the futurists in peering into their crystal ball.

THE tricky thing about staying alive forever is that it just takes one little fatal accident and it is all over. Surviving is not something you do once then take it easy; you have to do it every day, every hour, every minute. You might feel you are just hitting your stride after your first few million years, but still anything from a faulty brake cable to a herd of angry elephants could end it all in a second. When it comes to ways to die, your imagination is the limit—as the infamous tramway authority sign reminds us: "Touching wires causes instant death—$200 fine."

One longevity researcher, Professor Steven Austad of the University of Texas, calculated in 2010 that the average lifespan of a medical immortal would be 5,775 years. In other words, if you were immune to aging and disease, this is roughly how long you could expect to live before you accidentally drove off a cliff or fell down a well. This figure is based on extrapolating the survival rates for nine-year-olds in the United States—chosen because they are least likely to die of illness, as they have survived the diseases of early childhood but not yet fallen prey to those that come with aging. The figure is very approximate—not least because nine-year-olds do not tend to drive or own guns, which are two of the major sources of accidental death. It is also only an average: you might live for over ten thousand years—equivalent to being around from the beginning of settled civilization, through the rise and fall of ancient Egypt, until now—or you might die in a plane crash at the age of twenty.

In societies that are either less accident-prone or better at repairing people afterward, the average lifespan would be higher—for example, it would be almost twice as high in safety-conscious Japan as in the United States. But in most of the rest of the world—especially those countries that suffer from war and deprivation—it would be much lower. Even in the United States, living to such a ripe old age would require something like the normality of contemporary American life to continue for thousands of years—and that in itself is extremely unlikely. The greater part of human history has not been spent in peace and prosperity with a stable climate—and the future does not promise to be any different. On the contrary, there are many threats to our existence—individually and as a species—that are likely to ambush us on the long road to eternity.

INDEED these threats are on the increase: as Linus Pauling was starkly aware, as our knowledge of the world has grown, so has our capacity to destroy it. Within living memory we have come terrifyingly close to the destruction of nuclear Armageddon. That we escaped is in part due to the tireless campaigning of men and women like Pauling who sought to ban irresponsible testing and stop the arms race. The Cold War is now long over, but it is more than likely that international alliances and enmities will shift again, one day returning us to a nuclear showdown. The weapons, after all, still exist—and even if they were disarmed, the technology would not be uninvented; for as long as civilization lasts, we must now live with the capacity for self-annihiliation.

We also today live in the shadow of terrorism. Despite all the media and political attention, your chance of being killed by a terrorist—especially in the developed world—is currently minuscule. But we can be fairly sure that there are terrorist groups who would like to change that. The world's security forces spend their time worrying that some hugely potent weapon—such as nuclear material or a lethal superbug—will fall into the hands of those described by former U.S. president George W. Bush as "evildoers," whether they be politically motivated or intent only on hastening the apocalypse.

The risks of war, terrorism and unrest are likely to be exacerbated by one potential consequence of the quest for immortality on earth: overpopulation. There are currently around seven billion human beings living on this planet—an entirely unprecedented number, more than four times as many as a century ago and thirty times as many as when the Roman Empire reached its height. Population levels are a function not only of how quickly people are being born but also of how quickly they are dying. This massive increase in global population in recent times stems from the first longevity revolution, which we encountered earlier: that is, the fact that we can now keep more people alive for longer.

Current projections for global population—for example, that there is likely to be well over ten billion of us by the end of the century—are based on our continuing to die at roughly the same rate we do now. If we attained medical immortality yet continued to have children, the population would therefore explode once again—to potentially catastrophic levels. In many parts of the world, crucial resources such as fresh water and reliable food supplies are already scarce, and we are already destroying our environment through deforestation, desertification and pollution. On top of this, more people demanding energy means more burning of fossil fuels, and the resulting global warming threatens to bring further extreme weather, rising sea levels and many localized effects that will impact ecosystems and agriculture.

There is a real risk that an ever-expanding population of medical immortals would push the biosphere over the edge, causing a collapse in its ability to sustain life as we know it. The pursuit of immortality on earth, in the face of these unsolved problems and at a time when millions do not even have clean drinking water, can seem like just another expression of the selfish ideology of exploitation that teaches that the whole world exists only to shore up the survival of a few privileged individuals.

When looking at the Tithonus problem, we noted that some crucial systems of the human body appear to have both good and bad effects. One example is the natural limits of cell division: our cells can ordinarily only divide a certain number of times before they stop—a phenomenon believed to contribute to aging. So it might be thought that we should prevent this control on cell division. But this sometimes already happens of its own accord: it is called cancer. Tumors are cells dividing uncontrollably, effectively making their own bid for immortality at the expense of the organism as a whole. When we humans make our bid for immortality, the effect on the planet could be just like the effect of cancer on us: the whole is put out of balance, dominated and consumed until it can no longer sustain life at all.

The transhumanists, of course, have answers to these arguments. They point to the fact that richer, longer-lived people tend to have significantly fewer children—perhaps medical immortals would choose not to reproduce at all. Or perhaps they could be made to face the choice: immortality or kids, but not both. They also like to point out that, despite global warming, it is by no means clear that we are near the limit of the human population that the earth can sustain: continually developing technology has so far allowed us to grow ever more food. Although there are billions more people alive now than ever before, most live in unprecedented comfort and security. These techno-optimists believe that we will similarly find solutions to any unavoidable problems of climate change. Plus, add some of the dreamers, we could always colonize space.

Some of the more honest transhumanists offer a different rebuttal to the overpopulation question: it is unlikely to become a problem exactly because it is the project of the privileged few. The medicines required to conquer aging and disease will be too expensive for the vast majority of people, so the new immortals will be a small elite——too few to impact global population levels. But this of course raises another question: that of social justice. Death is the great leveler, to which even the rich must currently succumb——in the *danse macabre* of medieval allegory, the dancing skeleton took both king and pauper by the hand. But if immortality can be bought we would have the ultimate apartheid: between those fated to die and those blessed with everlasting life. On top of the intrinsic injustice of this situation, the undying elite might also be able to use their longevity to accumulate vast wealth and power, creating an eternal hierarchy of immortal rulers and their perishable subjects.

The transhumanists have an answer for this too: that money can already buy you a longer life——wealth is today closely correlated with longevity——yet we all seem to accept this. Nor do we ordinarily think that the fact that only a few can afford a life-saving treatment is a reason to ban that treatment altogether. Anyway, given that any future elixir of life is likely in fact to be a host of different interventions against the different diseases and symptoms of aging, the reality of who can access which treatments will be much less black and white than the skeptics suggest——most people will be able to afford some of the new medications, even if only a rich few can afford them all.

Yet even if we see off the problems of overpopulation and a bloody war between the immortality haves and have-nots, there are countless catastrophes that could strike on our way to eternity. Specialists in "existential risks"——risks to the very existence of the human race——point to a terrifying Pandora's box of fatal scenarios that ought to be keeping us awake at night. Many of these, as Linus Pauling foresaw, are by-products of the very technologies that are supposed to save us.

We earlier saw that genetic engineering would be essential to attaining medical immortality. But our ability to manipulate life with such precision would not only allow for the creation of strong and healthy babies—it could also be used to create monsters. These are unlikely to be the man-eating beasts of film and legend: far more deadly would be viruses and bacteria engineered to be more virulent, more contagious and impervious to existing vaccines. Such pathogens could arise unintentionally—or equally be developed as weapons of terror or war.

Nanotechnology looks to be even more dangerous. Much of its promise rests on the capacity for nanobots to reproduce—so for example repopulating your bloodstream with oxygen-carrying medi-bots. But exactly this ability could prove our undoing: a slight change in design—intentional or otherwise—could unleash a sea of minuscule replicators that could consume all organic matter, sweeping through cities and fields alike, replacing plants and animals with a gray goo of microscopic robots. Whatever precautions we take, human history to date suggests that any new technology will be exploited for military use—so rapidly reproducing, flesh-eating mini-bots are as likely to be part of the future as their lifesaving cousins.

But the ultimate risk is what the transhumanists see as their ultimate salvation: the godlike "superintelligence," an enhanced person or computer that is so clever it can solve all our problems, including how to live forever. It does not take the most vivid imagination to see how the creation of an all-powerful being could go badly wrong. The potential hazards are the stuff of all our favorite sci-fi films, from *2001: A Space Odyssey* to *The Terminator*. Whether due to a programming glitch or because he/she/it develops mysterious intentions of its own, it seems entirely possible that the superintelligence might decide to do away with us. If Linus Pauling were alive today, it is likely that he would be very worried indeed.

THEIR EXITS AND THEIR ENTRANCES

ALTHOUGH Pauling dedicated himself entirely to applying his new theories to cure his ailing wife, Ava Helen's condition worsened. The hemorrhages grew more painful and debilitating, until finally she could take no more. She ordered the transfusions to stop. Pauling had failed; all he could do was hold her hand as she slipped away. On December 7, 1981, she died, and one of the greatest scientific minds of the twentieth century found himself alone and in disgrace.

Linus Pauling was a titan of twentieth-century science—a hugely productive innovator, a scientific Midas who could bring new insights to any field he touched. But he had dedicated the last quarter of a century of his long life to promoting his panacea—vitamins. He ran up against the views of the medical establishment and, say many, against the facts. After a career at the forefront of science, he increasingly indulged in savage attacks on the studies that proved him wrong—and on the scientists behind them. In 1990, when he was eighty-nine years old, the leading scientific journal *Nature* described him as "viewed as a lonely crank" whose fall from grace was "as great as any in classical tragedy."

Linus Pauling contributed more than anyone else to the science behind anti-aging and to the belief that science, diet and lifestyle can together deliver extreme longevity, but he also stands as a warning to would-be immortals, a foretoken of a society dominated by ancient yet ageless grandees whose ideas long ago became fixed. His career shows that there is a time to stand in the limelight but also a time to leave the stage.

Of course, it was not simply any idea that preoccupied Pauling's final years; it was the belief in something close to an elixir of life. He thought he had found the solution to all mankind's ailments and that science would soon bear him out. But history is full of people who have believed just that, and the one thing they have in common is that they all died sooner or later—and usually their theories with them. Pauling had an immense depth of scientific knowledge, yet as he began to feel the effects of his own mortality, he allowed himself to believe in the impossible: a universal cure for humanity's many flaws. This should make us skeptical of those today who claim that antioxidants, green tea or growth hormones will deliver eternal youth.

THE first of our four fundamental forms of immortality narrative—Staying Alive—looks like it is here to stay. It is part of the promise on which civilization is founded, and it is integral to the idea of progress that is at the heart of the modern Western worldview. The hope of staying alive that little bit longer—and longer, and longer—is what has driven the development of almost all the material aspects of human society, and today it motivates the massive industries of science and medicine. These fields are delivering advances that really do make our lives longer and better.

But the science that promises to take us still farther also has other lessons: that the processes of aging and decay are deeply embedded in our bodies, that the very technologies that could help us could also prove our destruction and that the world we live in will not tolerate human life forever. We might stay alive a little longer than our parents or grandparents; we might one day defeat cancer or grow replacement organs. But none of us will succeed in staying alive forever—neither our fleshy frames nor the planet on which we live will allow it. This narrative is both seductive and productive, but it will not deliver on its promise.

When we started on this path, we said that staying alive in these bodies on this earth would be the most straightforward route to immortality. But we have now seen that the Reaper will catch us, no matter how much we try to jog away. We are, of course, not the first people in history to realize this—though we might be the first to really understand why it is so. Like the First Emperor, the wise or the pessimistic have therefore always sought a backup plan.

Okay, we must die, they reasoned, but surely we can rise again. First time around this flesh and blood might fail, but there could be a second run—and perhaps then we will be transformed into something eternal. For thousands of years, this view has given hope to countless people. And now it is inspiring a new generation of scientists who refuse to accept that death itself or even the end of the universe is an obstacle on the road to immortality.

This is our second strategy—Resurrection—and its popularity is owed largely to a man who almost single-handedly transformed this belief from that of a small Jewish sect into orthodoxy for the mightiest religion the world had ever seen.

PART II

RESURRECTION

4

ST. PAUL AND THE CANNIBALS

The Rise of Resurrection

S AUL watched with satisfaction as the heretic was dragged from the courthouse and took his place in the small procession that led the condemned out of Jerusalem's gates. Once beyond the city walls, he took the robes of the executioners as they stripped for the hard, hot work of stoning the blasphemer to death. All was going according to his plan. It was a year since the crucifixion of the rebellious Nazarene, but his followers continued to cause trouble; soon there would be one less.

Saul was a passionate believer in the one God and the law that he had given to Moses. "I advanced in Judaism beyond many among my people of the same age, for I was far more zealous for the traditions of my ancestors," he later boasted (Galatians 1:14). The execution he oversaw—of Stephen, the first recorded Christian martyr—was the signal for the cleansing of the holy city to begin. "That day a severe persecution began against the church in Jerusalem," the Bible tells us. ". . . Saul ravaged the church by entering house after house; dragging off both men and women, he committed them to prison" (Acts 8:1–3).

Saul was a Pharisee, meaning he belonged to a particular brand of Judaism that was devout but populist, in contrast to the austere religion of the Jewish aristocracy. Although he was born in Tarsus, a cosmopolitan coastal city on the southern edge of what is now Turkey, he was educated in Jerusalem by the best teachers of his time and was a citizen of the Roman Empire. This vigorous, clever and committed young man was destined for the highest ranks of the Jewish Temple hierarchy.

Such was his success in persecuting the latest charismatic cult to threaten Judaism that its few remaining adherents scattered throughout the surrounding lands. Determined to prove his devotion to the faith, Saul went to the high priest, "breathing threats and murder against the disciples of the Lord" (Acts 9:1), and asked permission to hunt down those blasphemers who had escaped to Damascus. Permission was granted, but famously, Saul was to arrive in Damascus quite a different man.

SAUL'S victims were the followers of Jesus, who had attracted an apocalyptic personality cult of a kind that was common among the Jewish subjects of the mighty Roman Empire. The Bible describes a few of these would-be saviors—such as Theudas, who "claimed to be somebody" and gathered some four hundred followers before he was slain, and Judas of Galilee, who "drew away many people after him" before he too perished (Acts 5:36–37). Evidently many Jews fervently hoped for the coming of the Messiah—the "anointed one" who would restore the line of King David to the throne and bring peace and justice to the land in accordance with the prophecies. And this is exactly how Jesus's followers regarded him: as a Jewish Messiah come to save the Jewish people in fulfillment of a Jewish prophecy. But many fellow Jews saw the Christians only as schismatics, dividing Judaism at a time when its very existence was already threatened.

On his way to Damascus to persecute these heretics, Saul was struck to the ground by a heavenly light. According to the book of Acts (chapter 9), a voice boomed: "Saul, Saul, why do you persecute me?" "Who are you?" Saul asked, to which came the reply, "I am Jesus, whom you are persecuting. But get up and enter the city, and you will be told what you are to do." Saul rose but found himself blinded and had to be led by the hand into Damascus. There he waited without eating or drinking until, after three days, he was visited by one of Jesus's followers. As soon as the disciple laid his hands on Saul, "the scales fell from his eyes," his sight was restored, he was filled with the Holy Spirit and was baptized.

Saul was certain he knew what this meant: he had become a witness to the first resurrection. Just as his disciples claimed, Jesus had truly risen from the grave and had now spoken to Saul directly. The significance of this was immense; the act of resurrection was the most awe-inspiring miracle of them all—the conquest of death itself. Saul was convinced that through this single act God had revealed his plan for all mankind: to grant them immortality. And now by appearing to Saul, Jesus had also chosen the medium by which this good news was to be spread.

Saul wasted no time before dedicating the same enormous energy and zeal with which he had once persecuted the new faith to furthering it: he went straight to the synagogues to proclaim that Jesus was risen from the grave. Those who heard him were amazed—"Is not this the man who made havoc in Jerusalem among those who invoked this name?" they asked. "And has he not come here for the purpose of bringing them bound before the chief priests?" (Acts 9:21).

As he continued in his new mission, Saul began using the Greco-Roman version of his name: Paul. Before long, his previous comrades, those pious Jews who remained skeptical of this latest Messiah, realized he had indeed abandoned them for the other side.

They conspired to kill him, as Paul had once conspired in the killing of Stephen. Believing he was planning to flee Damascus, his enemies lay in wait at the city's gates. But Paul had gotten wind of the ambush, and his disciples "took him by night and let him down through an opening in the wall, lowering him in a basket" (Acts 9:25). It was only the first of many times that an angry mob—whether of kinsmen or strangers, Jews or pagans—would attempt to stop Paul from spreading his newfound belief in the resurrection—and launching one of the world's great religions in the process.

DYING TO RISE AGAIN

IN the previous two chapters, we looked at the first fundamental form of immortality narrative—the promise that we can stay alive on this planet forever. And we saw that, even with the longer lives promised us by the scientific revolution, eternity on earth remains an unlikely prospect. Death is meticulous in collecting every living thing sooner or later.

But the earth is not a barren wasteland: all things die, yet the world is virile, green and blooming. Spring's bluebells wither all too soon, but the next year they rise from the ground again. In nature, dying is not the end but only part of a greater cycle—a cycle of life, death and rebirth. This observation has given hope to many who are otherwise resigned to the infirmities of the flesh. They recognize that we, like other living things, flourish only briefly before fading away. But they hope that, as with the bluebells, this fading is merely a prelude to our rising again. This is the hope of resurrection—the second basic form of immortality narrative.

We saw in chapter 1 that our culture and beliefs are attempts to satisfy the will to immortality and reconcile the tension created by the Mortality Paradox—that on the one hand it seems clear we are perishable and will die like all creatures, yet on the other hand this prospect seems unimaginable or even impossible. The Staying

Alive Narrative simply denied the necessity of the first part of the paradox, promising that we can avoid physical death. But clearly there are many who find this claim implausible—it is, after all, contrary to the evidence we see around us. The Resurrection Narrative, in contrast, takes death on the chin and admits that we will go the way of all things; it accepts the truth of the objective view that we flawed, fleshy beings must die. But, say the resurrectionists, that is just the beginning, and one day, with the selfsame bodies, we can rise to live again.

Until now, we have focused on how the will to immortality has driven progress in the material aspects of civilization, as it is this that enhances our prospects of Staying Alive. The idea of resurrection, however, straddles both the material and the symbolic aspects of human culture: it is deeply embedded in many ancient religious traditions, but it is also a motivating force in a hugely influential narrative about the power of science and material progress. In this chapter we will begin at the beginning: with resurrection's symbolic importance—including how it has inspired the most powerful religious tradition in history—before going on to look at whether the resurrection story is a plausible one.

It might seem obvious that religion has, at least in part, arisen to satisfy our will to immortality. Certainly, almost all religions have a clear account of how it is that we in fact survive bodily death ("If you believe in no future life, I would not give a mushroom for your God!" as Martin Luther said). And equally, it might seem obvious that religion and its siblings, ritual and myth, have contributed hugely to the development of civilization. But the story of just how religions function as immortality narratives—and in particular as Resurrection Narratives—is much subtler and more interesting than these first appearances suggest.

The practice of ritual and religion in the broadest sense is as old as our species—which is to say, at least 150,000 years old. Evidence for this is centerd, unsurprisingly, on what people did with their dead—burying them in particular ways with particular tools or weapons as if they might have a life beyond the grave. Burial sites in Qafzeh, Israel, for example, that are at least 100,000 years old have been found containing shells and deer antlers, and burials from between 100,000 and 200,000 years ago involving the use of the pigment red ocher are widespread in Africa. These finds led the historian of religion Karen Armstrong to conclude that belief systems are "nearly always rooted in the experience of death and the fear of extinction." By the time recognizable civilizations emerged, with writing, agriculture and so on, the afterlife had already long been a fundamental part of the human experience.

Rituals are found in all cultures. What makes them distinct from other activities is both that they are highly rule-bound—they must be performed by certain people, at certain times, in certain places, in certain ways—and that their effects are indirect, unseen or symbolic. A man slaughtering and roasting a goat is not performing a ritual; he is just preparing dinner. But if that man first takes that goat to a temple, sings incantations to the animal's spirit, cuts off the goat's head in a single blow, then leaves certain choice cuts of meat for "the gods," he is doing far more than what is required just to fill his belly. This "more" is ritual.

Rituals are the physical manifestation of a particular religion or mythology; they are what make a set of beliefs practical and real. In a worldview in which spirits or gods influence every aspect of daily life, rituals to appease, befriend, charm or fool them are common. Not all rituals are in themselves an expression of a yearning for eternity—some are simply about getting on with the business of life, such as eating a goat without incurring the wrath of the goat god. But there are deep-lying aspects of many rituals and religions that should lead us to think that they are very much driven by the will to immortality.

There are many different approaches to understanding ritualistic behavior, but there are two important themes that stand out. The first is that ritual is very often about control. Sigmund Freud first pointed out the similarities between the obsessive behaviors involved in religious ceremonies and the behavior of neurotic obsessives. In both cases, actions are performed that make little practical sense but that bolster a belief that everything will be all right—that some danger or bad luck will be avoided and purity or peace achieved. Subsequent research has borne out this link, suggesting that ritual behavior, like that of obsessive-compulsives, is often a response to the same overactive scenario-generating systems in our brains that cause us to imagine danger—and death—around every corner.

Which links into the second important aspect of ritual and religion. Freud wrote that "the gods . . . must exorcise the terrors of nature, they must reconcile men to the cruelty of Fate, particularly as it is shown in death." In part, this is achieved by ritual's generation of the sense of control. But fully reconciling us to death requires more than this; it requires the possibility of transcending the smallness and frailty of our lives. This is the function of religion at its grandest: enabling mere mortals to attain cosmic significance, to become one with their gods and so to attain immortality.

In early religions, the line between this world and that of gods and spirits was a fine one, and much of their ritual was about intentionally crossing it. Shamans, for example, would seek union with the spirits of animals in order to benefit from their powers. In the mystery cults of ancient Greece and Rome that persisted unchanged for many centuries before being pushed aside by Christianity, participants engaged in complex rites often lasting for days and including all-night feasts, processions, drunkenness, sex, music and dancing, role-plays and secret props all designed to unite the worshipper with the god or gods, affording a transcendent experience that promised wisdom, strength and the key to immortality.

Such rituals offered the humble mortal a chance to partake in the power of their deities and to imbue their actions with the magic of a cosmic drama. Still today, every Sunday, just such an immortality rite is repeated around the world, when Christians take Holy Communion: many of them believe that they are literally consuming the blood and body of their god, and all consider themselves to be reliving a crucial moment in his story. And the result? The Gospel of John explains: "I am the living bread which came down from heaven: if any man eat of this bread, he shall live forever" (6:51).

Religions and rituals, with their hymns and incense, do not merely add color to a civilization——their practitioners regard them as the heart and soul of their worldview, that which gives meaning and shape to their lives and deaths. To the extent that they offer the possibility of transcending our ordinary, fleshly selves, many rituals offer a glimpse of eternity and triumph over death. But there is one particular recurring pattern in beliefs worldwide that shows the importance of the Resurrection Narrative in the development of the religious story.

All ancient cultures were keen observers of natural rhythms—— they had to be, as those rhythms determined the success of the crops on which their civilizations were completely dependent. They recognized many such patterns, from the daily rising and setting of the sun, to the four-weekly moon cycle, to the turning of the stars and the migrations of the birds. They saw that the turning of those elemental wheels brought about that great miracle of nature: the annual renewal of life.

In contrast to these cycles of nature, the life of an individual man or woman seems starkly linear. We are born, we mature, we grow frail and die. Left to its own devices, a corpse does not rise again—— the earth does not sprout a replacement of your fallen comrade in the way that it sprouts new flowers in springtime. Many ancient peoples, such as the Egyptians, were well aware of these two opposing conceptions of time——the cyclical and the linear——and the threat that the latter posed to their prospects of living forever. If our time is linear, they believed, then life for the corpse lies behind it and ahead is only the unending blankness of death. Therefore their most important rituals, with all their elaborate and expensive trappings, served one goal: to break that linearity and to bind their human fates to the cycles of nature—the cycles that promised life, death and life again.

The pioneering anthropologist Sir James Frazer was the first to suggest that the pattern of death and resurrection was a universal in human mythology, with his hugely successful but still controversial book *The Golden Bough* citing countless examples from around the world. He argued that the story was usually told in the form of a god or king whose own passage through death and back to life was thought to have cleared the way for ordinary mortals. Osiris, the Egyptian god of the afterlife whom we met earlier, is a classic example: he is murdered, only to be put back together and resurrected, thereby opening the way to immortality for his people. His rites were also closely associated with the return of life to the land—they even involved growing plants in mummy-shaped pots, in ways that explicitly associated the cycle of the seasons with the possibility of immortality.

Gods that disappear and reappear, that descend to the land of the dead and reemerge, or that actually die only to rise again appear in many ancient religions. In the Greco-Roman mystery cults mentioned above a key figure was the goddess Demeter, credited with bringing agriculture to the Greek people. She was also thought to disappear into the underworld for a time (in pursuit of her daughter, Persephone, who had been kidnapped by Hades); her cult both served to persuade her to return in order to bring life to the land each spring and by extension offered the possibility of rebirth to the cultist.

The claim of resurrection—that lifeless bodies, on their way to feeding the maggots, can somehow breathe again—is an extravagant one. It requires a great deal of faith in powerful magical intervention to think the processes of death and decay can be undone. It was the role of these path-breaking deities—known in the study of ancient religion as "the dying and rising gods"—to provide this power; their example broke the stark linearity of human biography, and so opened the way to connecting with the cyclical rhythms of nature and subverting the finality of death.

The worship of such gods frequently involved rites of mourning and reinvigoration. Because of their association with the seasons, these ceremonies were often around the winter solstice, at the end of December, the time of the birth of the new year, and around the time of the spring equinox, when plant life begins to return in the Northern Hemisphere. With these dates in mind, it is now time to return to the most famous dying and rising god of all and his standard-bearer, St. Paul.

RAISED IN GLORY

IN 30 CE a small group of women—friends and fellow believers—went to the tomb of their charismatic leader to anoint his corpse three days after his martyrdom. But the tomb was empty. As they stood "perplexed," a man (or possibly two men or possibly angels) appeared to tell them that the one they sought, Jesus of Nazareth, was not to be found among the dead: "He is not here; for he is risen."

The women rushed to tell the menfolk, who thought their report "idle tales, and they believed them not" (Luke 24:11). But they—in particular "doubting" Thomas—were finally persuaded when Jesus appeared among them and demonstrated that he was not a mere ghost but the full man, risen again to new life: John (20:27) reports that Jesus said to Thomas, "Put your finger here and see my hands. Reach out your hand and put it in my side." According to Luke (24:42), he even ate before them "broiled fish and honeycomb" in order to demonstrate that he was truly "flesh and blood."

For Jews of the time, the claim that an actual physical resurrection from the dead had taken place was immensely significant. Alongside established Jewish factions such as the Pharisees, to which Paul belonged, there were many apocalyptic and revolutionary groups preaching the coming of the Messiah and the end of the world. They were awaiting any sign that the age of liberation and justice was drawing near. That a martyr had risen from the dead was just such a sign: Jesus's resurrection meant the End Times had begun.

THIS message was embraced by the most influential interpreter of the Jesus story: St. Paul. The apostle had been busy since his escape from Damascus in a basket. A man of remarkable energy, drive and intellect, he had been spreading the word of Christ throughout Asia Minor and even to mainland Greece, the heartland of the most sophisticated philosophical culture of the day. Wherever he went, he established churches of those he had converted——congregations for whom he remained the spiritual leader. The letters he wrote to those churches were the earliest Christian documents to be considered canonical, written even before the Gospels. They total half of the New Testament and strongly influenced the other half. Christianity as we know it is therefore largely Christianity as it was understood by Paul——remarkable given that he himself never met Christ and had once ruthlessly persecuted those who had. And it was a Christianity based on the promise of resurrection.

Perhaps because Paul had never met him, it was not Jesus's sayings that guided the apostle's letters, but rather what Jesus symbolized. For Paul, there were only two really significant events in his Messiah's life: the death on the cross and the resurrection three days later. These and these alone were proof of the prophecies; they heralded the coming of the End Times and revealed God's plan for humanity: to raise the faithful from the grave to eternal life.

In focusing on the resurrection, Paul set about transforming the biggest problem of Jesus's followers into their greatest selling point. The problem, simply, was that Jesus had been executed. At first glance, the killing of its leader should have put an end to this fledgling movement, just as it had for countless other charismatic cults in the region. It certainly seemed to disqualify Jesus from the role of Messiah, whom pious Jews expected would lead them in battle to reestablish the kingdom of David. And it disqualified him from the role of a hero for the Greeks and Romans, who saw crucifixion as the most disgraceful and unheroic of ends. He was therefore a most unlikely savior, as Paul acknowledged at the beginning of his first letter to the faithful in Corinth when he wrote, "We proclaim Christ crucified, a stumbling-block to Jews and foolishness to Gentiles" (1 Corinthians 1:22–23).

But Paul believed that if Jesus had risen from the grave, then his humiliating execution was meaningful after all. By focusing on the resurrection, he could claim that Jesus had defeated death, not just for himself, but for all humanity; the crucifixion and resurrection had undone the curse of the Fall that brought death to mankind—"as all die in Adam, so all will be made alive in Christ" (1 Corinthians 15:22). Just as with the heroes, deities and kings of many earlier religions, Jesus's rising again paved the way for us all to rise again. In other words, Paul claimed for Jesus the role of the dying and rising god, a symbolic figure whose life, death and rebirth enabled resurrection for all those who followed him. In Paul's hands, the historical Jesus story was transformed into a living myth, a narrative with the power of the legend of Osiris, yet set not in a legendary past but within the here and now.

PAUL, the pious Jew, took the doctrine of resurrection directly from his sect, the Pharisees. The Judaism of the earliest books of the Old Testament lacked a clear narrative of personal immortality, focusing almost exclusively on the survival of the tribe of Israel as a whole. But over the centuries, a belief developed that God, in his goodness, would raise the dead to live again in paradise. However, the supposed circumstances of this resurrection were vague, and it was by no means universally accepted within Judaism. Paul's genius was to use the Jesus story to develop a vivid and satisfying narrative of how and when this resurrection would take place, then to spread it not only within Judaism but far beyond.

To the sophisticated Greek Gentiles whom he was trying to convert, however, resurrection was an alien and surprising claim. The predominant view in the Greek world was that people survived death as a soul—a purely spiritual entity that left behind the degraded, decaying body for good. Resurrection, by contrast, was an earthy, this-worldly belief centerd entirely on the body. To the Greeks, the idea of reviving their flawed and rotting flesh was risible and appalling. If Christianity was to be anything more than a minor Jewish sect, Paul had to persuade this urbane audience to overcome their revulsion at the very idea of rising from the grave.

He was well aware of his audience's doubts, as he acknowledged in the New Testament's most famous passage on immortality—chapter 15 of Paul's first letter to the Corinthians: "Someone will ask, How are the dead raised? With what kind of body do they come?" He answers with a poetic image that would be instantly recognizable to the alchemists we considered in chapter 2 as a description of transformation: a worldly body is like "a bare seed . . . sown in dishonor, it is raised in glory. It is sown in weakness, it is raised in power . . . For this perishable body must put on imperishability, and this mortal body must put on immortality." In other words, having been raised, we will be transformed so as to be fit for eternal life. Paul then builds to his crescendo: "When this perishable body puts on imperishability, and this mortal body puts on immortality, then the saying that is written will be fulfilled: 'Death has been swallowed up in victory.' 'Where, O death, is your victory? Where, O death, is your sting?'"

It is a testament to this powerful passage that it is still read daily, some two thousand years after Paul wrote it—mostly, of course, at funerals to give hope and comfort to the bereaved. Yet many who hear it seem to hear an altogether different message from that which Paul intended. The majority of Christians today have sided with the Greek belief that we have a soul, that it lives on after our death, and that it goes straight to heaven (or hell). But this is the opposite from what was preached by the early Christians, including both Jesus and Paul. Indeed, it is opposed to the sentiment that we find throughout the Bible: that death is terrible—"the last enemy" as Paul calls it.

If we have souls that go straight to heaven, then we would have no reason to dread death. Being made mortal would hardly have been a punishment for Adam at all. It would have been a matter of little consequence that he and Eve were barred from eating from the Tree of Life in Eden if they could have expected shortly thereafter to float off to heaven. But this is not the Bible's message: it teaches that death is the end—or rather *was* the end, until the moment when Jesus redeemed Adam and Eve's sin and so opened the way to resurrection.

The original Christian view of death can clearly be seen by comparing the last moments of Jesus with those of Socrates some four hundred years earlier—as the great theologian Oscar Cullmann did in the 1950s, causing considerable upset at the time. Socrates welcomed his coming execution: as described by Plato in the *Phaedo*, he explained to his followers that death was the liberation of the soul from the body; it was a transition that was to be welcomed. He then drank with serenity the poisonous hemlock and died in peace. In contrast, the Gospel of Mark tells us that Jesus was "agitated and distressed" at the prospect of his execution; he told his disciples that he was "deeply grieved" (Mark 14:33–34). He did not want to be alone but continually woke his companions when he thought his enemies were coming. Finally, when hanging on the cross, he cried, "My God, my God, why have you forsaken me?" (Mark 15:34). This is not the behavior of one who believes death is liberation of the soul; for Jesus, unlike Socrates, it meant dread and extinction.

Indeed, it is only if death ordinarily means dread and extinction that we can make sense of the Jesus story at all. If we all have immortal souls that by nature live on after our deaths, then there would have been nothing special about Christ subsequently appearing to the apostles. The belief that people live on as spirits that could return to visit the living was common at the time. There would therefore have been nothing new or distinctive in the Christian message if, as the Greeks would naturally interpret it, Jesus had died but his soul had lived on and returned to visit his disciples. Jesus's resurrection only has the enormous significance that Christians ascribe to it if it would have taken a great miracle for him to have returned. This is the case only if death normally means oblivion. In other words, in its early days Christianity *needed* a belief in death and resurrection—*as opposed to* belief in an immortal soul. That was, in modern marketing parlance, its unique selling point.

What Paul offered with his version of Christianity was the promise of a real, tangible paradise in which we could experience joy as we can on earth. This was possible because of his claim that we would be resurrected with real, physical bodies—these very same bodies we know now, yet improved and made imperishable. This was a significant contrast to the vague and shady spirit existence widely believed in by the Greeks and Romans of his day. Paul then combined this claim that we would rise again with the apocalyptic beliefs also common in the Judaism of his day: the belief that there would very soon be a final reckoning, when good would triumph over evil and the world would be turned into a heaven on earth—at least for believers.

Paul expected the End of Days, as the Old Testament called this event, to come in his lifetime, as he told the congregation in Thessalonica: first the dead will be raised, then "we who are alive, who are left, will be caught up in the clouds together with them to meet the Lord in the air; and so we will be with the Lord forever" (1 Thessalonians 4:17). Here he was following the apocalyptic preaching of Jesus, whose core message was "The kingdom of God is at hand" (Mark 1:15) and who according to the Gospel of John proclaimed, "The hour is coming in which all who are in the graves shall hear his voice and shall come forth: they that have done good, unto the resurrection of life, and they that have done evil, unto the resurrection of damnation" (John 5:28–29).

Therefore alongside his promise of a joyful immortality (or threat of a dreadful one), Paul introduced an idea of progress—of movement toward a better future—that would also have been new to most of his Gentile audience. And the conclusion of this historical development was imminent: those who wanted an eternity of bliss had better sign up now.

Much of the Christian message would consequently have been novel to the Greco-Roman world, yet it built on ideas they could recognize. As we have seen, the idea of a dying and rising god was already common in the Mediterranean and Middle East. Indeed, the narrative parallels between Christianity and the Greek mystery rituals were so close as to have to be explained away as the devil's work by early church leaders. As Christianity developed it absorbed other widespread rituals, allowing its followers to partake in the cosmic drama of the Christ story: the two central Christian celebrations are both based on older rites—Christmas on the Roman celebration of the birth of the new sun after the winter solstice, and Easter on aspects of the Jewish Passover festival and on pagan spring festivals of rebirth, from which the name "Easter" comes.

The complete package offered by Christianity was therefore a set of rites that had already stood the test of time, but overlaid with a very concrete promise of imminent eternal life in paradise. We have seen that worldviews succeed by reconciling our will to live forever with the Mortality Paradox, in particular our awareness of death. This Christianity achieved spectacularly well, with enormous consequences for the development of Western civilization.

. . .

THE centrality of physical resurrection—both of Jesus and of us all at the end of time—is why it remains dogma throughout the Christian church. The Nicene Creed, the profession of faith written by the first ecumenical council in 325 ce to unify the church, states, "We look for the resurrection of the dead." This is recognized as the core expression of Christian belief by Catholics, Lutherans, Anglicans, the Eastern and Oriental Orthodox Churches and many others. And the ritual, mentioned earlier, of Holy Communion or Eucharist, which practicing Christians perform every Sunday, is, according to the official *Catholic Encyclopedia*, "a pledge of our glorious resurrection and eternal happiness," following the promise of Jesus: "He that eateth my flesh and drinketh my blood, hath everlasting life: and I will raise him up on the last day" (John 6:54).

Christianity is here not alone: as we have seen, the belief in physical resurrection came from Jewish tradition, and what is now orthodoxy for Jews—known as Rabbinic Judaism—evolved from the teaching of the Pharisees, the tradition of St. Paul. The most widely accepted of the Jewish statements of faith, that devised by the medieval rabbi Moses Maimonides, ends with a resounding commitment to resurrection: "I believe with perfect faith that there will be a revival of the dead at the time when it shall please the Creator."

Similarly, the youngest of the Abrahamic religions, Islam, is just as clear, as the Qur'an says: "It is God who gives you life, causes you to die, then gathers you together for the Day of Resurrection, of which there is no doubt" (sura 45, verse 26). There is also no doubt that Muhammad's vivid descriptions of the very physical pleasures awaiting believers in paradise—especially for those who died in battle—helped to motivate them in spreading their faith. Indeed, one scholar of Islamic history, Nerina Rustomji, has described how this new religion was defined by its graphic images of the afterlife, which was as novel to the pagans of the Arabian Peninsula as it was to the Gentiles to whom Paul preached.

Thus half of the world's population—some three and a half billion people—*officially* subscribe to the physical resurrection of the bodies they have known in this life. In reality, however, the figure is much smaller. One 2006 survey showed that, although 80 percent of Americans belong to one of the three Abrahamic religions, only just over 30 percent of Americans believe they will be resurrected. This means a majority of believers—totaling half of all Americans—do not believe one of the core dogmas of their faith. Responding to a survey, one Christian said that she associated the idea of resurrection with "bad horror movies," while Jon Levenson, professor of Jewish studies at Harvard, recently wrote that the historical centrality of resurrection to their faiths "comes as a shock to most Jews and Christians alike."

The reason for this astonishing gap between doctrine and actual belief is simple: despite its initial atractions, the idea of physical resurrection is a rather problematic one.

OF BOARS AND CANNIBALS

ANYONE believing that a Resurrection Narrative will satisfy his or her will to immortality must believe that it really is he or she, that selfsame person, who will rise again. Paul did not expect that someone merely *like* him in certain respects would rise from the grave on the Day of Judgment—he expected that *he himself* would. Indeed, only if the people who rise from the grave are really the selfsame people as those who once lived does the judging part of the Day of Judgment make sense: it would be grossly unfair to condemn anyone to hellfire unless that person really was the one who had committed the sins in question. This might sound obvious, but it in fact presents the resurrectionist with a problem.

If Paul believed that *he* would rise again, then he must have believed that he could somehow pull through the ordeal of being killed, buried and then revivified. This is, after all, what happened in the Jesus story: he is supposed to have pulled through being crucified, entombed and brought back to life. And many millions of people accept this story. Partly, they accept it because it *seems* not hard to imagine: we think it easy enough to picture a person dying and somehow a short time later reawakening to live again. But what we imagine is only the surface—someone becoming pale and cold, then magically warm and rosy-cheeked again. There is, however, much more to death than this.

Experts argue over the exact moment when we cross the boundary from life to death (or whether there is such a definite moment), but we can still sketch the outlines of what is usually involved. First, your heart stops beating, depriving other organs of life-giving oxygen. With no oxygen, your brain stops regulating your body's functions and stops supporting consciousness, and individual cells throughout your body begin to die. Bacteria in your gut take advantage of the cessation of your immune system and start consuming you from the inside. Before long, although you may still be recognizable from the outside, on the inside, whole parts of your body, including the brain, have lost their complex, delicate structures and have begun to turn to mush. After a week, much of your insides will have putrefied; after a month or so, you are a liquefying, bloated, unrecognizable mass. It might seem easy to imagine a corpse once again becoming rosy-cheeked, but it is much more difficult to imagine how putrefied lungs can breathe again or how a liquefied heart can beat.

The details of Jesus's resurrection are not described in the New Testament—only its effect, the risen Christ, and even that in contradictory terms. Diarmaid MacCulloch, the Oxford professor of church history, has described the failure to describe what really happened in Jesus's tomb as "the blank" at the center of Christianity. It is a blank that is very hard to fill. The process of death and decay does not sound like one that any human being could possibly pull through—and even Jesus, the Son of God, died as a man. Yet if the story of Jesus and the hopes of millions are to make any sense, then this total dissolution of the body can be no more than a temporary setback on the journey to eternal life.

The ancient Egyptians were well aware of this problem and had a whole battery of answers to how someone could survive the shock of being killed. Of course, they did their utmost to preserve the physical body and believed that this was important for a satisfactory existence in the next world. But they also believed in the importance of numerous souls, a person's works and the memories they left behind, their names and their families. All of these things provided ways of surviving even without a beating heart. So even before the mummification process was complete, although the deceased might be in a kind of limbo, they weren't really dead and gone.

But resurrectionists such as the Pharisees and early Christians did not posit the existence of mysterious, nonphysical substances like souls—indeed, that was the view against which they defined themselves. So when people died, they really were dead. And what was death like? Well, a bit like sleep. The dead, according to the Old Testament, were "those that sleep in the dust of the earth" awaiting the resurrection (Daniel 12:2). But waking up from a long sleep is something we can all understand; waking up from death is a different matter.

WITH cunning use of natron and linen stuffing, the Egyptians might have preserved mummies that looked a bit like human bodies, but these things no longer had brains, blood or many other features we ordinarily consider crucial to a *real* human body. Yet those who were mummified had it good compared to the Christian victims of Roman persecutions. The Romans were well aware of the Christians' belief that they would one day rise bodily from the grave and did everything they could to mock and hinder those hopes. A report of a persecution in Gaul in 177 ce records that the martyrs were first executed, then their corpses left to rot unburied for six days before being burned and the ashes thrown into the river Rhône——"Now let us see whether they will rise again," the Romans are reported to have said. Such barbarous acts did little to dampen the Christians' missionary zeal——but they did pose something of a challenge to early theologians. Just how was a handful of ashes supposed to rise again?

Early Christians at first thought the answer simple: all God had to do was gather the bits that made you up before you died (atoms, elements or whatever) and put them back together just as they were. As he is omnipotent and omniscient, this should not be too big a job, they thought. It is no different from dropping a precious statue and so causing it to break into pieces, then putting the pieces back together with such skill as to make the statue as good as new. Seeing the fully repaired statue, would anyone doubt that it had survived the little accident? Surely not. So seeing the newly repaired you on the Day of Judgment, no one would doubt that you had survived your sojourn in the grave.

This way of describing resurrection was defended by the church fathers for many centuries after Jesus emerged from his tomb and still has advocates today. But also, even in Jesus's time, this view had its critics, and subsequent developments in science and philosophy have only compounded its problems. As it involves a person being effectively dismantled by death and then put back together again, it is known as the Reassembly View of resurrection. It faces at least three major challenges.

The first of these is what I will call the *Cannibal Problem*. Imagine that before you had a chance to repair your broken statue, I grabbed a bit and used it for a statue that I was making. If you wanted to make your statue whole again, you could only do it by breaking mine and taking your bit back. We could not both at the same time complete our statues. Similarly, if the same atoms were at different times part of two human beings when they died, we (or even God) would have a problem fully reassembling both of them. And this is by no means unlikely: during the Roman persecutions, many Christians were fed to wild beasts in the arenas. Some of those beasts—wild boars for example—might then have been served up for the post-circus feast. So people would have been eating animal flesh that was in part made of human flesh and that in turn became part of their flesh. Or simpler still is cannibalism. If a cannibal comes to be made up of bits that once belonged to another human, then even God could not re-create them both whole on the day of the resurrection.

We now know that we do not even need recourse to such dramatic examples to make this point: we are continually acquiring and losing atoms that are then recycled by nature—one estimate suggests that we replace 98 percent of our particles every year. Given the sheer number of atoms involved (approximately seven billion billion billion in an average human body), odds are—even if you are not tempted by cannibalism—that you are now in part composed of atoms that once were part of others as they breathed their last.

Theologians have thought hard about this problem and come up with many innovative solutions—but none that have yet found widespread acceptance. One early attempt was to flatly deny that a human being can actually digest and assimilate the flesh of another human being—of which the skinniness of cannibal tribes was allegedly evidence. Others have argued that the matter will belong to that person for whom it formed the most essential part, others still that it will belong to the person who had it first—and in both cases that God would simply fill in the gaps in the person left short. But these solutions rather undermine the idea that your claim to be identical to the resurrected you depends on your being made of exactly the same bits. Despite two thousand years of trying, the Cannibal Problem remains without solution.

The second problem with which the resurrectionists struggle is just what the resurrected body is supposed to be like. I will call this the *Transformation Problem*; like the Cannibal Problem, it is almost as old as Christianity itself. The argument runs like this: on the one hand, resurrectionists claim that your resurrected body is made of the same bits as you, put together in the same way. This, after all, is what makes the old you and the new you one and the same person. But on the other hand, when you die, you might be old, withered, arthritic, senile and riddled with cancer. Yet this is not how believers imagine the inhabitants of the resurrection paradise. On the contrary, St. Paul promised that our bodies would be made glorious and incorruptible, fit for immortality. Indeed, most Christian resurrectionists are convinced that there will be no sickness in paradise, nor any need for eating and drinking, and everyone will be beautiful and perfect.

But this is rather like my smashing my clay statue, then casting one in the same shape but made instead of gold. Would we really say that these were the same statues—that my original statue had survived being smashed and "rebuilt" out of gold? Or would we not be more inclined to think that I had destroyed my old clay statue and made a new gold one in its place? The early theologians suggested we might keep some of our bodily features that would strictly be obsolete, such as teeth (because we would look silly without them) or even redundant internal organs. But even these features that are supposed to link us to our original, this-worldly selves would be somehow transformed to be made incorruptible. The resurrectionists have therefore run into a contradiction: on the one hand, your survival depends upon exactly the same atoms being reassembled just as they were before you died; yet on the other hand, the postresurrection you is supposed to be a different creature altogether, made of invincible stuff and arranged so differently that you no longer require even a metabolism. Just as with the gold statue, this sounds more like replacement than resurrection.

If this was not already enough, there is an even more serious problem with the idea that you could just be put back together again like Humpty Dumpty. I will call it the *Duplication Problem*, and it too has ancient versions, though it is still much discussed in the philosophical and theological literature. One modern rendition goes like this: we have just seen that we replace roughly 98 percent of our atoms every year. It is indeed entirely possible that, through this process of replacement and renewal, you now do not have a single atom in common with yourself as a five-year-old. But if that is so, then God could not only reassemble the current you, were you now to die, but he could also simultaneously reassemble the five-year-old you. And the reassembled five-year-old would have just as much claim to *be* you as the reassembled adult version: both would be made from atoms that composed you at a certain time and would be put back together just as you were.

This is a big problem for the Reassembly View of resurrection. As we will see in the next chapter, any theory that allows multiple versions of you to appear at the same time breaks the rules of logic—and even an omnipotent God cannot do what is logically impossible. One might argue that God would not attempt to pull off such a mean trick as to reassemble both the adult you and the child you—but that is not the point: the very fact that our criterion for survival allows for the appearance of multiple versions of you is enough to tell us that something is badly wrong.

These three problems show that even God would have great difficulty in physically putting you back together again on Judgment Day in a way that would mean it really was *you* rising from the grave. If we are just these fleshy bodies, then death and disintegration are high hurdles to overcome on the way to immortality. But we will see in the next chapter that there are other ways of seeing resurrection besides the Reassembly View, so the idea that we might rise again has life in it yet.

THE END IS (STILL) NIGH

"FIVE times I have received from the Jews the forty lashes minus one. Three times I was beaten with rods. Once I received a stoning. Three times I was shipwrecked; for a night and a day I was adrift at sea; on frequent journeys, in danger from rivers, danger from bandits, danger from my own people, danger from Gentiles, danger in the city, danger in the wilderness, danger at sea, danger from false brothers and sisters; in toil and hardship, through many a sleepless night, hungry and thirsty, often without food, cold and naked" (2 Corinthians 11:24–27).

This is Paul's own description of the tribulations he had endured on his mission—though when he wrote it they were far from over. Everywhere he went plots were hatched against him, mobs rose up and ambushes were laid. But his enemies were mostly not the Greeks and Romans whose ways he condemned as sinful— they were his fellow Jews and even fellow Christians.

St. Paul is famous today for his self-appointed title, "apostle to the Gentiles" (Romans 11:13), but he was not the only or even the first follower of Jesus to preach to non-Jews. What was unique about Paul's mission was that he argued faith in the risen Christ was enough to be accepted into the new church. In contrast to the other apostles—those who had in fact known Jesus in his lifetime— Paul believed that converts did not have to be circumcised or follow all the (many and detailed) laws of Moses; in other words, he believed that you did not have to become a Jew to become a Christian. Salvation and eternal life awaited all who had faith in Jesus. This was a declaration of war on the special status and traditions of the people of Israel.

When Paul returned to Jerusalem after many years of missionary activity a trap lay in wait for him. He had previously argued bitterly with the other apostles—who still regarded themselves as pious Jews—and had even accused St. Peter of hypocrisy. Despite an official truce, these apostles continued to regard him as a trou-blemaker: when he arrived in Jerusalem, they told Paul that he must prove to the Jews that he was still one of them and was not really preaching that they should abandon the law of Moses. The book of Acts describes how they suggested he escort some pil-grims in a ceremony of cleansing in the temple—and how when he followed their suggestion an angry mob lay waiting to lynch him. Only the intervention of a large detachment of Roman soldiers saved Paul from being beaten to death on the spot.

He spent the rest of his life in Roman custody. But he had already sown the seed of a religion that could transcend the provincialism of the Old Testament. Judaism contained within it a contradiction: it claimed both that its god, Jehovah, was a tribal god, *their* god, but at the same time that he was the one true God, the God of all. Paul resolved this contradiction by declaring that the age when Jeho-vah revealed himself only to the Jews was over; through the death and resurrection of Jesus, he had sent his message to Jews and Gen-tiles alike, who were both now free from the old law. This was the last stroke needed to release Christianity from its Israelite moorings and allow it to become the world religion it is today.

IN one of the most extraordinary cliff-hangers in literary history, the Bible simply leaves Paul in Rome awaiting his trial—we are not given a heroic martyrdom, inspiring valediction or final revela-tion. A rich hagiographic tradition has sprung up to fill in this gap, according to which he was beheaded—as a Roman citizen he would have been spared the torture of crucifixion—during Emperor Nero's persecution of the Christians following the Great Fire of Rome in 64 ce. If he was disappointed that the kingdom of God had not already arrived, he would at least have died convinced that he would not have to wait long.

That was nearly two thousand years ago, and believers are still awaiting the End Times. The clues Jesus gave for how we should know the last days—when "nation will rise against nation, and kingdom against kingdom, and there will be famines and earthquakes" (Matthew 24:7)—are unfortunately rather vague; indeed some might say they are a generic description of the human condition. Thus people of all ages have believed the end was nigh. Some denominations, such as the Jehovah's Witnesses and Mormons, argue they are right now upon us—and have been doing so for some time.

Others, however, have become disillusioned in their wait for the second coming and the resurrection. As a consequence, many have turned to a belief in the soul—which has since become part of orthodox belief for many Christian denominations, including Catholicism. However, not all have given up the ambition of resurrection—but instead of praying for an act of God, these optimists are increasingly putting their faith in an act of science. We are used to technology nowadays achieving what once would have been considered miraculous: in the next chapter we will see that there are those who believe it will soon allow us to raise the dead. And they are paying good money to ensure they will be among the risen. Yet one of literature's most enduring classics describes what monsters we might create in our quest to overcome death; penned by a teenage girl, it is a story that more than any other captures the fears of our time: *Frankenstein*.

5

FRANKENSTEIN REDUX

The Modern Reanimators

"**D**REAM that my little baby came to life again; that it had only been cold, and that we rubbed it before the fire, and it lived." So wrote the seventeen-year-old Mary Shelley two weeks after the death of her first child in February 1815. She went on: "Awake and find no baby. I think about the little thing all day. Not in good spirits."

It might have been more common to lose a child in the early nineteenth century than it is today, but as Mary Shelley's words show, it was still deeply upsetting for the parents. This was already her second experience of the caprice of death: her first happened when she was herself only two weeks old, although she was to feel the loss throughout her life. Her own mother, the notorious radical thinker Mary Wollstonecraft, had died of an infection contracted while giving birth to the daughter who was to eclipse her in fame. Mary Shelley, while still only a teenager, knew that death was always lying in wait, ready to destroy our fragile attempts at happiness.

Throughout her life, she was haunted by the dream of resurrection—of returning the dead to life, like her little baby, warmed by the fire. It was a dream that the new science promised to make real and that both fascinated and terrified her. A dream that, through her, would come to fascinate and terrify all of us.

THIS was in the time shortly before the breakthroughs in hygiene and medicine that brought about the first revolution in human longevity. The intellectuals of the day knew that something was about to happen—that science was on the verge of remaking their world—and the latest experiments were the talk of the salons. Two such intellectuals were the poets Lord Byron, already by then infamous for his many love affairs, and the young Percy Bysshe Shelley—Mary's lover and soon-to-be husband. The three spent the summer of 1816 together in the Alps around Geneva, in a self-imposed exile from the censure of British society—Percy Shelley was already married when he and Mary ran off together, and Byron was fleeing accusations of adultery, incest and sodomy. They were accompanied by Mary's half sister Claire—who was pregnant by Byron—and Byron's young doctor John Polidori.

This was the "sunless summer" of cold and incessant rain caused by a series of volcanic eruptions around the world. Crops failed across the Northern Hemisphere and a persistent fog clung to the land. Sheltering from the constant drizzle, the outcast writers discussed philosophy, composed poetry and read a collection of gothic tales that suited the gloomy weather. To pass the time, Byron challenged them all to write ghost stories of their own—a daunting challenge for a young girl in the company of such eminent authors. Every evening the party was carried away in debating great questions, but each morning Mary would be asked, "Have you thought of a story?"

But one of the "many and long" nightly conversations seized Mary's imagination, as she later wrote: "Various philosophical doctrines were discussed, and among others the nature of the principle of life, and whether there was any probability of its ever being discovered." Byron and Shelley speculated that "perhaps a corpse would be re-animated; galvanism had given token of such things: perhaps the component parts of a creature might be manufactured, brought together, and endued with vital warmth."

The "galvanism" that so excited Byron and Shelley referred to the work of the illustrious Italian scientist Luigi Galvani, who had discovered that severed frog's legs could be made to hop by the application of electricity. In 1803 his nephew Professor Giovanni Aldini had toured England to publicize these wonderful powers. In one widely reported demonstration he applied electricity to the corpse of a freshly hanged murderer: according to a local newspaper, "the jaw began to quiver, the adjoining muscles were horribly contorted, and the left eye actually opened." Applying the electricity lower down the body, "the right hand was raised and clenched, and the legs and thighs were set in motion." The audience was amazed and appalled by the demonstration, believing the murderer was at any moment going to be "fully restored"; science seemed on the verge of harnessing the power to resurrect the dead.

These thrilling ideas merged in Mary's mind with her own anxieties, the visions of her lost baby and her fantasies of resuscitation. When she went to bed that night she could not sleep, giving herself over to a reverie—a "waking dream." Her eyes closed, she saw a "pale student of unhallowed arts kneeling beside the thing he had put together . . . the hideous phantasm of a man stretched out, and then, on the working of some powerful engine, show signs of life, and stir with an uneasy, half-vital motion." In horror at what he has done, the scientist "would rush away from his odious handiwork . . . He would hope that, left to itself, the slight spark of life which he had communicated would fade." But it does not; on the contrary. The scientist goes to his bed, exhausted, but is woken by a sudden noise and "behold, the horrid thing stands at his bedside, opening his curtains and looking on him with yellow, watery, but speculative eyes."

Mary was terrified by this vision and preoccupied all night. The next day, she announced that she had found a theme for her "ghost story" and began writing. She was eighteen years old. Under the encouragement of Percy Shelley what she had planned as a short story grew within a year to a full-blown novel. The book's title: *Frankenstein; or, the Modern Prometheus.*

Mary Shelley's most famous work is a profound study of the scientific quest to control nature—and a scathing critique of the hero who pursues that quest, the lone scientist who dares to claim the power of the gods for mankind. In its many forms and retellings, *Frankenstein* has become a modern myth—essential to our understanding of ourselves and the world. It is the first great work of science fiction and a warning that we continually confront anew.

But most of all, *Frankenstein* is an exploration of the fantasy of conquering death—a fantasy that Mary, like all of us at one time or another, had herself indulged. Her tragic hero aspires to take on the power that for thousands of years had been reserved for God alone—to "renew life where death had apparently devoted the body to corruption." In other words, to resurrect the dead.

THE CONQUEST OF NATURE

WE saw in the last chapter that early Christianity flourished by promising that God would shortly raise the faithful to live again in eternal happiness. But the wait for the End Times has been a long one, and many have come to doubt whether we can be so sure of God's good intentions, or indeed whether he is out there at all. The impatient and the skeptical have therefore been working on a resurrection narrative of their own, a secular version of the apocalyptic tradition with its promise of paradise. It is a narrative that has been enormously powerful in driving human progress and shapes much of the way we see the world today. Its claim is simple: that we do not have to wait for God to raise us from the grave; it is a power that we humans can claim for ourselves. We must only discover "the principle of life," and then we can conquer death forever.

But we have also seen that the early attempt to make sense of resurrection—the Reassembly View, according to which your component particles would simply be put back together—is deeply flawed. In this chapter, we will explore an alternative theory of how resurrection could ensure that it really is *you* clambering out of the grave and not some doppelgänger. But first we will look at what led Mary Shelley and her companions to believe that science was on the verge of claiming control over life and death, and how this belief has shaped our world.

As Mary Shelley was penning *Frankenstein*, science was beginning to establish itself as the new authority on nature's laws. In the preceding century, the scientific method of careful observation and experimentation had fully emerged from the obscurantism of the alchemists. Secret meetings had given way to public scientific societies, and coded tomes to published journals. But although the methods had changed, the aims remained the same: the mastery of nature and conquest of mortality.

In her novel, Mary Shelley has the career of her young scientist hero, Victor Frankenstein, reflect these developments: he first dabbles with alchemy and the search for an elixir of life before being convinced instead of the power of physics and chemistry. At college, he learns that the scientists who "pore over the microscope or crucible, have indeed performed miracles," and "have acquired new and almost unlimited powers; they can command the thunders of heaven" and "mimic the earthquake."

This is the language of the new immortality narrative, which claims for science the powers of the gods. In chapter 4, we saw that earlier civilizations sought to control their fate through the performance of ancient, orderly rituals; the early success of science promised a much more active and effective means of taking charge of our destiny. It is a narrative of control and conquest, one that Mary Shelley captures in her description of these masculine scientists as those who seek "to penetrate into the recesses of nature, and show how she works in her hiding-places." Frankenstein is convinced by the new ethos of the age that through force of will and reason, we can become masters of nature.

It is nature, after all, that decrees that we must die—that causes our joints to seize up, our skin to wrinkle and cancer to strike. In order to live forever, we must, like the gods, rise above these natural limits. This therefore is the grand project of science, its answer to the Mortality Paradox: death and disease might be what nature intends for us, but we can master nature and thwart her plans. The founding fathers of the scientific method were quite explicit about this. René Descartes, for example, talked openly of seeking knowledge that would "render ourselves the lords and possessors of nature" and was considered by his contemporaries to be obsessed with the extension of life. And Francis Bacon pursued what he considered this "most noble goal" of life extension to his death— in 1626 from pneumonia, which he contracted when experimenting with the use of snow to preserve corpses. Throughout its history, science has sought to make life unending and death reversible.

In chapter 3, we saw that scientific progress is driven forward by the Engineering Approach to mortality, the modern version of the Staying Alive Narrative, which attempts to break down the challenge of death into a list of potentially solvable problems like curing cancer, harnessing stem cells or stopping smoking. We can now see that this is part of a broader ideology of mastering nature—a belief that there are *no* natural limits that cannot in the end be overcome by reason. This belief extends beyond the hope of staying alive to encompass also its Plan B: resurrection.

This drive to mastery of nature is often regarded as the very essence of modernity. As the sociologist Zygmunt Bauman has noted, with the advent of science, death came to be seen as an insult to our newfound powers—"the last, yet seemingly irremovable, relic of fate in a world increasingly designed and controlled by reason." Death is a humiliating natural restriction from which we must be emancipated. The young scientist Frankenstein is inspired to break this final shackle and so embodies the arrogance and ambition of this new narrative. His successors today are a growing group of technophiles who, in the words of the leading authorities on science and society Braden R. Allenby and Daniel Sarewitz, "explicitly embrace the pursuit of immortality, of human perfectibility, of dominion over nature, and of transcendence over the limits that time and space impose on the individual."

The belief that we can conquer death through scientific mastery of nature is often set up as being in opposition to the religious tradition but in fact closely follows the Resurrection Narrative of apocalyptic Christianity. The prophets of scientific progress—including both Mary's husband, Percy Shelley, and her father, the radical philosopher and writer William Godwin—promised the imminent arrival of a utopia in which the frailties of the human condition would be transcended. This is of course just what was preached by Jesus and St. Paul, who prophesied the Day of Judgment and subsequent arrival of heaven on earth. The only difference was that instead of a miraculous act of God bringing about the resurrection, we would achieve it ourselves through science.

I, AVATAR

MUCH of the energy of those inspired by this narrative is spent on research that offers to extend our days—that is, the pursuit of staying alive. But, as Victor Frankenstein recognized, the real prize for those who could learn to subjugate nature is not simply postponing death; it is the power of resurrection—bringing the dead back to life. After all, although some might hope to achieve the "longevity escape velocity" we met in chapter 3, many will recognize that there is a good chance that nature will get them before science has completed its conquering. Luckily, the narrative of endless progress reaches even beyond the grave.

We saw in chapter 4 that resurrecting the dead requires something extraordinary; it is not as easy as a certain energy company inadvertently suggested when they wrote to one recently deceased customer, "We are very sorry to lose your valued custom. Should you like to return at any point, please just let us know." But the astonishing advances in technology in the past decades have given many hope that it will indeed be just this straightforward, that there will soon be companies offering that if you would like to return, then "please just let us know." There are three theories in particular that are inspiring cutting-edge research in the promise of transcending our final limit: cryonics, mind-uploading and, once again, superintelligence.

Francis Bacon was onto the right idea on that fateful winter night when he decided to stuff a dead chicken with snow: freezing can indeed halt the decay that otherwise quickly turns a fresh corpse into a heap of stinking goo. Mary Shelley was well aware of this when, two hundred years after Bacon's chilly death, she wrote her short story "Roger Dodsworth: The Reanimated Englishman," about a man frozen by an avalanche while returning across the Alps to England from Italy in 1654, only to be dug out and revived in 1826. Again presaging modern science fiction by generations, she explains that the ice and snow put him in a state of "suspended animation." Rumors of such cases were rife in the 1800s—such as folktales from New England of how poor families struggling to feed the household through the harsh winter months would give the grandparents large quantities of homemade liquor, lay them in a coffin and bury them in a snowbank. When spring finally came they would be hauled out, defrosted and (allegedly) revived—perhaps with the help of a little more moonshine.

Whether modern techno-utopians believe these legends or not, they are convinced there is something in the idea of freezing bodies in order to ward off decay. At temperatures below −276°F, they argue, biological structures could be preserved for hundreds or even thousands of years without decomposing. Cryopreservation (that is, preserving things at extremely low temperatures) is already used for storing small samples of human tissue such as eggs and sperm. So it should be an ideal way of ensuring you are still around when scientists have worked out the finer points of resurrection. The leading prophets of the future scientific utopia are therefore signing up to have themselves supercooled. This is the practice known as *cryonics*, and already there are metal vats in numerous sites around the world containing the bodies of techno-optimists bobbing gently in liquid nitrogen.

Cryonics is of course not itself a recipe for resurrection; it is only a way of preserving corpses until the day when resurrection is supposed to become possible. It is, if you like, the modern equivalent of mummification, but the doctors and scientists have yet to work out the modern equivalent of the various spells that are supposed to return these modern mummies to life. Given the enormous damage caused to our cells when they are supercooled, on top of the damage of whatever it was that killed the person in the first place, they have their work cut out for them. Skeptics therefore see cryonics as just an eccentric form of burial. But it has nonetheless captured the popular imagination, featuring in countless science fiction stories and shaping our vision of the future.

It is, however, currently rather pricey: cryonics institutes charge around $150,000 to look after your body in perpetuity. Some aspiring resurrectionists find this a little much, and they also reason that by the time they are ready for the icy thermos they might anyway be disillusioned with their old and creaky bodies. Perhaps, therefore, it is not worth preserving the *whole* body. After all, many believe that what matters is just the brain: that is what supports a person's mind—memories, plans, hopes. Therefore, instead of signing up for the whole hog, they choose to have only their dead, severed head put in the freezer—for a mere $80,000. Such techno-optimists conclude that by the time technology is sufficiently advanced to defrost and repair a person, it will surely also be possible to grow or build a new body.

BUT the belief that it is only a person's mind that really matters has led some futurologists to more extreme conclusions. Many people see the mind as essentially a set of information—memories, desires, dreams et cetera—encoded in the brain. They argue that it is only this information that matters, not how or where it is encoded. Brains are useful because our minds run on them like software on a computer, but if we found some other way of running that software, then the squishy gray matter would be dispensable. Given the amount of damage caused to the brain by lying around dead for a few hours, then being filled with antifreeze, then supercooled and, one day, thawed, some cryonicists believe it would be best if they left their old heads behind. The route to resurrection, they argue, is for their brains to be scanned, all their psychological data recorded, then a new brain built to encode it—like running the same software but on a spanking-new computer.

The process of scanning and recording all the psychological information in a brain is known as *mind-uploading*. Even advocates admit that it is currently impossible—the data-storage capacity of the human brain vastly exceeds that of the most powerful existing computers, and scanners do not yet exist that are accurate enough to map the brain neuron by neuron. This is why those who consider mind-uploading to be the route to immortality still have to sign up to have their heads frozen—at the moment, the human brain is the only structure capable of encoding a human mind. But many modern utopians confidently expect that to change—one leading futurologist, Ian Pearson, predicted that "realistically by 2050 we would expect to be able to download your mind into a machine, so when you die it's not a major career problem."

If it does become possible to digitize all the information contained in a human brain, then indeed a whole new world of sci-fi routes to immortality would open up. Your mind could be assigned to an avatar—a virtual person in a virtual world who would have all of your recollections, opinions and quirks. Or, if your mind can be turned into software, then it could be installed onto a robot—who might even be made to look just like the old you. Or, as many immortalists dream, it could be downloaded onto a new brain in a new biological body—but a superbody, immune to aging and disease.

Philosophers call this "computational resurrection," the rerunning of the software that is your mind on a new piece of hardware so that you might live again. The resulting being—whether avatar, robot or human—would be psychologically identical to you: it would remember your first day at school, support your favorite football team and think it was married to your spouse. According to the techno-utopians, it would therefore *be* you; after years lying dead in a freezing thermos, you would live again in a new and improved form.

Mind-uploading has some important advantages over merely finding a modern elixir of life, which, as we saw earlier, would still leave you vulnerable to catastrophic accidents—your airplane crashing, for example, or being at the center of a nuclear explosion. You could make daily backups of yourself on your home computer, which would be linked to a central immortality factory. Within minutes of your plane falling from the sky, a new you, based on your latest scan, would be rolling out of the factory conveyor belt.

If this all sounds rather far-fetched, it is worth considering that companies already exist that offer primitive forms of personality uploading, even attempting to animate these personalities with avatars. Currently the amount and quality of information these avatars use is so small in comparison to the amount preserved in a human brain that few people would be willing to say that the avatar really has the same mind as the original. The goal of bridging this gap is driving forward research in many fields. And with the continued rate of increase in processing power and the involvement already of major corporations such as Microsoft, it might be rash to dismiss the idea that we will soon(ish) be creating digitally based entities with human-like psychologies.

The idea of digital immortality with its various resurrection options fits neatly into the ideology of mastering nature. Digital worlds are ones of our making—we are therefore necessarily their masters, setting the limits and determining what is possible. In such worlds resurrection is a commonplace idea: in video games, you always have more than one life, and you can always start the game again. (As the old joke has it, "My heart had stopped beating; I felt like I was flying down a tunnel toward a circle of light when I heard a voice: 'Insert coin to continue. Ten . . . nine . . . eight . . .'") There is no limit that cannot be transcended with the right programming. At the cutting edge of these technologies, research is motivated by the belief that this need not only be true of our electronic alter-egos, like Pac-Man or your avatar, but can also be true of you.

The digital age, however, promises even more radical reinterpretations of the Resurrection Narrative. We encountered earlier the idea of superintelligence—computers, robots or cyborgs whose intellectual capacities vastly exceed our own. Once we have built one such thing—an eventuality many consider to be inevitable—it would then take over from us the business of further technological innovation. Because it would be so much cleverer than us, the rate of further development would increase exponentially. Soon enough, it, or some even more super superintelligence that it has built, would become all-powerful and all-knowing. Effectively, it would be like God.

The futurists optimistically speculate that such a superintelligence (let us call him "DigiGod") would also be benevolent—that is, well-disposed to the humans that created his primitive digital ancestors. In that case DigiGod would want to make all the humans who have ever lived as happy as possible. Being all-knowing, DigiGod would also have the information required to create beings with psychologies identical to those of all the humans who have ever lived, and being all-powerful, he would also have the capacity to do so. DigiGod, according to these optimists, would therefore resurrect all of us—and create a fine paradise in which we can all live happily ever after.

This is the most extreme version of techno-utopianism, and its debt to the Judeo-Christian tradition is obvious. It is a wonderful demonstration of human ingenuity in weaving an immortality narrative from scraps of science, myth and speculation. This vision has reached its clearest expression in the work of the theoretical physicist Frank Tipler, who has gone as far as arguing that something like DigiGod is inevitable according to the laws of physics, *and* that he will be able to take advantage of certain specific features of the final stages of the universe to create the perception of living for eternity for the universe's inhabitants (Tipler calls this "the Omega Point"). In other words, if you do not believe in the traditional God of religion, don't worry: scientists are going to build him anyway, and he will resurrect us to immortality at the end of time, just like Jesus promised.

NATURE'S REVENGE

BUT as speculations about the prospects of scientific immortality go, we might doubt whether Tipler's vision is any more convincing than Mary Shelley's. When we left Victor Frankenstein, he was inspired by the science of his day to "explore unknown powers, and unfold to the world the deepest mysteries of creation." He throws himself into examining these mysteries until eventually he realizes that "what had been the study and cause of the wisest men since the creation of the world was now within [his] grasp."

Frankenstein toils day and night in his attic laboratory, leaving only to collect human parts—as large as possible to make his work easier—from "vaults and charnel-houses." In a passage of muted horror, we read how finally, "on a dreary night of November," he manages to "infuse a spark of being into the lifeless thing that lay at [his] feet." With language that parallels the reports of Aldini's "galvanic" experiments, Frankenstein tells us, "By the glimmer of the half-extinguished light, I saw the dull yellow eye of the creature open; it breathed hard, and a convulsive motion agitated its limbs."

Just as in her dream, Mary Shelley has her scientist hero rush from the room, overwhelmed with "breathless horror and disgust" at what he has done. Expecting the spark of life to fade from his creation, he collapses exhausted onto his bed, but the "demoniacal corpse" follows him, its arms outstretched. In the belief that he has created a hideous, evil monster, Frankenstein flees into the nighttime street.

From that moment on, things begin to go badly wrong. The poor abandoned monster, in search of his creator, attempts to befriend Frankenstein's five-year-old brother but accidentally kills him when the boy screams out. Shortly afterward monster and creator confront each other in the mountains above Geneva. The creature offers to quit the world of man and leave Frankenstein in peace if only he creates for him a companion—a female just as hideous who would provide him with some affection and sympathy. The scientist, torn between guilt, pity and revulsion, consents, and begins again what has become for him the "most abhorred task" of creating life.

But with his work already advanced, he begins to have doubts:

the female monster might be even more wicked; together they might breed, and "a race of devils would be propagated upon the earth." Overcome with revulsion at these ideas and "trembling with passion," he tears the half-finished woman apart. The monster, feeling betrayed once again, swears that he will be avenged, and so he is. The scientist returns to Geneva and attempts to resume his life, marrying his childhood sweetheart. But on his wedding night, while securing the house, he hears a scream from the bedroom. By the time he arrives, his bride is "lifeless and inanimate"—murdered. Frankenstein might have acquired the power to create life, but his abandoned creature still has the power to take it away.

Victor Frankenstein swears at all costs to destroy the monster and sets off in pursuit of his creation and archenemy. The chase takes them across Europe, into Russia and north to the Arctic Circle, the monster taunting his creator as he eludes him but leads him on. Eventually, worn out and adrift on an ice floe, the scientist is picked up by the ship of an explorer. Seeing in him a fellow spirit, Frankenstein recounts his adventure. But just as the ship is set to return to England, the young scientist dies of exhaustion and fever; that evening the explorer enters the cabin to find the monster standing over his creator's body and lamenting, torn between triumph and grief. Vowing to take his own life, the creature springs from the ship and disappears into the darkness.

THIS, then, is Mary Shelley's portrayal of the modern man of progress who believes he can conquer nature: reckless, self-obsessed and liable to bring destruction on himself and all those around him. In daring to usurp the powers of nature, Victor Frankenstein, the arrogant young scientist, becomes defined by his act of creation, his fate bound to that of his creature. His dream of conquering death takes on a literal life of its own in the form of the monster that he is unable to control and that in the end destroys him.

Mary Shelley was well placed to write this critique: both her father and her husband were just such "men of progress," and she had suffered from their egotism and willingness to sacrifice the interests of others in pursuit of their principles. Her message is that it is an illusion to think we can become like the gods, able to rule over life and death; we are a part of nature, not her master——and if we violate her she will destroy us. It is the perspective of an insightful young woman on the male-dominated world of scientific adventure.

Equally, the nameless monster is also defined by his relationship to his creator——to such an extent that in popular culture, he is often referred to, mistakenly, as "Frankenstein." His unnatural birth leaves him without parentage, role or identity; he is forced to stalk his maker in the hope of finding some kind of meaning or sympathy. After repeated rejection, his goal becomes solely his maker's destruction. When that is complete, there is nothing left for him, as he exclaims over Frankenstein's corpse: "The miserable series of my being is wound to its close!"

The lasting impression is not of the dumb monster of film legend but of a thinking being in search of itself. Its entire journey throughout the book is spent confronting the questions it poses as soon as it learns to formulate words: "Who was I? What was I? Whence did I come? What was my destination? These questions continually recurred, but I was unable to solve them."

THE DUPLICATION PROBLEM REVISITED

THE monster's questions are profound and challenging. He was stitched together from the rotting matter of the charnel house, created from parts that were once human but whose owners were now dead. What was his relationship to these others who once inhabited his body? Was he somehow all of them born again, or one of them, or someone new? This is the fundamental question that hangs over the prospect of resurrection——the question of the identity of the deceased and the risen again. It is the question we must answer in assessing whether there is any plausibility to the Resurrection Narrative.

As we saw in chapter 4, if you die in the expectation of resurrection—whether by an act of God or of science—then you expect that it really will be *you* who rises again. But we saw when looking at the traditional Christian version of resurrection—the Reassembly View, in which God reassembles you atom by atom—that this is not as straightforward as it might seem. That view suffered from three major worries: the Cannibal Problem, which asked what would happen if your matter had also belonged to someone else; the Transformation Problem, which asked how you could both be put back together exactly as you were yet at the same time be made invulnerable and immortal; and the Duplication Problem, which asked what would happen if God re-created both the child and the adult you.

These problems partly stem from having to gather the particular atoms that composed a person on his or her deathbed. But we might anyway ask what difference it could make if we use one particular carbon atom or oxygen atom instead of any other. It is difficult to see how it could be important whether a particular oxygen atom in your resurrected body was once in your original body—an oxygen atom is an oxygen atom. Atoms do not acquire special tags or magical properties from once having formed part of a particular human. The resurrectionist might therefore conclude that we should abandon this troublesome idea of using particular particles: it is not individual atoms that matter but only how they are put together.

This view suits very well the visions of the cryonicists and others whom we met above. We saw that many people believe that what is essential for them to survive into the future is that their mind or psychology be preserved and that someone's psychology can be seen as a set of data, as information about a person's beliefs, memories and so forth. The immortalists who dream of uploading and downloading their minds do not worry about whether their new body will have the same atoms as their previous body. In fact, we saw that they often dream of shiny *new* bodies made of much more reliable stuff than carbon-based flesh and bone. All they think matters is that a newly created brain has the right psychological "software" running on it.

The modern resurrection-hopefuls therefore believe that a person can be created anew if the right blueprint exists, even if that person's original body was completely destroyed in some terrible catastrophe. Let us call this the *Replication View* of resurrection. It says that you could be resurrected by replicating your psychology, regardless of the materials used. So it would not matter if the original you was eaten by lions, who were then eaten by cannibals, who were then atomized in a nuclear explosion. A new, resurrected you could still be made of brand-new atoms, or St. Paul's imperishable stuff, or silicon, or anything else; what would matter is only that this stuff be put together in the right way so as to create a person with your memories, quirks and opinions. If this view really does describe a way in which you can survive death, then you would have good reason to join the optimists and take out a cryonics insurance policy: the only obstacle to your one day living again would be the technical one of developing the immortality factory that can scan you and churn out your replica—a mere engineering problem, as the transhumanists might say.

Whether or not we can be resurrected by simply following a kind of blueprint is a hot topic in modern philosophy, as the answer tells us a great deal about just what kind of things we really are. Serious thinkers defend both sides of the argument. But even those who believe that replication can guarantee survival admit that it forces us to accept some unpalatable and troubling consequences. We will focus on just one of these, as it is the most telling: it is the Duplication Problem, which we met when looking at the Reassembly View.

We saw that in the Reassembly View, God could theoretically create both the five-year-old you and the eighty-year-old you because they could be made of different particles. This is a problem, but at least in the Reassembly View the problem is limited by the need to have a complete separate set of particles from the old you in order to make a new you—God could not create two eighty-year-old versions of you, because there is only one set of particles that made up the eighty-year-old you. In the Replication View, however, this problem is much worse. This view says that individual particles don't matter—it is only the blueprint that counts. So our future immortality factory, which stores the latest scan of your brain, could in theory churn out any number of duplicate yous. Each one would believe himself to be the real you just as much as you now believe yourself to be the real you.

This is a big problem. Let us take a candidate for high-tech resurrection called Frank. He dies in a dramatic midair explosion while crossing the Atlantic. Luckily, an automatic transmitter immediately alerts the immortality factory back on land, which within minutes produces a single new replacement—Frank 2, based on his latest brain scan. Frank 2 thinks, walks and talks just like Frank—apart from amnesia about his recent flight, but that is probably no bad thing. Frank 2 is told that the last version of him was killed in the plane and thinks, "How lucky that I did that brain scan just before leaving for the airport. But perhaps I'd better stay on land for a while, as having to be replicated is terrible for my no-claims bonus. Now best get back to the wife and assure her I'm okay." His friends and family quickly accept that, despite the midair mishap, Frank is back—that he has in fact been resurrected.

But imagine instead that the factory malfunctions. The instructions for a new Frank get sent to more than one of its many assemblers, and as a consequence the factory churns out two new versions—a Frank 2a *and* a Frank 2b. We can call this the *Duplicate Case*. Now, in this case, who is Frank?

It is tempting to say that they both are. But that cannot be right. For a start, it would violate a fundamental rule of logic (called the transitivity of identity) that says that if Frank 2a is the same person as Frank, and Frank 2b is the same person as Frank, then Frank 2a must be the same person as Frank 2b. Yet this is clearly not the case, as the two new Franks are in fact two separate individuals, perfectly capable of going their separate ways.

And if we look at it from the original Frank's perspective, it is even clearer that he cannot be both of them. Imagine he sees one of the plane's engines catch fire and knows he is about to die. He remembers that he has recently been scanned and so thinks that he need not worry about dying high over the ocean, as his psychology will simply be transferred to a new brain and body. He is reassured, believing he can reasonably look forward to waking up in the new body, just as he might look forward to waking up from a night's sleep—that, after all, is what we would usually expect if someone told us that we were going to live on.

But the factory has produced two new Franks. We can imagine that Frank 2b on emerging from the factory is shocked to see a mirror image of himself on the other side of the road and accidentally walks into an oncoming car, causing terrible pain and injury, while Frank 2a looks on. If it were true that Frank *is* both Frank 2a *and* Frank 2b, then this means he would experience *both* being hit by a car, as happens to Frank 2b, *and* seeing the collision from the other side of the road, as happens to Frank 2a. But there is no person having *both* of these experiences. Indeed, these experiences are mutually exclusive—one cannot simultaneously both be in terrible pain and not in terrible pain.

So Frank cannot be both of his replacements. Is he, then, just one of them? But how could this be? The relationship between Frank and Frank 2a is just the same as the relationship between Frank and Frank 2b. Both new Franks have just the same claim to be the original—there is no reason to think Frank might *be* one of them rather than the other. The immortalist could perhaps try to argue that Frank is whichever was produced first—but we can just as easily imagine that the factory produced them simultaneously, so this argument won't work either.

Yet if Frank is not both of them and not either of them, then he must be *neither* of them. In other words, he has not really survived at all. It looks very much like the immortality factory has not actually resurrected Frank but just produced two duplicates of him. It is as if someone made two new versions of a Vincent van Gogh painting that had been burned to ashes: no matter how true to the original they were, we would not think that van Gogh's work had come back into existence. And if someone tried to claim that the two new paintings really *were* the original, we would consider that person a fraudster.

To make this problem for the Replication View even clearer, let us imagine a slightly different malfunction: the message is sent to the immortality factory that Frank is about to die, but then the plane suddenly rights itself, and he does not die after all. But the factory has already started producing Frank 2, who duly rolls out of the machine based on Frank's latest brain scan. Now Frank has survived his flight, and he has not even noticed that a replica was being produced of him in the distant factory—it has had no direct impact on him at all. Frank might not find out that he has been replicated until he returns home from his travels to find Frank 2 in bed with his wife. In this case, in which the original Frank still exists, it is clear that the factory has just made a copy of him—so let us call this the *Copying Case*.

The relationship of this copy to the original Frank would be like that of identical twins—they would be extremely similar, but they would not literally be the same single individual. If Frank was about to die, it might provide some consolation for him to find out that his duplicate was living happily in Peru—Frank could even telephone him to be reassured that Frank 2 would continue his life's work for him or look after his children. But Frank would not when he died literally *become* Frank 2; he would not literally live on as him, any more than someone literally lives on as his or her identical twin.

In all these cases, the relationship between the original Frank and the new Franks is exactly the same——the new ones are freshly minted persons made to the mold of Frank's psychology. But what the Duplicate Case and the Copying Case show is that this relationship of psychological similarity does not suffice to make Frank literally exactly the same person as the replica. And if this relationship does not suffice to guarantee literal identity in these cases, then we have no reason to think it would guarantee literal identity in the original, straightforward case, where Frank dies and a single new version rolls out of the factory. What the immortality factory does is produce copies, just as much as if it were to produce copies of a van Gogh painting.

Which means you could not evade death by having your mind uploaded onto a hard drive and downloaded onto an avatar or a new body after all. The problems with digital immortality, computational resurrection and immortality factories are not merely technological: they are also conceptual. These would all just be high-tech ways of producing a counterfeit you. When you closed your eyes on your deathbed, you could not expect to open them again in silicon form. Even if DigiGod made a perfect copy of you at the end of time, it would be exactly that: a copy, an entirely new person who just happened to have the same memories and beliefs as you.

Which is bad news for techno-utopians and science fiction fans. This kind of replication is very common in sci-fi——for example, in the classic series *Star Trek*, it is the main mode of transport. Called "beaming," it involves Captain Kirk and his colleagues being "converted into energy," then "rematerialized" at the target destination. One real-life theoretical physicist and futurist, Professor Michio Kaku, has predicted that such a technology could really be attainable within a century. But there is a snag: "converting someone into energy"——which is taken to

involve at the very least pulling him apart into individual atoms—
would, by any reckoning, kill him. This might be forgivable if he
was then genuinely resurrected at his destination, when his atoms
were put back together again. But we have seen that such a recon-
structed person is really only a replica—a copy, like an identical
twin, not literally the same person come back to life. The tragic
truth is that Captain Kirk, poor man, died a long time ago—and
countless duplicates of him have gone the same way since.

Many philosophers consider the Duplication Problem to be an
insurmountable obstacle to accepting anything like the Replication
View of resurrection. But if that is so, then there is *no* plausible
account of resurrection. There is a deep reason for this, which is also
the true lesson of the Duplication Problem. All versions of the Resurrection Narrative start out by accepting that we really do die and
decay. But it is very difficult to make sense of how someone can
return from this kind of utter extinction. The first route to
immortality—Staying Alive—straightforwardly avoided this problem. And the third narrative form, which we will explore next,
claims that although our *bodies* die and rot, our *souls* live on, so we do
not really die at all. Resurrection is alone in taking death on the
chin—and this is the problem: most philosophers believe that if
something has completely ceased to exist—like a person who has
died and rotted or a painting that has been burned—then any new
version that is made, however similar, is nothing more than a copy.

Even many Christian philosophers who actually believe that
we will all be resurrected recognize this problem. They have
therefore tried to come up with imaginative theories that deny the
apparent fact that we die and rot—one respected philosopher, for
example, has argued that for resurrection to work, God must actually steal our real bodies just before we are about to die and store
them somewhere in suspended animation to be reawakened on
Judgment Day. The corpses we see rotting or being cremated are
fakes that God leaves in place of the real thing. Alas, the philoso-

pher in question does not explain why no one has ever seen a dying person being carried off to the storage space in the sky (or wherever it is), or why God would want to be an arch-deceiver. Needless to say, this view has not gained widespread acceptance. If it is the best account of resurrection going, then it is no wonder that millions have set their hopes on a soul instead.

This problem of the identity of the resurrected person is also reflected obliquely in the Resurrection Narrative's dystopian side. Ample works of film and fiction spin a story of what happens when your once-friendly neighbor rises from the earth, not as his wise-cracking old self but as a shambling, blood-hungry monster. Mindless, soulless and infested with maggots, such reanimated creatures are, of course, zombies. They are the true children of Frankenstein, a countercultural mockery of our claims to master life and death. Their message from the other side is that we lack the power, wisdom and maturity to conquer the grave and that what is dead and buried is better left that way.

THE LIFE WITHIN

THE dream of rising again haunts the human imagination. Throughout history, many immortality narratives have promised that death need only be temporary and that we will have a second shot at life. This dream of Resurrection, the second fundamental form of immortality narrative, has forged new faiths and is helping to drive forward our current technological revolution. Its intuitive appeal is in reflecting the natural cycles of life, death and rebirth that humans have long observed all around them. This has provided the basis of countless religions and rituals—including the Abrahamic tradition that has so much shaped the world today.

But the distinctive strategy resurrection offers for overcoming the Mortality Paradox is also its weakness. We have seen that in accepting that we really do die—denying only that it need last forever—the Resurrection Narrative runs headlong into a conceptual quagmire. The lesson both of *Frankenstein* and of philosophy is that the resurrection world would not be a paradise of happy reunions but more akin to a land of doppelgängers and zombies.

Awareness of these problems, in one form or another, is as old as the belief in resurrection itself. We saw in chapter 4 that the early Christians had great difficulty in persuading the sophisticated Greeks that they would bodily rise again. We would do well to follow the Greeks' example and be equally skeptical about the offers of digital immortality that promise you could soon be transferring your mind to a new and improved silicon body.

Many of those who recognize the frailties of the body and are skeptical of its capacity to die and rise again have therefore turned to another vehicle for eternal life: the soul. Most people on earth think they have one, and most of those think it will take them to an afterlife. And many hold the view, passionately advocated by many ancient Greeks, that the life of the soul is a much nobler thing than the messy life of the flesh—a view clearly expressed by Mary Shelley in yet another of her meditations on eternal life, "The Mortal Immortal":

> I yield this body, too tenacious a cage for the soul which thirsts for freedom, to the destructive elements of air and water . . . and, by scattering and annihilating the atoms that compose my frame, set at liberty the life imprisoned within, and so cruelly prevented from soaring from this dim Earth to a sphere more congenial to its immortal essence.

In the next two chapters we will see how the idea of the soul has shaped civilization and whether it does indeed provide us with an immortal essence. We will begin in heaven, then pass through purgatory and hell on our way once again to the most modern laboratories. And for the first part of our journey, we will take as our guide that master of the afterlife Dante Alighieri.

PART III

SOUL

6

BEATRICE'S SMILE

What Happens in Paradise

IN the manner of young Italian poets, Dante Alighieri was deeply in love. That he had seen the object of his adoration only a handful of times only fueled his ardor. At their first meeting they were both children: "She appeared to me dressed in a most noble color, a rich and subdued red, tied and adorned in a manner becoming to her very tender age," he later recalled. Her tender age was eight, and she was Beatrice Portinari, daughter of a wealthy banker; Dante was nine but evidently old enough to experience the most burning passion.

Nine years later, he came across her on a street in his native Florence, then an independent city-state; as he timidly stared, she glanced over and politely greeted him, at which point he immediately "saw all the bounds of bliss." This modest salutation sent the love-stricken young man into such paroxysms of passion that he had visions of the god of love feeding his flaming heart to the semi-naked Beatrice. So consumed was he with thoughts of his lady that he began to waste away, and only the writing of sonnets could give him solace.

But then something happened that was not in the script of courtly romance that Dante had earnestly been following: Beatrice died. She was just twenty-four and had recently married another man when "the Lord of Justice called this most gentle one to glory." Dante wept until he could weep no more, writing that the whole of his beloved Florence seemed to him "left as if widowed."

For the young lyricist deprived of his muse, this seemed a tragedy. Who now would inspire his verses? The answer came to him in "a miraculous vision": Beatrice was not dead and gone but with him, the Lord of the Heavens. Her soul lived on and, freed of its earthly shackles, was purer and more beautiful than ever. This was surely a worthy subject for the ambitious poet. No longer needing to be true to a living image, his artistic imagination was free to take his idol to a whole new realm. Dante undertook "to write of her what had never before been written of any woman." And that is exactly what he did, in an epic account of the life of the soul that shaped Western ideas of the hereafter for generations to come.

THE SOUL ASCENDING

NO one likes to imagine their loved ones simply rotting in the grave. But this is what the Resurrection Narrative has in store for them, until God or science should summon them to live again. We have seen, however, that these stories are not only unsatisfactory for their zombie-movie undercurrents—they also have deep-reaching philosophical difficulties.

The problems of resurrection are largely those of ensuring the deceased and the risen again really are the same person. The solution to these problems leads naturally on to the third fundamental form of immortality narrative: the Soul. The soul bridges the gap between this world and the next; it keeps an essential part of us out of the grave even when our bodies fail and permits us to fly directly to the next world without an embarrassing interim as a hapless pile of bones.

The soul hypothesis has proven intellectually and emotionally satisfying for countless cultures across the globe. Even in today's increasingly secular and scientific world, it remains hugely attractive: in America, for example, 71 percent of people believe they have one, whereas Europeans are only slightly more skeptical—in the UK and Germany, for example, polls suggest around 60 percent of people believe in a soul. In Africa and India, that figure is much higher—over 90 percent in India, and close to 100 percent in, for example, Nigeria. And even in communist or former communist countries, despite decades of official atheism, millions believe they have a soul. All in all, the overwhelming majority of the world's nearly seven billion inhabitants subscribe to this particular immortality narrative.

In the next chapter, we will look at whether these billions of people are right. But first, we will look at how the soul emerged from the murky world of the mystery cult to become perhaps the most influential single idea in the history of Western civilization. We will look at how the Soul Narrative succeeds in flattering our aspirational side with its promise of transcendence and how it has given us a sense of self that has fostered individualism, democracy and the demands for rights, equality and freedom that have shaped the modern age.

Of all the narratives, the Soul should be best able to deliver an immortality worth having. It promises an eternal life that takes place in a fantastical realm—whether heaven or hell, the halls of Valhalla or the Isles of the Blessed. This has provided visionaries and poets with the chance to imagine an ideal afterlife, without the limitations of physical existence. In this chapter, we will examine some of these visions to see if they offer an eternity to die for.

. . .

THE idea of the soul is both ancient and intuitive. It claims that
there is some part of you that is spiritual or immaterial in nature—
and that this part is the *real* you. Being immaterial, this soul is not
subject to decay and destruction like your physical frame, and so
when your body dies, your soul can continue its journey—to the
next life and immortality.

In dreams and visions, people of many cultures have had what
seemed like the experience of floating free of their physical self to
visit other places and times. They often regarded this as evidence
that their real essence was some spiritual thing that can function
independently of their fleshly frame. This incorporeal self goes by
many names, with accompanying variations in the account: astral
body, subtle body or etheric body; psyche, pneuma or mind; ghost
or spirit. But wherever we find the belief that the real you is separate
from your body and can outlive it, we have the Soul Narrative.

Many cultures ritualized these experiences of dreams and
visions, enhancing their meaning as journeys to the spirit world,
where wisdom and power were sought and natural limits could be
overcome. But their ideas of the soul were not necessarily much
like the ideas prevalent today. The Egyptians, for example, believed
in two souls, which played subtly different roles in making up a
human. Such notions of multiple or composite souls were common;
to many ancient peoples it seemed obvious that such faculties as
breath, consciousness, intellect and appetite were all essential to
human life yet were nonphysical and therefore dependent on different spiritlike aspects of the self. As not all of these "souls" were immortal by nature, the postmortem life of the spirit was inevitably
shadowy and incomplete.

In the Greek-speaking world, one movement in particular led the
way in uniting these disparate elements of the self: the mystery cults,
which we mentioned earlier as offering the participant a chance to
become one with their deity. They believed their rituals would bring
them a happy and full afterlife, in explicit contrast to the dark and

partial existence that awaited the uninitiated. Instead of going to dank, dark Hades, their souls would rise up to the stars to live with the gods. These cults were very influential in certain educated circles, and one thinker who came under this influence was Plato.

This Athenian philosopher, working some four hundred years before Jesus preached, developed a theory of the soul that was to prove very attractive to the Christian mind. Plato was the first person in the West to clearly defend the claim that the soul was the essential part of us—the true self—and that it was by nature immortal. In keeping with his broader philosophy, he argued that the physical body was only an imperfect imitation of the true person. Like other physical things, the body was subject to change and, ultimately, destruction. The soul, on the other hand, belonged to the unchanging realm of the divine—it was incorruptible and therefore eternal.

However, this heavenly immortality still had to be earned. In a view that sounds to modern ears remarkably Eastern, Plato suggested unworthy souls would be reincarnated into new bodies. In order to attain a more glorious immortality, one had to do what Plato did: contemplate the true, the good and the beautiful. Developing your intellectual side in this way strengthened your soul and brought it closer to the divine, ultimately allowing it to soar free from bodily existence.

Plato brought the idea of the soul out of the obscurity of the magico-religious mystery cult and into the realm of rational discourse. His belief in the soul was not the product of some mystical experience but was a philosophical theory, based on reasons and arguments available to all. By virtue of having a soul, each of us, he claimed, was intrinsically immortal: no complex rites or miracles were required to make us live on or rise again.

. . .

FOR many later defenders of the Christian faith, this account of immortality was irresistible. We saw previously that early Christianity depended for its success on the promise of the physical resurrection of the dead. The dominant view in the Mediterranean lands at the time was that people had a soul, but few were so confident as the Greek philosopher that it would fly up to join the divine; most expected instead the joyless underworld portrayed in Homer. They were therefore very receptive when St. Paul and his fellow missionaries promised the imminent arrival of a paradise on earth, which believers would enjoy as fully and physically as they do the pleasures of this life.

But that paradise did not prove to be quite so imminent as Paul had hoped. As one generation of martyrs followed another, the graves filled up without a Second Coming in sight. Christian thinkers were therefore challenged to come up with a plausible account of where the dead were supposed to be, what they were doing while waiting for the End Times to come and what would ensure that the risen faithful were really the same people as those who died. As we have seen, these proved to be hard questions to answer. But the promise of the afterlife was so central to Christian teaching that it could not be allowed to stand or fall with the problematic Resurrection Narrative. Some shoring up was therefore needed, and Plato held the answer.

The process was a natural one. The missionary zeal of the early believers, with their promise of eternity in paradise, proved enormously powerful. They won so many followers that over the course of the fourth century, Christianity became first accepted, then encouraged, then finally the established religion of the Roman Empire. No longer did the new faith have to fight to distinguish itself from the Greek and Egyptian mystery cults or the sects of other apocalyptic preachers. Now Christianity was in a position of power from which it could afford to pick and choose the best insights of the pagans to strengthen its own story, and converts from the intellectual classes of Greece and Rome brought their formidable learning to bear on the theological conundrums of the day.

The most famous of these converts was the towering figure of St. Augustine, a well-to-do Roman citizen and highly educated philosopher in the classical tradition. As a young man he explored a number of religions and philosophies and led a hedonistic life, famously praying, "Lord, give me chastity and self-restraint, but not yet." But eventually, under his mother's guidance, he converted to Christianity in 387 ce, just as it was becoming the official religion of the empire. His genius in applying his philosophical training to Christian doctrine made him probably the most influential theologian in history.

Augustine accepted the biblical story of our bodies physically rising from the earth when the last trumpet sounds, but he believed that we each have a soul too. Both body and soul were essential for a fully human existence, he believed, but—as Plato suggested—the soul was the better part of us, associated with our intellect and conscience. Most importantly, it would live on and preserve our identity after death. Then when the End Times arrived and the graves were opened, the body would rise again to be reunited with the soul; only then could the complete person lead a full afterlife—whether with the saints in heaven or burning forever in the fiery lakes of hell.

Although Augustine found room for the body in keeping with Christian tradition, he favored the Platonic ideal of an eternity of intellectual contemplation over fleshly pleasures. Body and soul would be reunited, but there was little bodily fun to be had in his idea of heaven. Women would be given back their bodies, complete with all their female parts, but he believed that these would not arouse lust in heaven's menfolk—rather, on seeing such beauty, men would applaud the wisdom and goodness of God. After his conversion, Augustine himself had become ascetic and celibate, and this was what he promoted as properly Christian.

Plato's theories rescued Christianity from the problems of the resurrection-only narrative: the persistence of the same single soul from the living person, through bodily death, to the resurrected person ensured that it really was the same person throughout. There was no risk that it would be a luckless replica who was being punished on the sinner's behalf.

The combined Resurrection/Soul Narrative remains the official doctrine of many Christian denominations, in particular the Catholic Church, defended by theologians from St. Thomas Aquinas in the Middle Ages to the German professor Joseph Ratzinger, who became Pope Benedict XVI in 2005. But in reality, the importance of the resurrection element of the story slowly withered—if souls of the departed are already experiencing their postmortem fate, whether in heaven, hell or purgatory, then being rejoined with their bodies seems at most a formality. For most Christians today, the soul alone is the route to immortality.

THE SOUL OF OUR CIVILIZATION

THE rise of the soul in Christianity is therefore a fascinating story of how one immortality narrative came to supplement and indeed largely replace another within a single religious movement. Of course, belief in a soul is both older and more widely spread than Christianity alone, and its attractions lie not only in filling in the gaps left by the Resurrection Narrative. Indeed, the appeal of the soul hypothesis runs deep: it speaks to an idea of ourselves as noble, transcendent and unique, an idea that plays strongly to our will to immortality, neatly resolves the Mortality Paradox, and as a consequence has been enormously influential—shaping, as the historians of ideas Raymond Martin and John Barresi put it, "the entire mindset of Western civilisation."

The Mortality Paradox arises because we observe objectively that our bodies will eventually fail and die, yet subjectively we cannot conceive of ourselves not existing. We therefore seek belief systems that can explain away the apparent fact of death and permit us to believe that it is not really the end. The Soul Narrative accomplishes this perfectly: it denies that the failing body is the true self, identifying the person instead with exactly that mental life that seems so inextinguishable. For believers in the soul, it is our very capacity to look beyond our corporeal being to imagine different bodies, different times, different worlds and ultimately the divine that proves that our true self must transcend the physical.

The claim that we are each of us fundamentally a soul therefore resolves the Mortality Paradox. But more than that, it connects each of us to what we believe is finest in the universe. For Plato, the soul was that part of us that could partake of truth and beauty in their unchanging reality. For the Christians, it is a spark of God, made in his image and capable of communion with him. This narrative is telling us that we are each part divine, something celestial and transcendent. It transforms the Mortality Paradox from a duality in our perception of death into a duality at the heart of our nature: not only do we seem part mortal and part immortal, but also part beast and part angel, part creaturely and part godly. Many poets and thinkers have seen this duality as the very essence of man. And of course, the story tells us that it is the angelic, the godly, the immortal that triumphs.

We saw earlier that ritual could create a sense of union between a person and his or her god and was fundamental to early religion. Such union would be achieved during elaborate rites, which would culminate in the participant experiencing a brief moment of what the anthropologist Ernest Becker called "cosmic significance." But the Platonic soul idea makes such complex ceremony redundant: it claims that we are by our very nature a spark of the divine and therefore by our very nature immortal. All we must do is live up to this nature—foster this better side of us, whether through contemplating philosophical truths or loving our neighbors.

This is a very gratifying story. It is a fine and effective antidote to the fear of death. But it also tackles the additional anxieties that spring from the view of ourselves inherent in the first half of the Mortality Paradox—the view that we are ephemeral creatures. The psychoanalysts realized that this not only causes death anxiety but also undermines our self-esteem and sense of the meaningfulness of life. It suggests that we are no more significant than other animals—than the worm or snail that briefly live their mean, functional lives before being crushed by an indifferent nature. All our questing for heroism and transcendence fights against this view, but the Soul Narrative simply explodes it: it claims that each one of us is essentially very special indeed—an immortal in the making. We are each of us born cosmically significant.

The way the Soul story has been adopted by the Abrahamic religions further bolsters the sense of individual cosmic significance of their believers. The soul is associated with consciousness and the life of the mind—the internal voice that we each have. And this internal voice, as a gift of the divine, is therefore able to communicate directly with its creator. St. Augustine, for example, having argued for the view of the soul as intellect, emphasized the importance of using this faculty to build a personal relationship with God. Simply by willing this communication in prayer, whether out loud or as internal monologue, each of us could and should enter into dialogue with the Almighty.

This communication has since become the basis of the Christian experience. But it is worth dwelling for a moment on the extent of the self-importance implicit in this view: once the gods were remote and capricious, only to be reached through complex rituals. Now suddenly the one true God is always on call; on the one hand, he is the Creator of the Universe, the lord of all, omnipotent and omniscient, he who sent the great flood to destroy a sinful humanity. Yet on the other hand, he wants to hear your every wish, regret and foible; all you have to do is think it, and he is there, all ears. The most powerful being there ever could be, dwarfing kings, presidents and prime ministers, is apparently interested in *you*.

Ernest Becker described this as "the most remarkable achievement of the Christian world picture: that it could take slaves, cripples, imbeciles, the simple and the mighty, and make them all secure heroes, simply by taking a step back from the world into another dimension of things, the dimension called heaven." From this new perspective, every man, woman and child, each one of the billions, is special and important, with a role to play in God's great drama and loved by him personally and individually.

The extraordinary claim that the creator of the universe knows and cares for each one of us has over the past two millennia become commonplace, almost a truism of the religious worldview. It is not unique to Christianity but has become a central feature of all the Abrahamic religions, especially Islam. In the places where religious conversions are still common——for example, prisons or programs for alcoholics and drug addicts——these narratives successfully offer to the convert a cosmic significance otherwise unattainable in a life regarded socially as a failure.

This is a radical departure from older worldviews that make mortals the playthings of a pitiless fate. In the polytheistic pre-Christian religions of Greece, Rome and the Middle East, the gods were indifferent at best, cruel, abusive and deceitful at worst. Cosmic significance could only be attained through the heroic deeds of men like Achilles and Odysseus, or through mastering the elaborate rites of the mysteries. But such worldviews offered only partial satisfaction of our will to immortality; little surprise, then, that they gave way to that version of the Soul Narrative that makes eternity our birthright.

THIS narrative has proved irresistible, even to those who do not accept its religious framework, and it has so suffused the modern—particularly Western—worldview that we can hardly imagine an alternative. This influence is the principle of individualism—the primary worth of each and every individual—which has come to be the supreme value throughout large parts of the world.

The full consequences took time to emerge: as the influential French anthropologist Louis Dumont wrote, it was "a transformation so radical and so complex that it took at least seventeen centuries of Christian history to be completed." Scholarly consensus is that this transformation arose from the unique combination of Greek philosophy and Judeo-Christian religion. Dumont's account of this development runs like this: initially, spiritually minded people discover their individual self by turning away from the collective that is society and defining themselves solely in relation to the divine. This can be seen in the spiritual traditions of Hinduism and Buddhism, and also in early Christianity: Jesus of Nazareth basically taught that we should leave our families and societies and wait humbly for the coming apocalypse. Outside of the distractions of society, a Christian could realize himself or herself as an "individual-in-relation-to-God."

Christianity's otherworldliness, however, began to be challenged when it became the official religion of the Roman Empire. Although in the form of the monasteries it maintained a tradition of those who spurned mainstream society, increasingly it was forced to find a way of permitting the millions of people who were suddenly within its purview some way of being both Christians and ordinary citizens. Dumont records two leaps forward in this reconciliation: in the eighth century, when the church accepted its active role in the political sphere, and then in the Reformation, when the individual believer powerfully reasserted his or her direct relationship to God.

It was Martin Luther, of course, in the early sixteenth century who initiated this second revolution, though it had been simmering for centuries. Each of us has an immortal soul with a direct line to God, he argued, and therefore each of us is a sovereign moral agent who must freely choose whether or not to put his or her faith in

Christ. This was a call for religious freedom, but Christianity was too embedded in the surrounding culture for its effects to remain contained in the spiritual realm. The assertion that each individual was equal before God quickly led to demands for economic and political liberties, causing revolutions both in thought and on the streets. In Dumont's terms, the individual *as opposed to* society had become the individual *within* society.

Individualism, with its belief in the absolute value and autonomy of the person, is therefore the political expression of the Soul Narrative. All ethical and political systems are grounded in some conception of what it is to be human. The claim of the Soul Narrative that each of us is a spark of the divine, and therefore sovereign unto him or herself, was a radical view of human nature that, once allowed to permeate social and political thinking, had far-reaching and dramatic implications. We were not merely one of the tribe, not merely Olaf-the-ax-maker, son of Olaf-the-ax-maker and latest in a long line of Olaf-the-ax-makers, not merely a weak body fated to briefly flourish and die like a spring flower. We were individuals, and as such deserved rights, equality, freedom and democracy.

The ethics of the soul reached its finest expression in the famous words of the American Declaration of Independence: "We hold these truths to be self-evident, that all men are created equal, that they are endowed by their Creator with certain unalienable Rights, that among these are Life, Liberty and the pursuit of Happiness." To most people in history, these truths would have been anything but self-evident. Indeed, to an ancient Roman patrician, a medieval serf, or an Indian "untouchable," they would have seemed self-evidently false—as they would have to the slaves kept by those free citizens of the new America. But once the view that each human being has a unique, immortal essence is brought into the social realm, then all the rest—eventually—follows.

After spreading beyond its religious origins this view acquired a secular vocabulary: the word "self" has now taken over from "soul," but it expresses the same essential idea that each of us has an irreducible core that makes us unique and special. Although this claim has been under steady assault for a century—from psychoanalysts and deconstructionists, behaviorists and neuroscientists—it continues to be the dominant philosophy of our age. Capitalism and consumerism, with their emphasis on economic autonomy, are dependent upon it, as are the political ideologies of human rights and liberal democracy, not to mention the modern cults of self-actualization and self-discovery.

The Soul Narrative, which is so successful at satisfying the will to immortality, has therefore provided the principal values of our civilization—even for those who long since abandoned its more mystical overtones. Ernest Becker, following the psychoanalyst Otto Rank, recognized that individualism and the aggrandizement of the self are not only products of this narrative but a continuation of the same quest for immortality. Whether or not we literally believe we have a soul that will go to heaven, the cosmic significance we ascribe to ourselves as unique individuals reassures us that we transcend mere biology. It convinces us that we are each special, possessing "infinite worth" as Dumont put it—not like the anonymous animals that live and die in their millions around us. In pursuing the cult of the self—building careers, actualizing our potential and acquiring ever more things—we are creating a myth of immunity to extinction.

WHERE IS HEAVEN?

DANTE had little reason to doubt either his own cosmic significance or that of mankind as the primary actors in God's great plan. He was convinced that the earth was at the center of the universal order and that heaven awaited the virtuous. Indeed, he claimed to have been there.

Dante boldly claimed that his epic was reportage—that his

descriptions were not merely a product of his judgment or imagination but what he had actually seen. Many seem to have believed
him: his fellow poet and admirer Giovanni Boccaccio reported
that those who passed Dante in the street would marvel at how his
beard seemed charred and skin darkened from his adventures in
the fiery realms of hell. Even those who may have regarded his
account as more like a religious vision than a report of a physical
journey found it so persuasive that they believed that, like the
Bible, it must at the least have been divinely inspired.

His masterpiece opens on the day before Good Friday in the year
1300, with Dante lost in a forest and being harassed by wild beasts.
He is rescued by the soul of the Roman poet Virgil, who offers to
guide him out—albeit via the spirit world. His guide then takes
Dante through hell, where the souls are "in such pain / That every
one of them calls out for a second death"; up to purgatory, where the
souls "though in the fire, / Are happy because they hope . . . to join
the blessed"; and thence to the very edge of heaven, but as a pagan,
Virgil can go no farther. He therefore hands his charge over to none
other than the beloved Beatrice to act as guide through the celestial
realm, where, in Dante's view, she clearly warrants a place.

Dante gives us a perfect picture of the medieval geography of
the afterlife, complete with maps: Hell, following convention, is in
the bowels of the earth. Its nine circles go deeper and deeper toward the core, with ever-more-terrible punishments being meted
out on increasingly wicked sinners. In the lowest pit of the lowest
circle, Satan is entombed to the waist in ice, futilely beating his
monstrous wings. As Dante, like most educated people of his time,
believed the earth to be a globe, he and Virgil are able to pass by
Satan and go farther through the earth's core, at which point they
begin ascending up toward the surface of the Southern Hemisphere. Emerging, they find Mount Purgatory, an island mountain
with seven terraces whose summit, high in the sky, is the Garden of
Eden. From here, heaven is within reach.

Dante's portrayal of heaven itself reflects the conflation of cosmology and religion that was normal at the time. In the Hebrew and Greek of the Bible—as still in many modern languages—the term "heaven" refers to both the sky and the abode of God. This for Dante and his contemporaries was a literal truth. They believed that the earth was at the center of the universe, and around this center turned layers of "celestial spheres" that held the heavenly bodies. These spheres *were* heaven, home of the souls of the righteous: the first sphere both held the moon and was the abode of those souls who had been virtuous but inconstant; the fourth sphere, for example, held the sun and was the residence of the souls of the wise, such as Thomas Aquinas. Then came various planets, until the eighth sphere, which held the fixed stars along with the saints and the Virgin Mary.

Beyond that was the "primum mobile"—the "first moved" sphere whose motion was controlled directly by God. It was the realm of the angels, and beyond it, in the empyrean, which transcended physical space, dwelled God himself. This was in keeping with Christian tradition: when the disciples watched while Jesus, forty days after his resurrection, "was lifted up, and a cloud took him out of their sight" (Acts 1:9), they would have understood this to be a literal ascension into heaven, physically situated beyond the sky. Dante claimed to have been there, and his fellow medieval Christians on reading his travelogue could look up into the clouds and dream that their souls might one day follow in his footsteps.

THE discovery a few centuries later that the earth was not the center of the cosmos—or even of our little solar system—came therefore as something of a shock. This view took more than a century to become accepted after Nicolaus Copernicus published his arguments in 1543 and was fought by the Catholic Church at every step. In the trial of Galileo, who provided further evidence for the Copernican view, it was condemned as "heretical, for being explicitly contrary to Holy Scripture." When the monk and astronomer Giordano Bruno added that the sun was just one of many stars in a potentially infinite universe, he was burned at the stake.

The Copernican view was a major blow to humanity's cosmic significance. In Dante's universe, we are at the center of creation, with God and his angels all around us. This is the reassuring image that Dante and his contemporaries would have had as they stared up at the stars. But in the Copernican universe, we are adrift on one of many planets, revolving around one of many stars in an enormity of cold, dark space. As C. S. Lewis observed, when we moderns now look up to the stars, it is not to the firmament of angels looking kindly back, but out——endlessly out——into the lonely void.

As telescopes grew more powerful and knowledge of cosmology improved, the prospect of finding the heavenly host receded. No matter how hard the astronomers looked, no angels could be seen plucking harps amid the stars. The advent of human space travel dispelled the illusion once and for all. Russian cosmonaut Yuri Gagarin, the first man in space, is reported to have commented, "I don't see any god up here." The American astronauts who landed on the moon, though fond of quoting Scripture, did not meet the souls of the "virtuous but inconstant" promised by Dante. We humans currently wandering the surface of planet Earth appear, as far as we can see, to be alone.

Some biblical literalists continue to believe that heaven is physically located in the distant realms of space, but the evidence of science makes this view nothing more than a curiosity. Most believers have instead taken refuge in the slippery language of "another realm," "other dimensions" or "alternate universes." Although these words are also used in science, the claim that heaven resides in such spaces is not based on scientific evidence or even compatible with it. The hypothesis about the nature of the universe called "string theory," for example, posits some number of extra dimensions beyond the usual four——a fact that has given hope to some of the faithful. But these dimensions are not alternate realities where paradise might be hiding; they are part of this universe and are (if they exist) very, very small—meaning many orders of magnitude smaller than an atom. Unlikely, therefore, to contain the New Jerusalem.

This is embarrassing, not only for our sense of cosmic significance but for the Soul Narrative itself. Before Copernicus, its advocates were always fairly sure about where their souls went: up or down, to the sun or the stars, beyond the horizon or under the earth. Now, however, we have searched all these places. Each time one of these sites is found to be empty of souls and angels, believers relocate heaven to the next place that we cannot so easily check— until we can, when it moves on again. It is not a track record that inspires confidence.

Souls, if they are to live forever, must live forever *somewhere*, but it is not at all easy to say where. Defenders of supernatural realms must explain what makes these supposed spaces more than just fantasy. Seeming to find it a little awkward, clever theologians invariably try to avoid the question of heaven's whereabouts as much as possible. When put on the spot, they tend to take something of a mystical turn. The aforementioned theologian Joseph Ratzinger, who became Pope Benedict XVI, for example, writes that heaven "lies neither inside nor outside the space of our world" but rather is "the new 'space' of the body of Christ, the communion of saints." Well, that clears that up, then.

BUT the Copernican was only the first of two revolutions that threatened both the Soul Narrative and our hopes of going to heaven. The second, of course, was Charles Darwin's theory of evolution by natural selection, which placed us humans firmly on the family tree with apes, pigs, lizards and plankton. This raised many difficult questions for the conventional narrative of our place in the universe, some of which we will look at in the next chapter when we consider the scientific search for the soul. One of the most pressing is what, if we are just one of countless species in the complex web of life, makes us so special that we think we have been picked out to live forever.

The Soul Narrative allows us to dream that we are part angel, part brute—and that the angelic part of us is both the more important and destined to live forever. The Darwinian revolution points to a different conclusion: that we are pretty much just brute. It is difficult to believe that God made us in his image when the evidence suggests we evolved very gradually over an immense time span. And biologically speaking, we are very similar to chimpanzees—not to mention other hominids such as Neanderthals. If God made us in his image, then he must have made them in his image too.

The assumption behind the worldview of Dante was that we humans are the point and purpose of creation, living in a world made for our moral and spiritual edification. But seen in the great sweep of the evolutionary history of life, this view seems madly arrogant. Most of the history of life has been dominated by single-celled bacteria, and indeed they form most of the organisms currently alive today. In fact, some biologists argue that multicellular organisms such as you and I *are* effectively just colonies of bacteria-like cells. Much more plausible, then, to think that a supreme being has made bacteria to rule the earth—perhaps, even, that they are in its omniscient but single-celled image.

As we are just one species among millions, it is not obvious why a supreme being would want to have every *human* soul who has ever lived hanging around his heavenly abode forever. Or why he might not choose bacteria, dolphins, or chimps for company instead. But assuming such a being would be so generous as to single us out for all this attention, we might ask just what such an eternity would be like.

BEYOND THE PEARLY GATES

FOR some ancient cultures, as we have seen, the next world was a dull, unchanging half-life. But for many others, it was very much like this world, only better. Vikings who died in battle, for example, would go to Valhalla—a large hall where they would drink beer and prepare for further fighting. Muslims expect a paradise called "the Garden" in which there will be all those things that are scarce in the Arabian desert from which Islam stemmed: rivers, fountains, shady valleys, trees, milk, honey and wine—not to mention, for the men, seventy-two female companions each.

The theologians who developed the Christian idea of heaven frowned upon such carnality. These were intellectuals and ascetics, and like Plato, from whom they borrowed their idea of the soul, they imagined a heaven fit for philosophers. This is the paradise of St. Augustine, in which a lifetime's study and worship would be rewarded with the chance to contemplate the divine forever. Throughout most of the church's history this has been the orthodox view, as it is in keeping with the modest descriptions of heaven in the Bible as a place of light whose inhabitants "are before the throne of God, and worship him day and night" (Revelation 7:15).

This is known as the "theocentric" view of heaven, as it is centerd on the adoration of God to the exclusion of almost everything else. It was the orthodoxy in Dante's day and is reflected in the exquisite poetry in the third part of his *Divine Comedy*, "Paradise." In Dante's vision, virtue in this world is rewarded with closeness to God in the next, and the most virtuous of all sit in a great rose-shaped amphitheater, gazing up to contemplate the glory of the Lord. Here they enjoy an eternity of happiness and tranquillity.

The theocentric heaven is, however, not everybody's idea of a good time. The ethnologist Élie Reclus writes of Christian missionaries attempting to convert a group of Inuits with the promise of a God-centerd heaven. After listening to the account of paradise, one Inuit asked, "And the seals? You say nothing about seals. Have you no seals in your heaven?" "Seals? Certainly not," replied the missionary. "We have angels and archangels . . . the 12 apostles and 24 elders; we have—" "That's enough," cut in the Inuit, "your heaven has no seals, and a heaven without seals is not for us!"

Seals might be a rather rare request, but many people expect more from heaven than an eternity of singing hosannas. In particular, they hope to be reunited with lost loved ones, to see again a child who died too young, converse once more with departed grandparents or feel the embrace of a husband or wife who went before them. This is the "anthropocentric" vision of heaven, one centered on the human. Throughout the history of the Soul Narrative, there has been constant tension between the mystical vision of the theocentric heaven and the more lively and recognizable afterlife promised by the anthropocentric version. This tension was a prominent theme in medieval verse, as the poets struggled to reconcile deeply felt worldly passions on the one hand with the prospect of an eternity of quiet contemplation on the other—a problem to which Dante, as we will shortly see, devised a unique solution.

In the West, the widespread acceptance of the theocentric vision was finally toppled in the time from the American Civil War in the 1860s to the First World War of 1914–1918. The advent of industrialized warfare left behind millions of bereaved wives, mothers and fathers, and they had clear expectations of their religion: to give them their boys back. This fostered the development of the Spiritualist movement, which portrayed the afterlife as a sociable community where people might pursue hobbies, look up old friends and generally live in an idealized version of small-town America or rural England.

This tension continues, with the theocentric vision largely defended by high-minded theologians—such as Pope Benedict XVI— and the anthropocentric view promoted by preachers keen to keep their congregations. The popular version has transformed with the times into a Hollywood heaven, a pick 'n' mix paradise where, according to the American evangelist pastor James L. Garlow, "your every desire is satisfied more abundantly than you've ever dreamed." This is a vision for the consumerist age when people are used to getting what they want—and what they want does not stop at a harp and a halo. Not even freedom from worldly suffering excites those in the West who now live in unprecedented ease. So we are lured into church with promises of a heaven containing, in Garlow's words, "buildings, art, culture, and music . . . goods, services, major events, transportation, and communications." But attractive (or dreadful) as such a vision might be, it raises some tricky questions.

ONE day when Jesus was preaching in the temple, he was approached by some Sadducees (who rejected the idea of an afterlife). They said to him: According to Jewish law, if a man dies leaving a wife but no children, then his brother should marry the widow. Now there were seven brothers: the first married, but died, so the second married the widow; but he too died, so the third married her, but he too died, and so on until the seventh brother was dead, whereupon the woman died too. In the afterlife, whose wife would the woman be? (Luke 20:27–33.)

Jesus's answer neatly avoids the problem: those who earn a place in the next world, he said, "neither marry nor are given in marriage . . . for they are like angels." But this reply is a blow to those who wish for an anthropocentric heaven, in which you might indeed expect relationships like marriage to continue, or at least be an option. But Jesus—like the skeptical Sadducees—was aware of the many paradoxes to which this would lead.

Take, for example, a husband who dreams of going to heaven to be reunited with his dear departed wife. A reasonable wish, you might think, to have fulfilled in paradise. But it turns out that his wife's idea of heaven is instead to be in the arms of her childhood sweetheart. How, then, will both husband and wife find eternal happiness? Transferring human relations to eternity does not magically solve their problems—indeed, it only exacerbates them, making them more painfully clear. We have desires that are simply incompatible—my idea of paradise, for example, might be to see you every day, yours to never see me again. You might think Grandpa is up there waiting for you, but perhaps he would rather be playing poker.

Advocates of heaven often claim that all its inhabitants will be happy and good and will somehow just get along: "there is no jealousy, no competition, no cheating, no corruption, and no scandal . . . and all residents like as well as love one another," according to one modern guide to the Christian afterlife. But it is difficult to see how this is compatible with their being real human beings. The reality of human psychology means that any community will experience conflict, dissatisfaction, frustration and, given a few billion years, boredom. It might be possible to imagine people who could live together for eternity without ever getting on each other's nerves, but such people would be very different from me and you. And if we are to be somehow transformed so as to be entirely immune to ill feeling, irritation and boredom, we might ask whether it really is still you or I at all.

The reality of the anthropocentric view is that in positing a heaven in human terms, it cannot avoid importing human problems. The Islamic afterlife, as we saw, is a particularly colorful one, with endless feasts on sumptuous cushions in beautiful gardens, with rivers of milk and honey. All of which sounds fine for a vacation but is unlikely to suffice for infinity. For the virtuous male Muslim there awaits the added perk of lovely-eyed virginal female companions. This, however, is unlikely to make the hereafter paradisal for female Muslims—though some traditions suggest they too will be given heavenly escorts. But even if, as one ancient commentary holds, there are seventy-two of these creatures per person, this still might seem thin gruel for a billion billion billion years—and that would not even be the beginning of forever.

Such escorts might, however, be necessary if spouses cannot recognize each other: presumably, if you died an old woman it would not be your idea of heaven to spend eternity frail, bent and with two artificial hips. You might therefore prefer that your soul take on the form of your sweet sixteen-year-old self. Other people will have become addled in their old age, their memories and reason consumed by dementia. Most soul theorists assume that everyone in heaven would be healed of earthly wounds and diseases, including presumably those of the mind—no one wants to spend an eternity with Alzheimer's. But we now have a soul in heaven that is radically different and discontinuous both in form and mind from the individual on earth. The claim that it really is the same person is again becoming increasingly tenuous.

We must also ask where these bodies are coming from. Souls are supposed to be nonmaterial—that is, not made of stuff. This is what makes them immune to the degradations to which bodies are prone, and so immortal. But all the images of the afterlife that we have looked at sound very physical—full of people, thrones, even "transportation and communications." Indeed, a next world devoid entirely of things, where even people have no form, is inconceivable. For Christians and Muslims, this problem is solved once the great resurrection has taken place and people have their bodies returned to them (though that, as we have seen, is a problematic notion in itself). But until then, it is a mystery how our souls are supposed to take on any form without losing their nonmaterial nature. Dante's poetic answer is that the surrounding air collects itself into the shapes of the people and their various rewards and punishments he claims to have seen in heaven and hell: "So the neighboring air there puts itself / Into the shape impressed upon it by / The virtue of the soul."

An anthropocentric view of heaven as celestial tea parties and shopping malls is widespread in the modern West as well as in the Islamic world. But it is fraught with difficulties, as Jesus well knew when he suggested rather that the next life would be like that of angels. The theocentric view, therefore, is likely to remain the heaven of choice for popes and theologians. However, there are challenges that it too must answer—challenges that take us back to the question of whether living forever is a good idea at all.

BACK TO ETERNITY

THE theocentric view takes an altogether different approach from that of the anthropocentric. Instead of a sensuous Shangri-la, it offers eternal exaltation of the divine. Its advocates say that this encounter with God *is* love and happiness, far exceeding anything we might have experienced on earth. The theocentric vision therefore defines away boredom and dissatisfaction: by definition heaven is pure, unending joy.

This view brings the Christian heaven closer to other mystical traditions such as those popular in Eastern religions. Its advantage lies in the claim that the afterlife experience will transcend anything we have or could experience in this world; it is therefore immune to the kind of criticism that says we would eventually tire of endless milk, honey or ginger ale. But this mysticism is a disadvantage too, for we are left wondering if such transcendence is really possible, whether it is an experience humans are capable of having—at least while remaining recognizably human.

To remain unchangingly joyful for eternity, the theocentric vision cannot itself depend upon some particular set of realizations, like a series of good jokes or profound insights. Whatever it is that first amazed or interested us in the divine vision would presumably at some point cease to do so. Even if it was like the very best of what we had experienced in this life—the sublimity of a grand landscape, the companionship of friends—we would tire of it eventually. So, advocates suggest, this experience cannot be one that fits into the usual categories of surprise, interest, learning, discovery or entertainment, as all of these have finiteness built into them. It must instead be more akin to a trance, an unending state of perfection in which time has become obsolete.

Perhaps such a thing is conceivable. Various mystics and religious practitioners claim to have had an experience close to this—although of course only for a limited time, not for eternity. Revealingly such experiences are usually described in terms of a loss of self or ego; all that is distinctive about the individual human personality fades from view—memories, preferences, dispositions are all irrelevant or even hindrances. Pope Benedict XVI's description of the final state of heaven comes very close to this: "It will be a single act in which, forgetful of self, the individual will break through the limits of being into the whole, and the whole take up its dwelling in the individual." What he and other sophisticated theologians realize—and Eastern religions have long known—is that eternal life could only be bearable if it is far removed from the pettiness and smallness of an individual life—indeed if it is not really individual life at all.

In support of this view, some theologians argue that eternity should indeed be understood not as endless time but rather as timelessness. Eternal life should therefore be seen not as a life that goes on forever but as one where time has ceased to apply, a life outside of time. For theologians such as St. Augustine, this reflected the idea of God as himself being beyond time. Dante attempted to capture the idea by describing how, in the empyrean, the flow of light moves from being like a river to being a circle, the symbol of eternity. The theologian Paul Tillich described this vision of the soul's future as "rest in His eternal presence."

This is the logical extension of the mystical, theocentric vision, and it also fully reveals the flaws in that view. For an after*life* without time is not really a *life* at all. Everything that makes up human life—experience, learning, growth, communication, even singing hosannas—requires the passage of time. Without time, nothing can happen; it is a state of stasis, a cessation of thought and action. The attraction of the soul view was the unique aura it gave to every individual life, but its logical conclusion is an eternity of nothing, with life negated altogether.

In the face of such difficulties, many people retreat behind the mantra "We do not know, we cannot know." But these difficulties are conceptual ones that challenge any idea of heaven or an afterlife of the soul. The problem is not simply that we do not know *which* version of the heaven story is true; rather, it is that none of them seem to offer a coherent, satisfying account. But Dante, at least, offered a poetic one.

BEATRICE'S SMILE

DANTE's challenge was to reconcile his pious love of God with his passionate love for Beatrice. He achieved this by making Beatrice his guide in heaven who escorts him up through the celestial spheres to the very empyrean. Instead of being the temptation that leads a weak man away from righteousness, his lady therefore becomes the grace that leads him to God. Beatrice's soul lived on, and through her beauty, Dante thought he saw heaven's glory embodied; in his love for her, he believed he came closer to the source of all love—Christ. Through Beatrice, Dante attains a spiritual state in which he is able to look upon the glory of the church, of Mary, Mother of God, and of the Father himself.

This was a daring attempt to resolve the tensions between this world and the next: in placing Beatrice's soul with the saints, Dante was steering very close to blasphemy. Here was a woman of no particular fame, not renowned for her virtue or with any particular accomplishments to speak of—indeed her sole claim to be placed in such godly heights was having been pretty enough to catch Dante's eye. And yet she sits in the highest heaven, alongside the likes of St. Augustine and John the Baptist. It is an extraordinary inflation of her significance—and of Dante's own, placing *his* beloved so close to God. And it is an extraordinary and risqué fusing of the sexual impulse—Dante's crush on a beautiful woman—with Christian piety. Yet he pulled it off with such verve and style that his work was accepted as inspired by the Holy Spirit.

Finally, before leaving him to return alone to earth and tell his story, Beatrice reconciled for Dante the theocentric and anthropocentric views of heaven. Of course, his paradise followed the theocentric orthodoxy of his day, with the ultimate satisfaction it offers of everlasting worship of "the eternal light." But the poet could not imagine an immortality in which his human love for Beatrice went unrecognized and unrequited. And so when Beatrice had returned to her seat in the great amphitheater surrounding the godhead, she had time for a final gesture that gave him all he needed of earthly satisfaction:

So I PRAYED; AND SHE, SO FAR AWAY
AS SHE APPEARED, SMILED AND REGARDED ME;
THEN TURNED AWAY TO THE ETERNAL FOUNTAIN.

In this chapter, we have looked into the heavens—and not found paradise so easily as Dante's great poem suggests. In the next chapter, we will look inside ourselves for the soul itself.

7

THE LOST SOUL

Reincarnation and the
Evidence of Science

AMID the mountains and steppes in the far northeast of the Tibetan plateau, a group of monks stopped at a small farm. They sought a boy, though they had no idea what he looked like or what his name was. For many months they had been walking the mountain roads and snowy passes until eventually they were drawn to this house by the unusual guttering, made of hollowed-out juniper wood. It reminded the senior monk of a vision reported by Tibet's regent in faraway Lhasa. After making inquiries, the travelers had been told that a boy had indeed been born two years before to the simple, pious family that lived there.

As they approached, the senior monk—a lama, from the Sera monastery—donned sheepskins and pretended to be a servant, while another monk acted as leader instead. They told the man of the house, who was clearing snow from the small yard, that they had lost their way and sought shelter for the night. The monks were taken to the front room, but the lama pretending to be a servant stayed with the mother and her young child in the kitchen, helping to make tea and carry firewood. The little boy, Lhamo Dhondup, immediately took to the kind stranger and climbed up onto his lap. He grabbed at the old rosary that hung from the man's neck. "You can hold it if you can say who I am," said the monk. "Sera Lama!" shouted the toddler.

The lama was astonished. The little boy apparently recognized him although they had never before met—and he seemed fixated on the rosary, which had belonged to the recently deceased thirteenth Dalai Lama, whose new incarnation the monks sought. When the party prepared to leave the next day, the little boy pleaded to go with them. They appeased him only by promising to return—which they did, a few weeks later, as an official deputation.

This time the party carried with them numerous objects that had belonged to the thirteenth Dalai Lama, along with similar items that had not. The little Lhamo Dhondup would have to pick those that had been the deceased ruler's to prove that he was his reincarnation. The items—black rosaries, yellow rosaries, walking sticks, prayer drums—were arranged on a low table. First, the boy picked up the correct rosaries and put them around his neck. The monks held their breath in anticipation. He reached toward the sticks—and put his hand on the wrong one. The watching monks felt a shock of disappointment, but quite suddenly the boy took his hand away and firmly grasped the right one. The monks' eyes filled with tears of happiness—they had found the fourteenth Dalai Lama!

All Buddhists believe in reincarnation, the idea that when a person dies their soul will be reborn in a new body. The form of that new body—which can be any living thing, man or woman, flea or octopus—is usually a direct consequence of how that person behaved in their previous life. This is the cycle of cause and effect known as karma. But Tibetan Buddhists believe that some highly spiritually developed individuals can choose the vehicle for their next life. The Dalai Lama, the most senior of Tibet's lamas, is one such enlightened individual. When the thirteenth incarnation died in 1933, his head was said to have turned to face northeast—indicating that it was there that he had chosen to reappear.

It was 1938 when his newest incarnation was found. For five years Tibet had been ruled by a temporary regent, while the Dalai Lama's soul was thought to travel through the "in-between state" before finding its next earthly vessel. The world below the mountainous plateau was on the verge of war, and new forces were emerging that would soon challenge Tibet's studied isolation. The country needed its figurehead; to the simple people, the Dalai Lama was like a god, said to be an incarnation of the bodhisattva of compassion, an enlightened being returned to earth to guide his people.

At the age of five, Lhamo Dhondup was initiated as a monk and given the name of Tenzin Gyatso, the fourteenth Dalai Lama. Taken away from his family home, he was raised with monastic austerity in a huge, cold palace. On the rare occasions he left it, accompanied by a long and colorful procession, people would prostrate themselves before him. In 1950, at the age of fifteen, he was enthroned as worldly ruler of Tibet, just as a large Chinese army was crossing the border.

THE SOUL OF THE EAST

IN chapter 6, we looked at the soul in the Western tradition, from Plato to Pope Benedict. The phenomenal success of this narrative is a direct function of the emotional and intellectual satisfactions it offers: each of us, it declares, has some core that is pure and immortal, a spark of the divine. Physical death is therefore merely a transition to a better place where our spirits will be free.

But we saw that, on closer examination, this better place proves somewhat elusive. Both where it is and what it is like are questions that are hard to answer without collapsing into contradiction. The Eastern version of the Soul Narrative, with its focus on reincarnation, has a partial solution to these problems: when you die your soul does indeed live on, but here on earth in a new body—at least until you reach enlightenment.

It is these Eastern traditions that we will explore in this chapter, in particular Buddhism and Hinduism, along with the reincarnation doctrine that they share. Reincarnation belongs to the Soul Narrative because it is something like a soul that is thought to survive bodily death and be reborn. To say that you were Napoleon or Cleopatra in a past life is just to say that the same soul that was in the Napoleon-body or Cleopatra-body and lived the Napoleon-life or Cleopatra-life is now in your body living your life. Reincarnation therefore depends on your having a soul to outlive your current physical frame—unlike, for example, the Resurrection Narrative, which claims that your current flesh-and-bone body will one day rise from the grave to live again.

We will also look at where the reincarnation doctrine meets the realm of modern science: in the giant brain-scanners of the world's laboratories and hospitals. It is in these machines that the scientific search for the soul is being conducted, and we will see what the very latest discoveries on the nature of the mind tell us about our prospects of living on.

No one better represents the encounter of ancient wisdom and modern science than the fourteenth Dalai Lama. Born into a culture that had changed little since the Middle Ages and trained in a religion older than Christianity, he was nonetheless from childhood fascinated by technology. As a teenager, he experimented with—and crashed—one of the three cars he inherited from his predecessor, the only automobiles in all of Tibet, and went on to acquire quite a reputation as a repairer of watches. As an adult, he has sought dialogue with top scientists in every major field. When reassessing the doctrines of his faith against the latest discoveries, the Dalai Lama frequently cites the teaching of the Buddha, who himself said, "Monks, just as the wise accept gold after testing it by heating, cutting, and rubbing it, so are my words only to be accepted after examining them, not out of respect for me!"

BUT much as the Buddha exhorted others to think for themselves, his own life story remains something like a founding myth for his followers such as the Dalai Lama. And as such this myth rivals Christianity for its explicit concern with confronting the fear of death. The boy Siddhartha Gautama was born to an aristocratic family in the foothills of the Himalayas, on the border of modern-day India and Nepal, sometime in the sixth century bce. Various omens surrounding his birth were interpreted to mean that the boy would grow up to be either a great spiritual leader or a great king. In order to ensure the latter, his father attempted to shield Gautama from witnessing the kind of human suffering that might turn someone to the priesthood.

But the fates intervened to foil his father's plan. On one rare journey outside of the family's palace, the youthful Gautama saw an old man; when his charioteer explained that all people must grow old, he was thunderstruck. On his next journey, he saw a man who was sick and was shocked and dismayed when his charioteer explained that disease was an inevitable part of life. Then on the third journey, Gautama saw a corpse being taken to the cremation ground. On learning that we all must die, he was devastated. When on his fourth journey he saw an ascetic holy man, he resolved himself to find a way to overcome the great problem of the human condition: mortality.

Although some Buddhists believe the story to be literal, many read it as a parable: Gautama's sheltered life in the palace represents self-delusion and denial of the grim realities of human existence——that we all age, ail and die. The first three of the encounters represent the dawning recognition of these realities——an experience we each have as we mature. And the fourth encounter represents a turning to religion in order to cope with these truths. This story is therefore a perfect allegory of the first part of the Mortality Paradox—the realization that we are all perishable, finite creatures who one day must die—and of how this realization leads us to search for immortality narratives.

Although he advanced rapidly under various holy masters, Gautama did not take to the life of the ascetic. After nearly dying of starvation, he realized such extremes were not the way to escape worldly suffering. So he sat down under a tree and resolved to meditate until enlightenment came—which it did forty-nine days later, from which point on Siddhartha Gautama was known as the Buddha—"the awakened one."

The particular realizations that came with the Buddha's enlightenment are known as the Four Noble Truths: that life is suffering; that suffering is caused by the unceasing tumult of selfish desires that bind us to an impermanent world; that this suffering can have an end; and that this end can be achieved by giving up these selfish desires and leading a life of compassion and calm. Those who achieve this have reached *nirvana*, the state of liberation from the tribulations of this world, described by the Buddha as "deathlessness."

MUCH as Christianity emerged from Judaism only to take on a life of its own, so Buddhism emerged from the much older family of Indian religious and philosophical traditions today known as Hinduism. The Buddha's Four Noble Truths drew on developments already well under way within Hinduism, as it moved from originally being a religion based on elaborate ritual and sacrifice toward being a philosophy based on each person seeking his or her own inner essence, the pure soul, or *atman*, that was the true self. Of all the teachings that Buddhism inherited from Hinduism, the most important is reincarnation, an idea central to all Indian philosophies.

Hindus believe that the part of us that is conscious—the mind/soul/self called atman—is an essential part of the universe: "It is unborn, eternal, permanent and ancient. It is not killed when the

body is slain," explains the Bhagavad Gita, one of the most important texts in Hinduism. This, of course, sounds a lot like an expression of the second part of the Mortality Paradox—our inability to
conceive of our own nonexistence. From the claim that this soul is
indestructible, it follows that it must go somewhere when its vessel,
the body, dies—and most naturally, this is another body. "Just as a
man casts off worn-out clothing and accepts new ones," says the
Bhagavad Gita, "even so the embodied soul discards worn-out bodies and enters into different ones."

But which ones? There is all the difference in the world between
being born a prince and a pauper—and that is if you are lucky enough
to come back as a human; you could just as well be a termite or a
mouse. We noted above that this, for most people, is determined by
one thing: karma, the universal law of cause and effect. Karma
means that if you do good, good things will happen to you, and if you
do ill, then bad things will happen to you. Although these good
things and bad things can take many forms, among the most important is whether you will be born into a handsome, healthy body high
up the food chain or some nasty creepy-crawly destined to be
squished. While some Hindus see karma as being dependent on the
will of a supreme being, Buddhists in particular see it simply as a
natural law, as inescapable as gravity.

For Hindus, the proof of reincarnation and karma is all around
us: some people clearly are born blessed with intelligence, riches or
looks, whereas others are born dumb, poor or ugly. This, they believe, can only be explained as the consequences of our actions in a
previous life. Lameness, poor teeth and a weak constitution are all
thought to be just deserts for some prior sin. And just as important
as your physical and mental abilities, your karma is believed to de-
termine which caste you will be born into, and so your station in
life. If you are born a dung shoveler, son of a dung shoveler, then
you have only your (prior) self to blame.

Some might see the doctrine of reincarnation as a fine immor-

tality narrative in its own right. But even though it could be pleasant enough to be reborn to some high station, you would still face
the prospect of eventually aging and dying again. The wise therefore hope to transcend this cycle of birth and death altogether;
their highest aim is not to come back as prince or beauty queen but
to attain what the Hindus call *moksha*, or liberation. In this state,
the atman, having realized its true nature, no longer has to return
to earth for another round but can live in eternal bliss, freed of the
tribulations of bodily life. For the Buddhists, this liberation leads
to nirvana, in which worldly concerns are extinguished, leading
(in theory) to perfect happiness.

Reincarnation depends on some idea of a soul that discards one
body to take on another, but the Indian idea of atman is not identical
to the Platonic-Christian tradition that we met in chapter 6. In the
West, your soul is usually considered to encompass at the very least
all aspects of your mind and personality. If you die and, as a soul,
travel up to Christian heaven, you expect to take your memories,
beliefs and painfully acquired wisdom and experience with you. The
Hindu soul carries much less psychological baggage. It may be that
when reincarnated you retain a few residual memories of your past
life, but usually not. And when you are reborn in the body of a baby
(let alone a worm or fish) it would seem a little precocious if you
started manifesting the accumulated wisdom of your previous lives.
Hindus and Buddhists therefore do not expect to take all their memories and beliefs with them—whether to the next body or to nirvana.
Your soul, they believe, is more like pure awareness: you as a subject
of consciousness, stripped of all particular traits and foibles.

The Buddhists take this stripping down of the soul to its
extreme, to the point where it is often claimed that they deny altogether that there is such a thing as the soul. But this is not quite
right. If nothing of you survived death, then there would be nothing of you to be reborn. The doctrines of reincarnation and karma,
which are crucial to all forms of Buddhism, would then not make

any sense. So when Buddhists argue that there is no such thing as the self or soul, they are denying that you have an unchanging core personality that could be described as "the real you." But there is still a mental/spiritual something through which you live on after your body dies—what the Dalai Lama calls a "capacity for awareness, a kind of luminosity."

They believe that this attenuated soul underpins all our experience but is so overlaid with the constant stream of thoughts and impressions that we cannot hope to perceive it until in the very last stages of the dying process, when the ephemera of this world have faded from view. Then our consciousness is reduced to this pure, self-less state, ready to move on to the next incarnation. This is a difficult idea to grasp or even express in clear terms. But one thing is clear: attenuated as it is, Buddhists consider this version of the soul robust enough to warrant your next incarnation being punished for whatever you got up to in this one.

COSMIC JUSTICE

THE doctrine of karma and reincarnation therefore does for Buddhism and Hinduism what heaven and hell do for Christianity and Islam and the "weighing of the heart" did for ancient Egyptians: it provides cosmic justice. In all these narratives, the structure is the same: an eternal life worth having is to be earned through good behavior, whereas wickedness, however defined, leads to annihilation or an afterlife of suffering.

Even when helping old ladies across the road, giving to charity, or loving our neighbor, we are therefore very often pursuing our bid for immortality. At least, this is so if we are induced into such moral behavior by these threats of eternal punishment or prospects of eternal reward. And the sheer pervasiveness of this link suggests we are: rare is the culture that does not use our desire for a happy eternity to ensure compliance with the group's ethical code. Ancient Egyptians, for example, in order to earn their place in the Otherworld, had to demonstrate that they had not committed any of the forty-two sins, which included stealing cultivated land and stopping up the flow of water.

We might not like to think that we only engage in ethical behavior in order to further our selfish prospects of living forever, but most cultures and religious worldviews assume that this is exactly how we behave. Particularly among elites, there has long been an assumption that the masses will only be stopped from rape and pillage if their will to immortality is used to leverage some discipline: eternal life for the restrained, damnation for rapists and pillagers. As late as 1934, one noted psychology professor, William McDougall, for example, was moved to write in response to the scientific attack on the doctrine of the soul that it was "highly probable that the passing away of this belief would be calamitous for our civilisation."

The order and cohesion that this brings to a group is undoubtedly very useful for such a group's survival. But the belief in cosmic justice also provides an excellent defense mechanism for the immortality narrative itself. Frequently built into a worldview's account of what is to be rewarded are those behaviors that further that worldview, and similarly behaviors that could undermine it are punished with hellfire. Three of the Judeo-Christian Ten Commandments, for example, are explicitly concerned with protecting the narrative (you shall have no other gods, worship no idols and not take the Lord's name in vain). Similarly, many religions forbid killing, except in the case of holy war to defend the faith, as seen in the Islamic idea of jihad or the Christian idea of the Crusade. Such norms, while contributing to the internal unity of a group, also ensure a steady supply of young men ready to die or kill to defend their worldview, helping to make the immortality narrative self-perpetuating.

But it would be wrong to see this as merely a crude system of carrots and sticks; there is more going on here than simply frightening us into good behavior with stories of demons frying our entrails. A great deal of recent research shows that we have an innate sense of fairness—that is, we have evolved to want to see goodness rewarded and wickedness punished. But all too often this world is not fair; selfishness and deceit can bring you to the top, while self-lessness and decency are merely exploited by others. What the ethical dimensions of these immortality narratives promise is that all will get their just deserts in the end. Bullies may flourish today, but tomorrow they will be ruing their ways in the fiery pit or when re-incarnated as an intestinal worm.

Such narratives therefore reassure us that, despite appearances, life is fair after all. This has close parallels to the way in which the Soul Narrative grants cosmic significance: there we saw how the message that every one of us has an immortal soul that is a spark of the divine allows us to believe in our unique importance. Similarly, the belief in cosmic justice reassures us that our deeds do not go un-noticed and that no matter how mighty our oppressors might now seem, they will eventually be punished for doing us little people wrong. This is a very satisfying message.

Certainly the reassurance of cosmic justice through the system of karma has contributed to the remarkable stability of the Hindu worldview, which is still flourishing after well over two thousand years. But this stability means conservatism, in particular with re-gard to social structures: the doctrine teaches that those who are born to high positions have earned them in past lives, and similarly those born to lower castes have only themselves to blame. There is therefore no incentive to permit social mobility—indeed, doing so could even be contrary to the workings of justice. Worse still, defor-mities, sicknesses and other disabilities are regarded as cosmic pun-ishment for previous ills, substantially reducing the sympathy and assistance they are seen to warrant. That is rough justice indeed.

Nonetheless, the belief in cosmic justice has become so firmly established that some thinkers have turned the argument on its head: rather than establishing first the case for their immortality narrative, then using this to explain cosmic justice, they argue first that the cosmos simply must be just, and that as a consequence we must therefore be immortal, as this is the only way that cosmic justice is possible. What was a by-product of an immortality narrative therefore becomes an argument for it. The circularity of this reasoning is thereby complete: eternal life guarantees cosmic justice, and cosmic justice guarantees eternal life. Such eminent thinkers as the great German Enlightenment philosopher Immanuel Kant have been taken by this dubious line of thought.

THE attractions of the Soul Narrative for the moralists extend even to its dark side: the belief in ghosts. There are countless tales of souls that do not go gently into the next world but stay here on earth to haunt the living. These ghoulish tales too have a didactic purpose, as the hauntings are very often portrayed as the result of some moral transgression. This is frequently some evil done to the deceased: in many cultures, improper burial is sufficient to set the spirit roaming, and violent murder is a surefire way to ensure a haunting—for example, as in the case of Hamlet's father, who walks the earth until he is avenged. But equally, the cause of the restless spirit might be some wickedness they themselves committed, condemning them to either make amends or haunt the earth forever like the ghost of Jacob Marley in Charles Dickens's *A Christmas Carol*, who was too miserly to deserve a proper place in the afterlife. Either way, such stories reinforce the message that we must be good in this life or we will get our comeuppance in the next.

Belief in ghosts has been found in so many different societies and worldviews that many anthropologists consider it a cultural universal. Even in modern, secular environments, this belief remains high—according to recent polls, for example, 42 percent of Americans believe in ghosts; in the United Kingdom it's 38 percent. Given the implications of such a belief—that bodily death, contrary to all the evidence, is not the end—these are remarkable figures. But we have already seen in the second part of the Mortality Paradox that we are predisposed to think of our own souls living on indefinitely; increasingly psychologists believe that similar cognitive mechanisms are at work when we think of other people.

We are used to imagining friends and family when they are not physically present, psychologists argue, and that same ability—very useful in ordinary life—causes us to continue to imagine them if they die. In other words, our sophisticated mental picture of the world includes these people, and we cannot so easily erase them from this picture overnight—especially if they have played a prominent role in our lives. The result is powerful feelings, even hallucinations, that the deceased are somehow still with us. Or in a word, ghosts.

It is tempting to think that the established religions frown upon such beliefs—certainly the clergy are often portrayed battling against the spirits of darkness. But wise priests have long recognized that belief in the Soul Narrative and belief in restless spirits go hand in hand. As early as 1681, the English clergyman Joseph Glanvill wrote a treatise denouncing skepticism about the existence of ghosts, suggesting it was the first step toward atheism and thence the end of civilization as we know it. Today, modern gurus in both the Eastern tradition, such as Deepak Chopra, and the Western, such as pastor James L. Garlow, mentioned in chapter 6, continue to cite ghost stories as evidence that souls are real.

SOUL, MIND AND BODY: THE EVIDENCE OF SCIENCE

THE question of evidence plays a central role in the Soul Narrative. Believers in the Resurrection Narrative expect a miraculous act of God; therefore only faith in him could justify their hope of immortality. But belief in a soul has always been different: the existence of the soul was a hypothesis amenable to reason; the logicians of both ancient Greece and ancient India considered it to be the best explanation for a host of empirical phenomena and puzzles of existence. So whereas Jesus, whose hope lay in resurrection, cried out for his God from the cross, Socrates, having rationally demonstrated that his true self was immortal and about to be set free, was able to drink the poisonous hemlock with utter composure.

But what is it that is supposed to prove the soul's existence? First, there is the fact of life itself. There seems to be an unbridgeable gulf between things that are living and things that are not. For many cultures, such as the ancient Greek, it seemed clear that living things had some extra component that gave them their vitality, something that rocks, dust and water lacked. This animating principle was the soul: being alive and being ensouled were one and the same.

Second, there is the fact of consciousness. Some living things are not only able to move or grow but to think, imagine and believe. Once again, there seems to be a great gulf between material stuff, which is graspable, measurable and visible, and the realm of ideas, which float in our minds. Clearly minds are not like other things in the world, and their existence requires a special explanation: for many, that is the soul.

Third, there is the more esoteric evidence: the young Lhamo Dhondup's ability to choose the rosary and walking stick that once belonged to the thirteenth Dalai Lama, for example. Even more elaborate stories of Indian children remembering past lives are regularly reported and are considered by many as proof that souls move from one incarnation to the next. And as we just noted, sightings of ghosts are believed by some to be evidence for the existence of the spirit and its survival beyond death.

These three arguments are no longer as obviously convincing as they were two thousand, two hundred, or even just twenty years ago. We saw in chapter 3 that the scientific consensus has long turned against the idea that an animating principle is required to explain life. The modern understanding of how life works, from the organism down to individual organs, to tiny cells and to DNA, leaves no room for spiritual substances. The first of the ancient arguments for the existence of the soul we can therefore leave aside.

The third argument, based on ghosts and other spooky sightings, is also best left to one side. Those who have attempted to investigate these phenomena in order to draw substantive conclusions have invariably come away disappointed. Rarely do ghost stories or past-life recollections bear much scrutiny, and even where no fraud or invention is involved, other explanations for what happened are usually at least as plausible as the existence of an active spirit world. If this sounds to some readers like short shrift, it is worth noting that the Society for Psychical Research, founded in London in 1882 by some of the most eminent thinkers of the day to explore paranormal phenomena in a positive spirit, failed in over a hundred years of open-minded investigations to find any widely persuasive evidence of supernatural happenings.

However, one source of purported supernatural evidence for souls is worth mentioning: that of so-called out-of-body experiences (OBEs). The classic case is that of a patient whose heart has temporarily stopped beating and who seems to experience leaving their body, perhaps looking down on it, or perhaps traveling down a tunnel of light where they are met by deceased family or other benevolent beings. These experiences can be life-changing for those who have them and are often interpreted as reinforcing their religious beliefs.

That people sometimes experience such things as traveling down a tunnel of light is not disputed. The popular perception of such experiences is, however, skewed: many people are not aware, for example, that the classic case described above forms only a minority of such experiences, which vary greatly in detail and intensity and do not occur only when a patient is near death. Indeed, experiences much like an OBE can be induced by certain drugs or by electrodes stimulating part of the brain. Attempts have therefore been made to test the veracity of claims to be floating outside the body—for example, by putting up signs in emergency rooms that could be read only from a vantage point above the patient. So far, no hard evidence of a person genuinely leaving his or her body has resulted.

In order to conclude that the existence of souls really is the best explanation for out-of-body experiences—or for haunted houses, or for a Tibetan child choosing one rosary over another—we would first need a plausible account of what the soul is and how it could survive the body. Given the ambiguity of the evidence, without a strong theory of the soul a naturalistic explanation is likely always to be preferable. This therefore brings us to the case for the second argument: for the soul as mind.

Although large numbers of people today profess belief in a soul, many are vague when pressed on exactly what they think it is. But if the soul is to be your vehicle to immortality, then it must capture some fundamental essence—the real you—such that if your soul lives on after the death of your body, you can be assured that *you* live on. In the West, this "real you" is usually taken to mean your mind—that conscious part of you that thinks, feels, remembers, dreams. When you float out of your dying body or arrive in heaven, you expect at the very least to have conscious awareness and intact memories and beliefs.

The case *for* the existence of the immortal soul therefore rests upon the mind being independent of the body and dependent instead upon some spiritual essence that can survive bodily death. If, on the other hand, the mind is entirely dependent on the body, then we would have to conclude that the mind dies when the body dies, and there would then be little of us left over to call the soul. The crucial question for the plausibility of the Soul Narrative is therefore whether your mind or consciousness can, like the captain of a sinking ship, leave your dying body to continue its existence, or whether, as one of Socrates's skeptical friends put it, your mind ceases with the destruction of your body just as the music of a harp ceases with the destruction of the harp. Let us consider the evidence.

THE doctrine of the soul stems from a time before the insights of modern science, when philosophers (Aristotle, for example) believed that the brain was nothing more than an elaborate cooling mechanism for the blood. The body seemed a crude and unreliable construction—clay roughly molded by the gods. It seemed inconceivable that this matter could be responsible for the richness of memory, the mystery of creative thought or the profundity of religious sentiment. Much more rational instead to attribute the glory of the human mind to the soul, the divine spark, than to the workings of the overcooked-cauliflower-like object in our skulls.

Nonetheless, some thinkers—including Aristotle—were skeptical about the mind outliving the body. We have seen that early Jews and Christians also believed immortality could only be granted through the reassembly of the complete man or woman, flesh and all. As science and medicine advanced, evidence for a very close relationship between mind and brain grew. The mischievous skeptic Voltaire, for example, said that he could not help laughing when told that a person's mental faculties could outlive their brain—a response most unwelcome in the Catholic France of the 1730s. In a treatise first published after his death, he wrote that "as God has connected the ability to have ideas to a part of the brain, he can preserve this faculty only if he preserves this part of the brain; for preserving this faculty without the part would be as impossible as preserving a man's laugh or a bird's song after the death of the man or the bird."

Some of the most compelling early evidence for the dependence of the mind on the brain came from cases of people with brain damage. Probably the most celebrated is that of Phineas Gage, a railway foreman working in the U.S. state of Vermont. A large part of the front of his brain, called the left frontal lobe, was destroyed in 1848 when a metal pole was forced by an explosion through his cheek and out the top of his head, landing some eighty feet away. Remarkably, Gage survived and physically made a full recovery. But more remarkably, at least to the scientific community of the time, the accident altered Gage's personality in surprising and dramatic ways. Whereas previously a responsible, diligent and respected worker, he is said to have become "capricious," "fitful" and "irreverent," unable to hold down a steady job. A localized brain injury seemed to have caused a change in Gage's moral character, a part of his personality about as closely associated with the God-given soul as any could be.

We do not in fact have enough details about the Gage case to draw substantive conclusions from it alone. But fortunately we don't have to: both the capacities of medicine to keep alive people with brain damage and of science to systematically study such cases have increased exponentially in the intervening decades. The result is a wealth of data on how injuries to particular parts of the brain can eliminate or substantially alter core aspects of the mind. It is now well documented how specific brain injuries can, for example, destroy a person's capacities for emotion, memory, creativity, language and, as in the Gage case, respect for social norms and decision-making, as well as a person's ability to process sense perceptions such as sight and sound. All these are model examples for faculties that would previously have been attributed to the soul. The crux of the challenge is this: those who believe that the soul could preserve these abilities after the total destruction of the brain in death must explain why the soul cannot preserve these abilities when only a small portion of the brain is destroyed.

To make this point clear, we can take the example of sight. If your optic nerves in your brain are sufficiently badly damaged, you will no longer be able to see—you will go blind. This tells us very clearly that the faculty of sight is dependent upon functioning optic nerves. Yet curiously, when many people imagine their soul leaving their body, they imagine being able to see—they imagine, for example, looking down on their own corpse or on their own funeral procession. They believe, therefore, that their immaterial soul has the faculty of sight. But if the soul can see when the entire brain and body have stopped working, why can't it see when only the optic nerves have stopped working? In other words, if blind people have a soul that can see, why are they blind?

This question has no satisfactory answer, and indeed some thoughtful theologians, such as Thomas Aquinas, have accepted that a soul without a body cannot see—seeing is something done by a body and brain with eyes and optic nerves in working order. But we now know that, just as damage to the optic nerve can destroy the faculty of sight, so damage to other parts of the brain can destroy faculties like memory and reason. Increasingly, evidence suggests that *all* aspects of the mind and personality are in this way dependent upon the brain. So, paralleling our question about the blind person, we can ask of someone with brain damage who is unable to think rationally or feel emotions: If they actually have a soul that is able to think rationally or feel emotions, why can't they think rationally or feel emotions? Why would localized brain damage stand in the way when destruction of the whole brain and body does not?

FOR a long time, students of the brain were limited to Gage-style cases. But in the past decades, a wholly new technology has revolutionized neuroscience: machines that can produce images of the living brain in action. Collectively, the techniques involved are known as "neuroimaging," and they enable scientists to closely study the correlations between the airy world of thought and the measurable, physical matter of the brain. In laboratories around the world, you can now watch live as various parts of your cerebrum light up when you engage in such typically mental activities as remembering your mother's face, imagining playing tennis or simply daydreaming.

The results show that for every mental process, there is an

accompanying brain process. Even more worrying for the Soul Narrative, they show that the physical brain process starts *before* the conscious mind is aware of it. So, for example, someone monitoring your brain activity could tell you which decision you have made (left or right, tea or coffee or whatever) before you even *consciously* know yourself. This makes no sense at all if the real you is a conscious soul. But it makes perfect sense if your mind is the product of the workings of a complex, physical brain.

In a way, of course, we are all aware of the intimate link between mind and brain: alcohol, for example, gets us drunk, substantially affecting our attitude to risk, respect for social norms and many other aspects of our personality. But alcohol is simply a physical substance; if our minds were dependent on a nonphysical soul, why would they be so radically altered by a particular molecule of carbon, hydrogen and oxygen? Similarly, we know that even a cup of tea or coffee can affect our mental states, not to mention drugs such as heroin and cocaine. Even the level of water in our bodies can affect our personalities. Neuroscience, along with a better understanding of our underlying biology, is beginning to explain these intimate bonds between mind, body and brain.

The world-renowned neuroscientist Antonio Damasio illustrates this with the example of hunger. He writes, "Several hours after a meal your blood sugar level drops, and neurons in the hypothalamus detect the change; activation of the pertinent innate pattern makes the brain alter the body state so that the probability for correction can be increased; you feel hungry, and initiate actions to end your hunger." Some of the actions you take to end your hunger might be unconscious, such as reaching for another cookie without thinking about it, and others may be conscious, such as deciding what to choose from a menu or following a recipe in a cookbook. But all those mental processes are themselves just part of the larger loop of biochemical activity that began with the drop in blood sugar levels.

What happens if your blood sugar level drops too low illustrates even more clearly the union of mental and physical: First, you will begin to feel anxious and become irritable, and your ability to concentrate—at least on anything not food related—will diminish. As diabetics know, if it suddenly drops lower still, you can become emotionally volatile, belligerent and confused. If, on the other hand, your hunger is prolonged, then you will eventually become apathetic and depressed. These are all profound changes to your personality—the part of you that is supposed to be the province of the soul—caused by chemical changes in the brain and body. Under the close scrutiny of modern science, the ancient distinction between mental and physical breaks down, and thought and feeling appear firmly grounded in biology.

CAN MATTER THINK?

THE main argument for believing that a mind requires a soul is that it is difficult to see how the fine and ethereal world of thought could arise from crude matter alone. Those who make this argument—known as dualists—maintain that mental events like remembering and dreaming are fundamentally different in kind to the workings of physical things such as brains. Physical things can, for example, be measured, weighed and located, but not so your memory of your first kiss or your dream of a place in the sun. Physical things are observable to all, whereas mental processes seem to have an irreducibly subjective quality—only you know what it is like to be you. Summing up this view one hundred years ago, the *Catholic Encyclopedia* asserted that "the chasm that separates psychical facts from material phenomena is intellectually impassable. Writers, therefore, who make thought a mere 'secretion of the brain' . . . may be simply ignored."

A century ago and earlier, such arguments were conducted largely in seminaries and colleges, on the basis of abstract principles. Even then, not all were convinced by the claim that only a soul could explain the mysteries of the mind. Thomas Jefferson, for example, third president of the United States and all-around Enlightenment man, wrote that he should "prefer swallowing one incomprehensibility rather than two. It requires one effort only to admit the single incomprehensibility of matter endowed with thought, and two to believe, first that of an existence called spirit, of which we have neither evidence nor idea, and then secondly how that spirit, which has neither extension nor solidity, can put material organs into motion."

Note that Jefferson is not denying that it is mysterious how "matter" such as a brain can produce thought. Rather, he is saying that the alternative soul-based view is even more mysterious: First, it requires us to accept the existence of some nonmaterial, spiritual stuff that can produce the conscious mind. No evidence is given by the soul theorists for this stuff's existence, nor an explanation for how it produces thought. It is taken to be obvious that spiritual stuff can secrete consciousness in a way that material stuff cannot. But this is not obvious—certainly no more obvious than how the brain could produce consciousness.

Second, Jefferson is pointing out that if we accept a soul-based explanation of the mind, we must additionally explain how this spiritual stuff can seamlessly interact with and control the physical body. When you make a decision to get up, your body usually responds by getting up—a manifestly physical event. But how does an entirely nonmaterial thing move around the atoms, molecules and cells of the brain and body in order to cause this physical event? If the mind is itself part of the physical brain, this is much less mysterious.

Such theoretical considerations have, as we have seen, now been supplemented by the evidence of neuroscience. Unlike Jefferson and the authors of the *Catholic Encyclopedia*, we can begin to appreciate the true magnificence of the human brain. Each one of us has in our skulls somewhere in the region of one hundred billion neurons, each of which in turn has on average seven thousand synaptic connections to other neurons. It is no surprise that we cannot envision how the brain produces the conscious mind, because such complexity is indeed quite literally far beyond anything we can imagine. It is not an exaggeration to say that the human brain is the most complex thing in the known universe. If this hugely intricate system involving trillions of connections forming millions of interconnected networks is *not* producing our minds, then we might wonder just what it is doing.

FOR the idea that your personality might survive your bodily death the situation therefore looks hopeless. This is not to say that all the mysteries of mind and brain have been solved; they have not. Neuroscience is still in its infancy, and there is a great deal about the intricate workings of the brain and the production of the conscious mind that is not yet understood. Perhaps indeed we will never properly understand how the mind arises. But *all* of the now-voluminous evidence so far accumulated points to the complete dependence of the mind on the body. The psychologist Jesse Bering sums it up so: "The mind is what the brain does; the brain stops working at death; therefore, the subjective feeling that the mind survives death is a psychological illusion operating in the brains of the living."

That illusion is of course generated by the Mortality Paradox. It is a testament to the success of the Soul Narrative in resolving this paradox and assuaging our fear of death that it remains so popular in the Western world despite the evidence of science. Nonetheless, in particular in Europe, this belief is thought to be on the decline (though accurate figures for earlier periods are hard to come by). Not so in India, for example, where religiosity remains high. But as we saw earlier, the Hindu and Buddhist ideas of the soul are abstracter and leaner than those of the Abrahamic religions common in the West. In particular the Buddhists strictly reject the idea that the entire personality, complete with memories, beliefs, dreams and dispositions, survives bodily death; this they have long believed to be dependent on the body.

When the Dalai Lama met with leading neuroscientists in 1989 for a symposium to discuss the implications of brain science, he explained, "Generally speaking, awareness, in the sense of our familiar, day-to-day mental processes, does not exist apart from or independent of the brain, according to the Buddhist view." The soul in the Western sense of an independent entity that supports the full personality, he accepts, is "thoroughly refuted." But Buddhists do believe in some essential part of you that survives the body in order to be reincarnated in accordance with the laws of karma. This is pure consciousness, stripped of all memories and convictions and the rest of the accumulated baggage of a lifetime. The Dalai Lama describes it as a "continuum of awareness that . . . does not depend upon the brain." Can this pared-down soul, this "continuum of awareness," survive the onslaught of neuroscience?

KNOCKING THE SOUL ON THE HEAD

THERE is one big problem with the idea that your consciousness or "awareness" can in some form survive the death of your body. It is something with which we are all in fact very familiar, not least from countless Hollywood films: simply that if you get hit on the head with sufficient force, you will be knocked unconscious. Your awareness of the world ceases; your lights go out. The hitting is itself a physical act, with measurable, physical effects on the brain, and its result is that your consciousness is temporarily extinguished. Similarly, if you are injected with general anesthetic—a syringe full of chemicals—your awareness will be extinguished. For anyone who thinks consciousness can survive bodily death, this is an embarrassing state of affairs.

The reason is this: the soul, which even in its pared-down form is supposed to maintain some minimum degree of consciousness, is supposed to be an entirely nonmaterial thing independent of the body—only thus can it survive the body's death. Now it is natural to suppose that a hard blow to the head would stop your *body* from working—we might expect you to collapse to the ground and even to seem, from the outside, unconscious. But if consciousness were being maintained by an entirely *non*material thing, we would expect your consciousness to continue regardless. If you have a nonmaterial soul, you should, after the ordeal, be able to tell us how frustrating it was that your body had stopped working and what you thought while you were waiting for your body to recover. But this is not what happens.

To return to our analogies: If a ship is damaged and is stuck for a time out at sea, once it is repaired and returns to port we expect the captain to be able to tell us what it was like throughout the ordeal. If captain and ship are quite separate things, then the ship not working should not affect the captain. And so if consciousness is in your body like the captain of a ship, immaterial and able to survive the body's destruction, then a failure of the body should not stop consciousness from working. But it does.

Believers in a soul can and do find ways of explaining away this uncomfortable fact. They can, for example, argue that we really *are* conscious when, for example, under general anesthetic—but because the brain is not working, we cannot create new memories, so it retrospectively *seems* like we were unconscious. This is a terrifying thought, suggesting we really do experience what must be the agony of, for example, invasive surgery. The eerie feeling of falling off into darkness only to emerge after what seems like a few seconds but can be hours would be just a trick of the memory.

Islam takes a different approach. According to the Qur'an, "God takes the souls of the dead and the souls of the living while they sleep—He keeps hold of those whose death he has ordained and sends the others back until their appointed time" (39:42); this argument could be extended to unconsciousness: when under general anesthetic, as when asleep, your soul returns to God. This is a wonderfully poetic retort but does not explain why we have no memory of going to, being with or returning from Allah.

Many more such explanations are possible, and they all have three things in common: they are ad hoc, untestable and pose as many questions as they answer. And this, as any philosopher or scientist knows, means we ought to be very skeptical. The basic fact remains: what happens when you are knocked hard on the head or injected with general anesthetic is exactly what we would expect if your consciousness is entirely dependent on your brain and not at all what we would expect if consciousness is dependent on an immaterial soul.

Therefore even the very pared-down soul of Buddhism is not a plausible doctrine. Reincarnation, like going to heaven, requires that some essential part of you can separate off from the corpse and carry on in some other form. But what the overwhelming evidence of science teaches, and what many have long suspected, is that there is no essential part of us that is not wholly dependent on the body. If you have a soul, yet it does not take your mind, personality or consciousness with it, then its survival after the death of your body should be of as much interest to you as the survival of your toenails.

THE problem with the Soul Narrative is therefore not that, having looked closely, science has not *yet* found the soul, nor that it has just not *yet* looked in the right place. Many scientists have indeed been believers who desperately hoped to find proof of an immortal core to their being. An American doctor by the name of Duncan Mac-Dougall, for example, constructed an elaborate hospital bed—cum—scales that weighed patients immediately before and after death. Assuming that any difference between the two measurements would be caused by the departing spirit, he concluded in 1907 that the soul weighed twenty-one grams. He later expressed the hope that he could use an X-ray machine to photograph the soul as it left the body. Needless to say, neither his results nor his hopes have been borne out by subsequent research.

But the problem is not that scientists have not yet looked hard enough. The problem is that everything the soul was supposed to explain—thoughts, consciousness, life itself—has been shown to be dependent on the body. We therefore have every reason to believe that all these faculties—from memory to emotion to the most basic form of awareness—cease when the body ceases. There is simply nothing left over for the soul. As a hypothesis, it is redundant.

Some people argue in response that the statement "You do not have a soul" is a negative, and it is not possible to prove a negative—we can therefore never really know if you have a soul or not. But this is of course a fallacy: we prove negatives every day. The claim that you do not have a carton of milk in your fridge is a negative, yet it would be very easy to prove. We know what would count as reliable evidence of your having a carton of milk in your fridge (we would be able to see it, touch it and so on). It can then quickly be established whether such evidence exists or not. Similarly, we can work out what would count as evidence for the existence of a soul that supports your mental life—for example, the various facets of your mind being independent of the functioning of your brain—and what would count as evidence against the existence of such a soul, such as your falling unconscious when hit on the head. And, as we have seen, the evidence is overwhelmingly against.

The more we know about ourselves, the less surprising it is that we have no souls. We have evolved over billions of years from simple creatures that had no mental life whatsoever—and before that from things that weren't creatures at all. We each of us arise from the physical meeting of a sperm and an egg and develop cell by cell. The mental life that emerges is one that is intimately linked at all times to the state of the body. Indeed, the best modern theories of consciousness tell us that the mind is just the representation that a physical organism makes of itself and its environment in order to help it survive in a complex world full of very physical dangers. And the evidence also tells us that this vastly intricate brain that produces everything from emotion to art, reason to religion, is a far more wonderful thing than the simple soul of Plato and the theologians.

DISSIPATION

THE Dalai Lama tries hard to be both modern and at the same time true to the traditions that he embodies. Being a good Buddhist, he daily considers the prospect of his own death as part of his religious practice—and indeed he has more reason to than most, as his death will spark the search for the next incarnation of this highest lama, which is likely to be a highly politicized affair given the dispute over Tibet's sovereignty. But he has also said that if his people no longer need him, then he might not return at all. And one day, as scientific education spreads and the evidence for the materialist worldview continues to mount, he surely won't.

The Buddha said that the doctrines of religion should be examined in the light of the evidence, and this we have done. There was a time when the existence of the soul was a very plausible hypothesis, when life and the mind were barely understood. But that time has passed, and the soul hypothesis has been superseded. That so many people continue to believe in the soul regardless has nothing to do with its credentials as a rational thesis, but rather everything to do with the satisfactions it offers as an immortality narrative.

We have seen in this chapter and chapter 6 that the Soul Narrative not only promises a route to eternal life but also comes with the significant perks of reassuring each one of us that we are unique and special, *and* that we live in a just and orderly universe. And all of that in a package that fits perfectly with the intuitions of the Mortality Paradox—that although the body may die, our minds will live on. This makes for a very attractive story that has been one of the most important ideas to shape our world and is very hard to give up.

Nonetheless, it is on the defensive. We have seen this already in Europe: the idea of the soul is slowly becoming thinner and thinner, as science shaves off the functions once claimed for it. Thus the soul has lost its claim to be the animating principle, it is losing its claim to be the bearer of the mind and it will soon lose any claim to be the maintainer of consciousness or awareness of any kind. When this happens, this third immortality narrative will have lost its power altogether.

In Hinduism and Buddhism there is an undercurrent of recognition that the individual mind cannot continue without the body. Beyond the theory of reincarnation, which requires a soul robust enough to be punished for its past sins, there are hints of something more radical. Nirvana, for example, literally means "extinguishing" or "blowing out." But what is it that is being "blown out" like a candle? Some Buddhists say worldly desires. Others, however, go further and believe it is the self that is extinguished. For some in the ascetic tradition, the source of worldly suffering is not just being in the world—it is being at all. Liberation therefore means to cease to be an individual altogether, or as the Hindus put it, to become one with the all, the Brahman.

The soul was supposed to be the real you that shed the body like tattered old clothes. We have seen, however, there is no real you other than the body and brain. But we have also seen, in our exploration of the first immortality narrative, Staying Alive, that your body and brain have no prospect of existing forever. And our consideration of the Resurrection Narrative suggested that if your body, once dead, is put back together, it will not be you but a mere replica that is brought to life. So as the Soul Narrative breaks down, it takes with it the hope that you can personally survive forever in a form much like your present existence.

What is left are the disparate parts of you that might go their separate ways, fragments or echoes of you that survive the dissipation that is death. This might mean an anonymous energy that rejoins some universal spirit, or perhaps the memories you have left in the minds of others. Some people might still call these "soul," but then it has ceased to mean a conscious, albeit immaterial, person and instead means something more like the imprint you have left on the world. When this point is reached, we have already left the Soul Narrative and begun instead the fourth path to immortality: Legacy.

PART IV

LEGACY

8

LOOK ON MY WORKS, YE MIGHTY

Everlasting Fame

ALEXANDER III, newly anointed king of Macedon, very much
wanted a prophecy that would endorse his impending attack
on the mighty Persian Empire. On his way back from crushing an
insurrection in southern Greece in 336 bce, he therefore passed
by the most famous of all oracles, that of Apollo in Delphi. But it
was late November, and the oracle was closed for the winter.
Alexander, however, was not a man to be denied: he sought out
the high priestess and dragged her physically into the sanctuary.
Recognizing that protest was useless, the quick-thinking proph-
etess proclaimed, "Young man, you are invincible!" Alexander
immediately released her—that would do just fine as a prophecy,
he decided. From then on, he took "the invincible" as one of his
titles.

And invincible he proved to be. Within ten years of receiving
the perfunctory prophecy, he had overcome the Persian Empire,
then the largest in the world, and gone far beyond. He is one of the
few campaigning generals in history who can genuinely claim
never to have been defeated—his conquests came to an end only
when his Macedonian veterans, some three thousand miles from

home, refused to cross the Ganges to invade yet another foreign kingdom. When he halted his eastward charge and turned back to make a new capital in Babylon, his empire included most of what are today Turkey, Egypt, Israel, Syria, Lebanon, Iran, Iraq, Afghanistan and Pakistan.

These extraordinary deeds, all achieved before he turned thirty, might at first seem to be sufficient to explain why we today call him Alexander "the Great" and tell his story in film, fiction and countless histories. But there have been many other great generals, conquerors and emperors through the ages, and most do not earn anything like the kind of attention reserved for this belligerent and short-lived ruler. And his lasting renown is no mere question of fashion; it is a remarkable fact that there has never been a period in the 2,300 years since Alexander's conquests when he has not been famous in East and West alike. There seems to be something special about his story, something that projects him beyond the struggles of other mortals and into the realm of gods and heroes.

Which is exactly how he wanted it to be. The reason the story of Alexander is still so popular after so many centuries is that he did everything he could to make sure this would be so—and he was as talented a mythmaker as he was a military strategist. He understood that greatness was the sum not merely of one's actions but also of how others saw them, and so he went out of his way to cast his deeds in epic terms. As when he cut the Gordian knot, prophesied to be "solved" only by the future king of Asia, at every juncture he ensured there would be ample material for the poets and chroniclers—first by emulating the legends of the past, then by creating new ones of his own.

Alexander was raised to have epic aspirations. His father, King Philip II of Macedon, claimed descent from the demigod Hercules, son of Zeus and a mortal princess, and was himself a hugely successful military leader. But more important still was his mother, Olympias, who claimed as a forebear the greatest of the Greek warrior-heroes——Achilles. She raised Alexander to believe that it was a hero's blood that flowed in his veins. As a teenager, Alexander learned the story of Achilles as told in Homer's *Iliad* by heart; years later when on his campaigns he slept with a copy annotated personally for him by his tutor, Aristotle, under his pillow.

When Alexander became king, Macedon was in the ascendance and was ready to challenge the might of the Persians across the Aegean. When he set sail with his fleet, he was conscious that he was leading the first Greek army into Asia since Agamemnon a thousand years before had led the Greeks to reclaim Helen of Troy. He sacrificed at the tomb of the first Greek to be killed in the Trojan war, then immediately went to the ruins of Troy to lay a wreath on the tomb of Achilles; there he took up what was said to be Achilles's shield and replaced it with his own. The message was clear: Alexander was following in his forebear's footsteps and would match his heroic deeds.

Which he did, and with remarkable speed. In defeating the mighty Persian army he triumphed over a force many times greater than that of the ancient Trojans and thereby surpassed the deeds of Achilles. Thence he needed a new role model and so turned to the feats of his other legendary forebear, Hercules, whose adventures were said to have taken him deep into Asia. Finally he outdid even this fabled hero——when on his campaign into India he heard of a fortress on an enormous rock that even Hercules had failed to conquer, he immediately laid siege to it and ensured that he was the first to get to the top.

No mortal, not even the heroes of old, seemed Alexander's equal; his greatness was more than that of a mere man. So it must have seemed to his ever-expanding number of subjects, and this was a belief that Alexander was keen to foster. On his way to the final battle with the Persians he took a long detour into Egypt to consult the great oracle temple of Amun, the Egyptian chief deity whom the Greeks identified with Zeus. The temple's flattering priest fed an idea that had been planted long before by his mother: that Alexander's real father was perhaps not Philip at all but the king of the gods himself, and that his all-conquering son might therefore count himself among the divinities.

Having completed his conquests, Alexander instructed the other Greek states that he was to be acknowledged as a god, and obligingly they instituted cults in his honor. Ironic, perhaps, that shortly thereafter a fever sent him the way of all mortals at the age of only thirty-two. When he lay dying, Alexander was asked to whom he left his sprawling empire: "to the strongest," he replied, and so opened the way for fifty years of bloody war as his successors fought to carve up the conquests of their departed god-king. He had done nothing to ensure that his kingdom would endure or prosper, nothing to ensure stable government or a secure inheritance for the children he had sired. He had all along only had one goal, for which in the end he sacrificed everything and won: everlasting fame.

HERO

IN chapter 7 we gave up the ghost of a hope that your mind might literally outlive your body and float to heaven—the conclusions of science are that there is no soul to save you from oblivion. But we also saw earlier that the chances of your dodging the Reaper and staying alive are vanishingly slim and that the very idea of physical resurrection is fundamentally flawed. Together these first three immortality narratives provide the core of all the world's religions, from Taoism to Catholicism, as well as the inspiration for much material, economic and scientific progress. But though they might point toward the Mount of the Immortals, all three fall a long way short of reaching the summit.

The prospects of your living forever as a full person—that is, continuing indefinitely to enjoy a life something like the one you have now—are therefore not at all good. But there are other conceptions of immortality that do not require the survival of the individual person as such. Such conceptions—which I have grouped together under the title of *Legacy*—are every bit as ancient and widespread as the first three immortality narratives and every bit as popular today. Indeed, many cultural commentators believe they are positively exploding.

I will distinguish between two forms of the Legacy Narrative— what I will call the *cultural* and the *biological*. This chapter will focus on the first, the pursuit of cultural immortality. Its influence is everywhere to be seen: alongside the effects of material progress, its products define the landscape of modern civilization. Paintings and poems, pop music and politics—all of these result from the effort of the individual to carve out some space in an undying cultural realm. And though Alexander's exploits show everlasting fame to be a perennial pursuit, the modern cults of film stardom and TV celebrity, mass-market magazines and instant communications have transformed it from an elite occupation to the career of choice of thousands.

WOODY ALLEN, an unquestionably famous man, was nonetheless blunt in his assessment of fame as an immortality vehicle; he once wrote, "I don't want to live on in the hearts of my countrymen; I want to live on in my apartment." There are many—even among those who have achieved celebrity—who are inclined to see the Legacy Narrative as nothing more than a metaphor. It cannot be *true* immortality, they argue, if the individual does not survive. But understandable as this skepticism might be, the Legacy Narrative has some surprising and sophisticated answers. And in the end, legacy might not be as good as living on in your apartment, but if the other immortality narratives are dead ends, then it might be as good as it gets.

This certainly was the view of the Greek heroes who inspired Alexander. If a surer route to living forever had come their way, they would have taken it. Standing on the battlefield of Troy, one nobleman fighting on the side of the Trojans admitted this to his companion: "My good friend, if, when we were once out of this war, we could escape old age and death forever, I should neither press myself forward in battle nor bid you do so," records *The Iliad*. "But death in ten thousand forms hangs ever over our heads, and no man can elude him; therefore let us go forward and win glory."

His message is clear: If there were some way of achieving eternal youth or cheating death, then he would gladly take it. But there isn't. The position this warrior has reached is therefore much like our own, now that we have examined the first three immortality narratives and found them all wanting. Yet despite his realistic appraisal of his mortality, still the will to transcend this short span of life drives his thinking. His conclusion: In the absence of better options, our only route to eternal life is by winning glory—even at the price of falling in battle.

Yet on the face of it, this is a very odd conclusion. After all, to die young in war is not the only alternative open to someone who has given up on the other immortality narratives—some might argue that, on the contrary, taking very good care of what life one has would be much the better option. Achilles, greatest of the Greek heroes, on the eve of battle weighed up this existential choice: "I carry two sorts of destiny toward the day of my death," he said. "If I stay here and fight beside the city of the Trojans, I shall not return home, but my glory shall be everlasting; whereas if I return home to the beloved land of my father, my glory will be gone, but there will be long life left for me."

It could be argued that many of the young men who go off to battle do not really believe that *they* will be the ones who take a spear to the neck. But Achilles *knew*—because it had been prophesied—that if he chose the warrior's path then his life would be short, albeit crowned with eternal glory; whereas if he turned his back on soldiering then a long and happy life of hunting, feasting and siring children awaited. He loved life, he said, "more than all the wealth of Troy," yet still he chose to stay and spill his blood on a foreign battlefield for glory's sake.

Alexander must have weighed up the same choice as his hero Achilles. He had every prospect of a long and happy life if he stayed at home to be king of his small but powerful state. But like Achilles, Alexander chose the path of glory. As Ernest Becker observed, "men seek to preserve their immortality rather than their lives." In contrast to those such as Woody Allen who might wish to live on in their apartments, Alexander set sail to invade the Persian Empire at the age of twenty-one and never set foot in his homeland again.

Why? What good is eternal glory to a corpse? Is a famous dead person any less dead? Such heroes thought so. They prized fame more than happiness, love, wealth, more than this life itself—because they believed it opened the way to an existence beyond the flesh. But the heroes also knew that they could not achieve this existence on their own, which is why when he set sail, Alexander made sure that his entourage included the scribes, historians and sculptors who would do for him what Homer did for Achilles. He knew that it was these, not the priests and alchemists, who were the guardians of eternal life—they were the ones who controlled the realm of the symbolic, and it is only there that immortality is to be found.

THE LIFE OF SYMBOLS

ALEXANDER THE GREAT'S achievement was to step out of the natural realm—quite literally through an early death—and transfer himself completely into the realm of legend, where he still thrives today. For the ancient Greeks, this was the recipe for eternal life: to escape the course of nature, with its death and decay, and carve out a space in the symbolic realm of culture, which might survive from generation to generation—and perhaps forever.

Nature, as we have noted before, is the bringer of decay and dissolution, which is why we strive so hard to transcend our natural limits. If nature takes its course, we die and rot back into the earth, and soon nothing is left of us. But we humans are not only creatures of nature: we live in two worlds. The first is the natural world that we share with other organisms, but the other is a world unique to us—that of the symbolic. And here, in this world of our own making, we can achieve the permanence for which we yearn.

Although the symbolic world is one of our collective making, it is every bit as real as deserts and mountains. Many of the things that govern our actions—success, status, even money—belong to this realm. Those who spend their days at desks or in studios, in libraries or offices, are dedicating their lives to the symbolic. Symbols are the component parts of language and culture, of what makes us different from each other and at the same time what we have in common as a species and makes us different from all other living things. Homo sapiens is, as the German philosopher Ernst Cassirer put it, the symbolic animal.

The societies of Achilles and Alexander, where no one worked in offices or at computers and food was frequently still hunted for, might at first seem to us simple. However, they were anything but: just as much as ours, they had complex status systems, poetic and musical traditions, religious beliefs and ideas of history and their place in the world. They might have been more sensitive to natural rhythms than we are, but this seems only to have heightened their awareness of the distinction between the natural and symbolic realms.

On the one hand, they knew well that the *bios*, the ordinary human lifespan, was finite—that, as one Trojan warrior put it, generations of men are like leaves on the trees: as one grows, another wilts and is gone. And in contrast, it was equally clear that the *symbolic* realm did *not* follow this pattern, that kingdoms, titles, wealth and honor survived to be passed from one generation to the next, that stories persisted to be told by new generations of min-strels and bards. Culture did not seem susceptible to the natural process of decline and death. As the Harvard classics professor Gregory Nagy puts it, for the ancient Greeks, "death and immortal-ity are presented in terms of nature and culture respectively." The natural way was mere death; immortality lay in transferring oneself entirely into the symbolic realm of culture.

This is just what Achilles and Alexander and the other Greek heroes achieved, thereby showing the way for Western civilization. Naively, we are sometimes tempted to see such heroes as the most courageous among us, as they seem to face physical danger so fear-lessly. But on the contrary, says the anthropologist Ernest Becker——"heroism is first and foremost a reflex of the terror of death." Heroes are motivated to sacrifice their natural life by the dread of utter oblivion, and their heroic deeds grant them instead a more permanent existence as part of culture. Heroism, in the words of the historian of fame Leo Braudy, "enables the individual to step outside of human time."

One might have thought that the long dominance of Christian-ity in Europe would have dampened this glory seeking; we have seen that the Soul Narrative grants cosmic significance——a kind of heroism——even to the lowly and obscure through a personal rela-tionship with God. But the literature of Christian Europe suggests otherwise: Dante's *Divine Comedy*, for example, is obsessed with the question of who in the afterworld properly deserves to be remem-bered by posterity, and Geoffrey Chaucer in 1380 dedicated a major poem to examining the inhabitants of the "House of Fame." Not even the prospect of heaven could reduce the desire for posthu-mous renown.

We might of course suspect that these works not only were *about* fame but also were attempts to achieve it. The Spanish poet and philosopher Miguel de Unamuno put it pithily when he wrote that "the man of letters who shall tell you that he despises fame is

a lying rascal." Clearly the attempt to impress posterity is a powerful productive impulse that has given us some of the pinnacles of
human achievement. One man of letters, John Milton, author of
Paradise Lost, was clear about what got him up in the morning:
"Fame is the spur that the clear spirit doth raise . . . to scorn
delights and live laborious days," he wrote in 1637.

The symbolic realm enables the projection of ourselves
beyond the biological with all its shortcomings, and so we scram-
ble toward it, proliferating images and artworks as we compete
for ground in cultural space. This is what drives civilization
onward, producing the *Mona Lisa* and the Taj Mahal, *Citizen Kane*
and the great American novel. A place in posterity can come
through invention, entrepreneurship or teaching—anything that
might either seem exceptional or last beyond the lifespan of the
individual to shape the future. As the philosopher and historian
Corliss Lamont wrote, "The economic and social effects of this
sentiment . . . have been and are immense and incalculable."

In the scientific community talk of immortality is largely
frowned upon, yet many are driven by the prospect of a great discovery that might etch their name in the annals, perhaps even a
theory named after them or the immortalizing epithet "Nobel lau-
reate." French thinkers are less circumspect: the motto of the pre-
eminent French learned society, the Académie Française, is "*à
l'immortalité*," and members are known as "the Immortals."

Of course, not all bids for renown are as worthy. The mass
media of film, television, radio and Internet have enabled a whole
new degree of instant, global stardom for those of dubious talent.
As a result, our society is drowning in a flood of celebrities, products of a fame industry of lavish scale. The media portrayal of their
glittering lifestyle seduces millions to see renown as the only measure of worth. The singer Morrissey reflected the aspirations of
millions of would-be pop stars when he admitted, "I always thought
that being famous was the only thing worth doing in life." Of

course, celebrity can have many fringe benefits, but the film star James Dean made clear what its real purpose is when he said, "To me the only success, the only greatness, is immortality."

James Dean is also notable in that his life parallels those of Achilles and Alexander for shortness and intensity, demonstrating how the cultural immortality narrative can cause people to act in ways entirely contrary to purely biological survival. Achilles and Alexander also not only died early but did nothing to ensure the well-being of the children they left behind. Their classically heroic behavior, which has inspired so many since, seems to have been deeply detrimental to their own prospects of living on. But we have seen that the will to immortality was not oddly weak in these heroes, such that they should happily die young—rather it was uncommonly strong, driving them to carve their names into our cultural space. Our craving to live forever has its roots in the most natural of all instincts but can take an entirely unnatural course when transferred to the realm of the symbolic.

The pursuit of the eternal through the Legacy Narrative can therefore explain a great many of the curious, often seemingly counterproductive things that humans do, from soldiers accepting suicide missions on the battlefield to artists wasting away in their garrets. There is nothing people have not sacrificed for a place in posterity—freedom, wealth, happiness. Or as Socrates put it, approvingly relating the words of his teacher and lover Diotima, "Think of the ambition of men, and you will wonder at the sense-lessness of their ways, unless you consider how they are stirred by the love of an immortality of fame. They are ready to run all risks greater far than they would have run for their children, and to spend money and undergo any sort of toil and even to die, for the sake of leaving behind them a name which shall be eternal."

HEROSTRATUS WHO?

WHAT Diotima saw as mere senselessness, however, can take on a darker aspect in the intense competition for space in the cultural sphere. Not everyone has the skill or patience to create something of value or beauty, and it is far easier simply to destroy what others have made. There is therefore a temptation for the fame seeker to brand his or her name into the cultural sphere with some heinous deed and so through wickedness to become the stuff of legend. So tempting indeed is this route to posterity that it has its own name: *the Herostratus syndrome.*

On the night of Alexander the Great's birth, July 21, 356 bce, a previously unknown man—a nobody—set fire to the temple of Artemis at Ephesus. This temple, 120 years in the building, was one of the Seven Wonders of the World. Visited by pilgrims, kings and tourists, it was over three hundred feet long and fifty feet high and on a site considered holy for millennia. The fire destroyed it utterly. The arsonist did nothing to hide his guilt but gave himself up freely. He was called Herostratus, and when asked why he had committed this terrible act, he replied: to become famous.

To discourage copycats, the Ephesians not only tortured and executed Herostratus but also subjected him to a *damnatio memoriae*—the damnation of a man's memory through banning (on pain of death) all mention of his name. Yet here I am writing about him two thousand years later, while the names of the temple's architects have long been lost. In a society such as his, obsessed with fame, the temptation was high to attain it through nefarious means: sacrilege, regicide, treachery. And equally, in a society such as ours, obsessed with celebrity, the temptation is high to immortalize one's name through some wicked but dramatic act: assassinating a president or pop star, blowing up a building or gunning down fellow high school students.

Ancient writers speculated that Herostratus was motivated by a sense of injustice—not injustice that the world was overlooking his great talents but, on the contrary, injustice that the fates should have given him no talents whatsoever. It was not fair that society should grant the immortality of fame only to those who were simply lucky enough to have been born with an artist's eye, the silver tongue of the rhetorician or the strong arm of the warrior. Psychologists' studies suggest that this combination of a sense of injustice and inadequacy is common to those who make their names by killing the talented or destroying their works.

This should be no surprise: the contest for cultural immortality is a highly competitive one that necessarily only rewards the exceptional. The "facelessness of the many gives meaning to the faces of the few," as the sociologist Zygmunt Bauman put it; the masses form the anonymous night sky against which the stars shine. Those who believe they have an equal right to a place in the firmament of fame but who do not have the talent to earn it are likely to become frustrated, neurotic and very, very dangerous—blazing comets crashing into the earth. We cannot all be heroes; most of us accept this fact, but some choose instead to be villains.

Still it is ironic—and a mark of our tendency to hero worship—that a figure like the pitiful Herostratus is necessary to hold up as a contrast to the great Alexander in illustrating the dark side of the quest for fame. Herostratus, after all, merely burned down a single building. This wanton act of destruction is child's play compared to the deeds of the mighty conqueror. The people whose lands Alexander hacked his way through could tell you all about the dark side of the quest for glory: for them, Alexander is the destroyer, the accursed one, bringer of death and destruction—Alexander the Terrible.

The "pacifying" of Greece with which Alexander's career began involved the utter destruction of the ancient city of Thebes, during which all the men were put to the sword and all the women and children sold into slavery. This established the pattern for how he was to deal with those who opposed him. The ruthless young king had many such ancient cities pillaged and razed, countless men summarily executed, women raped and made slaves, civilians slaughtered, priests killed, temples sacked, show trials held, assassinations arranged, opponents tortured, whole peoples destroyed. His legacy is written with the blood of others.

We find those contemptible who feed their desire for notoriety by killing a handful of innocents, but Alexander, who cut and burned his way across a continent at the cost of hundreds of thousands of lives, we call "the Great." As the French biologist and philosopher Jean Rostand wrote in 1939, "Kill one man, and you are a murderer. Kill millions of men, and you are a conqueror. Kill them all, and you are a god."

Of course, the desire for cultural legacy has contributed much that is positive to civilization. Many people seek a place in posterity by building bridges, curing disease or painting pictures. But what Herostratus and Alexander understood is that doing something saintly is by no means the most important entry requirement to the hall of fame. Rather, it is doing something *extraordinary*— whether extraordinarily good or extraordinarily wicked.

A TWO-STEP GUIDE TO POSTERITY

THIS was also well understood by a famous couple who predate even Alexander and Achilles—two figures whose bid for immortality combined every form yet devised, including the cultural, and who unquestionably had a flair for the extraordinary: Akhenaten and Nefertiti. Their example provides a nice introduction to the two steps for achieving the transition into the symbolic realm.

In 1905, the American Egyptologist James Henry Breasted, one of the first scholars to examine the career of Akhenaten, astutely described him as "the first *individual* in human history." All pharaohs were exalted as special, divine even—but their specialness came from their fulfilling the eternal role of the god-king. It was precisely *not* their individuality that made them special——indeed, their own personalities were entirely subsumed by their endless performance of ancient rituals and carefully prescribed duties. Their monuments make this clear: from the anonymity of the pyramids even to the colossal granite statues, it is their conformity to type that is emphasized——each pharaoh is as broad shouldered, square jawed and devoid of distinguishing characteristics as the next.

And then came Akhenaten. His statues not only portray but exaggerate his distinctive characteristics——a thin chest and bulbous belly, weak arms and a feminine chin. Frescoes even show naturalistic scenes of his relaxing at home with Nefertiti and their children. And, as we have seen, he abolished the ancient rites and, with Nefertiti, established his own——to an abstract god with whom only he could communicate. Akhenaten used the power of the pharaoh to break free of all the role's traditional constraints and to become extraordinary even by pharaonic standards——to become therefore unique and individual. Thus he took the first step to symbolic immortality.

At a biological level we are born individuals: we are each a distinct organism. But at the symbolic level, we have to fight to carve out a distinctive identity in a space of shared words and ideas. This begins with a name——and it is noteworthy that Akhenaten chose this *unique* name for himself, rejecting being simply the next Amenhotep (the fourth) as his father had intended. We still talk about the acquisition of a reputation in terms of "making a name for oneself"——a name that serves to stake out space in the symbolic sphere on which a legend can then be built. The above-mentioned Spanish philosopher Miguel de Unamuno called this the "tremendous struggle to singularize ourselves," and "it is this struggle," he believed, "that gives its tone, color, and character to our society."

But to establish oneself as an individual is only the first step. It is entirely possible that your name and individuality will still die with you when your biology fails; many an eccentric has gone this way.

The second step, therefore, is to project this individuality into the undying cultural realm and fix it there. This Akhenaten also attempted with estimable vigor: the evidence recovered from the new capital he and Nefertiti founded at Amarna suggests their images, statues and deeds adorned every spare space, public and private. The royal road was lined with huge statues of the heretic pharaoh, the royal couple alone were pictured in the temples to their god and even in private houses and tombs they appear, granting riches and eternal life to their loyal followers.

These statues, pictures and records are all what the psychologist David Giles calls "reproductions of the self." We who are now awash with images—of ourselves, celebrities, models advertising toothpaste—find it difficult to appreciate the power these reproductions once held. Throughout history, access to the technology of cultural reproduction has been jealously guarded, the right to it a continual source of controversy. Alexander, for example, was the first man to feature his own face on official coinage—previously this was a privilege of deities; Julius Caesar was later to follow suit. With the upsurge of portraiture in the fifteenth and sixteenth centuries, ruling elites fought to control the uses of this technology, in particular as it applied to themselves. Elizabeth I of England, for example, redefined herself through a public image that mixed the symbolism of majesty, piety and power with elements proclaiming her as a unique and irreplaceable individual. Meanwhile you could be boiled alive for reproducing her image in the wrong way.

Today opportunities for symbolic reproduction are no longer available only to pharaohs and emperors. We are each reproduced in hundreds of baby photos, holiday snaps and home videos. Indeed, with the digital revolution, we are now living through the greatest opening of the cultural sphere since the invention of the printing press in the fifteenth century. It has never been easier to leave an impression in the shared space of symbols: with the minimum of computing power and know-how, it can be achieved in minutes.

At the start of 2011, there were 158 million blogs (personal Web pages that are—in theory at least—updated regularly with the views of the blogger), with tens of thousands more being added every day. On top of this, there are hundreds of thousands of other personal websites on which people display their wares—photos, thoughts, stories, products. But even these are eclipsed by the number of people using online social networking services, which also allow the user to create a personalized space in the digital realm, connecting it to the similar spaces of friends and acquaintances. By spring 2011, Facebook, the most popular of these sites, had over 600 million active users and counting. One 2010 consumer report found that 92 percent of American children had an online presence by the age of two.

Some of these pages are known to no one but their creator; they are the digital equivalent of the fading holiday photo in the bottom drawer: not enough to earn symbolic immortality. But others attract hundreds of thousands of visitors or followers, allowing people with meager resources but a good idea to reach massive audiences. The paradox of this new ease of access to the cultural realm is that achieving significance requires a whole new scale of self-reproduction and exposure. Fame now requires vastly more than a few carefully painted portraits; to count as a celebrity, you must be virtually reproduced many thousands or even millions of times. This is a scale that might even have astonished Alexander.

Of course, all this activity brings this-worldy satisfactions, and social media websites have become part of everyday interactions. But there is also an underlying awareness that the digital realm has opened up a new dimension to posterity. Most social networking sites offer some kind of "memorialization" facility, which will preserve a user's activity even after they have bodily departed this world. More sophisticated services offer to collect your data from across the Internet—blogs, photos, videos, Facebook posts and any other digital musings—to create a comprehensive memorial site. One company even enables you to have this digital legacy embedded into a real, physical gravestone, whence it will be beamed to interested passersby. The increasing popularity of these services suggests that those who spend their time transmuting their thoughts and images into digital form hope that something of this will outlive their frail flesh. Those who are determined to achieve Alexander-like status today have no choice but to master the means of digital reproduction.

A major advantage of cultural reproduction in all forms is the possibility of creating a kind of ideal self. Early portrait artists knew well to flatter their powerful patrons, just as models present their best side to the camera and wise users think twice about what they post to their website. And crucially, these images, once made permanent in cultural form, do not age. That of course is the point, as the ancient Greeks recognized——that the symbolic realm does not suffer from the inherent decline and decay of the biological. Achilles and Alexander, James Dean and Marilyn Monroe, Jim Morrison and Jimi Hendrix all therefore in their ways achieved what the First Emperor and Linus Pauling could not——eternal youth.

ALEXANDER THE BUNDLE

"WHY should I care about posterity? What's posterity ever done for me?" asked Groucho Marx. It is an important question: before we sacrifice too much taking the two steps to cultural immortality, we ought to be sure that they are taking us to an immortality worth having.

Despite all the thousands of would-be Alexanders, Elvises and Marilyns, few thinkers have attempted to provide a thoroughgoing defense of the idea that fame or glory really can deliver everlasting life. There has been no equivalent of Plato or St. Paul to map out just how this path is supposed to lead up the Mount of the Immortals. The Homeric heroes and their successors seem to have gone to battle on the basis of powerful intuitions rather than persuasive arguments. But a philosophical case could run something like this:

We have already concluded that you have no soul—no unchanging essence or immutable inner core. We could go farther and say that there is, in fact, nothing that is the "real you." You are just a collection of disparate thoughts, memories, sense impressions and the like, all bundled up together in a package we conveniently label a person. What is more, all these disparate parts are continually changing, as some things are forgotten and others learned, opinions changed and new memories formed. The question is, then, if you are such an ever-changing bundle, what does it mean for "you" to survive?

One answer might be that you survive if enough of these disparate parts survive. So what makes me the same person as the Stephen Cave of last week is that I have inherited enough of that person's bundle of ideas, memories et cetera. Following philosophical tradition, let us call this the "bundle theory" of the self.

Now, anyone pursuing cultural immortality is taking various bits of themselves and replicating those bits in the symbolic realm—say, for example, by ensuring that their deeds, thoughts and sayings are recorded by court historians and their images captured by statue makers. This can be seen as a way of ensuring that various bits of that particular bundle live on. And if enough of the bits of the bundle live on, then the person lives on—even if entirely in the world of symbols.

So if Alexander had not (biologically) died in Babylon in 323 bce, there would have continued to be a human being with certain ideas and memories more or less continuous with those of the earlier Alexander, and so we would say that he had survived. The physical, human Alexander, however, did die—but many aspects of the Alexander-bundle continued, for example, in the records of his deeds and sayings, in the many engravings of his image and in the minds of the hundreds of thousands whose lives he touched. Indeed, his image, ideas and reputation were replicated to such an extent that we can argue the Alexander-bundle survived just as fully as it would have done if the original flesh-and-blood human being had survived.

And these images, these ideas and this reputation have survived to this day: Alexander therefore lives, albeit in a rather diffuse form, spread around the libraries, museums, video collections and Web servers of the world—and of course in the minds of other human beings. The route to immortality, therefore, is to ensure that as many of the component parts of your current self-bundle are continued in forms that are more robust than flesh and blood, and the more such parts that survive, the better. This might not sound much like really living on, but the supporter of this view might argue that it is just as good as ordinary day-to-day living on, which is itself just a mishmash of such overlapping continuities.

So might argue a metaphysically inclined celebrity. Of course, most celebrities are probably not quite so metaphysically inclined, but nonetheless some of the experiences they regularly describe fit well with the bundle theory of the self. David Giles, the above-mentioned psychologist of fame, notes that the famous often talk of a fragmentation of their identity as they increasingly find it difficult to distinguish between their public and private, real and manufactured selves. As they see themselves on television, read their own views in magazines—or what the PR people told them should be their views—or see their images on album covers, their sense of having an irreducible self over which they alone have ownership is rapidly eroded. For some, such as Ernest Hemingway, this is a problem that challenges their authenticity: Hemingway's suicide was therefore his final attempt to reclaim and bring cohesion to a fracturing self. But to others, such as Picasso, this endless proliferation of perspectives on the self and reality is exactly what makes art possible and life interesting.

The idea that images or records capture something real and alive is an old one. Images in the form of statues have long been worshipped in the belief they contain some aspect of the divine. In all three main Abrahamic religions such image making has been deeply controversial, as it mimics the act of creation that is the prerogative of God, thereby implying both hubris and idolatry. Yet even in Christianity, icons continue to be objects of veneration. Similarly, before such technologies as film and photography became ubiquitous, the idea that they and other image-making techniques actually captured a part of the person was widespread. In many cultures, from China to Native America, photographs were initially thought to peel off a layer of the person's self and trap it on paper.

The bundle theory is therefore not as odd as it might at first sound. Indeed, the idea of a coherent, unchanging self has been under sustained attack for over a century, starting with the speculations of the psychoanalysts who divvied up our consciousness into various conflicting parts, and continuing with the revelations of neuroscience, which emphasize the brain's multiple systems and structures. So is Alexander the Bundle still among us?

IT MIGHT BE ART, BUT IS IT LIFE?

THERE are good reasons to think not. Though it is a respectable idea, the bundle theory is controversial and has ample critics. Many philosophers argue, for example, that there cannot be memories, beliefs, desires etc. without there being *someone* doing the remembering, believing and desiring. Desires don't just float about in bundles or any other way. But if there is a person doing my remembering, believing and desiring, then surely I am that person and not just the memories, beliefs and desires. In which case, I am not a collection of memories, beliefs, desires etc. after all, but rather I am *a person with* memories, beliefs, desires etc. That person might be a soul or a biological organism or something else. But it is not a book or a statue—no book or statue is a person. In which case, Alexander does not really live on in the history books after all.

But even if we accept the highly controversial bundle theory of the self, there are problems with trying to survive purely in the symbolic realm. The bundle theory claims that you live on if enough of your memories, beliefs, desires etc. do——but it is deeply questionable whether your memories live on in a literal sense just because they are written down in a book. Memories and desires are, after all, mental states, and a book does not have mental states. A book does not actually *remember* or *desire*. It merely has *descriptions* of mental states, and a description of a thing is not the same as the thing itself. A description of Alexander's ambitions is not the same thing as Alexander's actual yearnings, just as a picture of Alexander's face on a coin is not really Alexander's face. The replications of ourselves that we make in the symbolic realm are simply the wrong kinds of things to constitute a person——you don't live on through pictures of you any more than you get fat by eating pictures of a hamburger.

It therefore looks very difficult to argue that cultural legacy can provide anything like literal survival. It is contentious enough to argue that your self is just a bundle, but even if it is, the things that make up this bundle do not themselves really survive in the cultural realm. But perhaps the greatest mystery with the pursuit of this kind of immortality is that the pursuers would mostly admit this. They *know* that they are not *really* living on in anything like the normal way by conquering foreign lands or painting pictures——yet they do it anyway.

David Giles, in his inquiry into the motivation of fame seekers, dismisses the possibility that famous people have some psychological or genetic trait that explains their quest for prominence——no such quality has been found. And other alternative theories, such as that we seek renown for the immediate wealth and status it brings, he concludes are "inadequate to account fully for the long-standing and desperate desire for fame." Of course, fame can bring significant this-worldly benefits——but, as we have seen, a mark in the symbolic realm is often made at the expense of a long and happy life, as in the case of Alexander or the countless pop and film stars who have lived fast and died young. Achilles, the paradigm of the Western hero, even *knew* that his pursuit of glory would cost him his life, so this pursuit cannot have been a means to this-worldly profit.

So what were the great names of history hoping for in dedicating their lives to eternal renown? It is highly likely that here the Mortality Paradox is at work—or rather, the second half of it, the inability to imagine our own nonexistence. Even if the aspiring hero claims to know rationally that he will not be around to reap the glory of some suicidal mission, still he cannot help picturing the laurels being heaped on his memory. That act of imagining, which makes him present as the observer, makes it *seem* like he will still be there in the future to receive the back-slaps and plaudits. So even if Achilles claimed to know consciously that he would die on his path to glory, a powerful, nonrational cognitive process made it feel to him that he would still be around to profit from it.

We might add to this that at a subconscious or emotional level we do not really distinguish between the material and symbolic realms. As symbolic animals, so entirely immersed in a symbolic understanding of the world, we transfer our will to immortality instinctively from the physical to the cultural. This is what Giles calls "the evolutionary rationale" for the pursuit of posterity: the urge to reproduce ourselves into the future is so strong that it will be satisfied even if that reproduction is only a picture in a magazine.

The reason why no Plato or St. Paul has attempted to show how cultural legacy can deliver a satisfactory immortality is therefore that the strong arguments are not to be found. The motivation for the pursuit of glory is instinctive and intuitive, and those instincts and intuitions are misled: the inability to imagine our own nonexistence suggests to us we will be around to reap the glory, but reason suggests the opposite. Achilles and Alexander succeeded in becoming extraordinary and succeeded in stamping their names onto the cultural sphere, but they are still as dead as their countless anonymous victims.

The conclusive damper on aspirations to cultural legacy has nothing to do with the bundle theory; it is the entirely practical point that memories are not forever. Indeed, very few people are remembered for long at all—the psychologist Roy Baumeister has estimated the length of time for which most of us can expect to be remembered as seventy years. He points out that not many people can even *name* their great-grandparents—and if their own progeny know nothing about them, it is unlikely that anyone else does.

Of course, some people like Alexander do achieve great fame. But the cultures that hold them in esteem will not last eternally. The glories of Greece still shine, but the heroes of countless other ancient cultures have long been forgotten. Marcus Aurelius was aware of this when he wrote in his journal in 190 ce, "Soon you will have forgotten the world; and soon the world will have forgotten you," and he was an emperor of Rome, with a good deal more reason to expect lasting fame than most of us.

We do still remember Achilles and Alexander and even Marcus Aurelius, despite his prediction. But one day they will have to contend with the end of the Western civilization that values their deeds, and beyond that the end of our species and the eventual end of the world. Culture might outlive a single human, but it will not outlive humanity. No matter how great our glory, it could only ever be a postponement of oblivion. Nowhere is this better expressed than in the 1818 poem "Ozymandias" by Mary Shelley's poet husband, Percy Bysshe Shelley. A traveler reports finding a ruined colossus in the desert:

And on the pedestal these words appear:
"My name is Ozymandias, king of kings:
Look on my works, ye Mighty, and despair!"

Nothing beside remains: round the decay
Of that colossal wreck, boundless and bare,
The lone and level sands stretch far away.

ACHILLES'S REGRET

ALEXANDER has been seen by many as the shining embodiment of ancient Greek values. We saw earlier that he was raised on the heroic myths, was tutored by Aristotle and carried The Iliad with him wherever he went. But despite this training in the classics, we might conclude that Alexander did not read his Homer closely enough.

Both *The Iliad* and *The Odyssey* are filled with pathos, as Homer chronicles the toll of the hero culture. The plot of *The Iliad* begins with Achilles being snubbed by the Greek commander Agamemnon and as a consequence refusing to fight, even calling on the gods to favor the Trojans. The grimly ironic result of Achilles's petulance is that his closest friend, Patroclus, falls to the spear of the Trojan prince Hector. At this, Achilles goes on a rampage, cutting down swaths of young Trojan warriors: "As a fire raging in some mountain glen after long drought . . . even so furiously did Achilles rage, wielding his spear as though he were a god, and giving chase to those whom he would slay, till the dark earth ran with blood . . . but the son of Peleus pressed on to win still further glory, defiling his invincible hands with bloody gore."

In his rage, Achilles loses all humanity, killing those who are unarmed, some who beg for mercy, and, when he finally kills Hector, defiling the corpse. Homer does not write of him with admiration but has the god of the river that Achilles is filling with corpses rise up against him with the words, "Achilles, if you exceed all in strength, so do you also in wickedness."

Later, in *The Odyssey*, while on his homeward voyage after Troy has finally fallen, Odysseus goes down to Hades to visit the shades—the gloomy spirits of the dead. There among them, he finds Achilles, who finally fell to an arrow shot by Hector's brother Paris, fulfilling the prophecy that if his life was glorious then it would also be short. Odysseus is shocked when Achilles describes his miserable existence in Hades amid the "mindless, disembodied ghosts." Odysseus remonstrates with him—surely Achilles, most renowned of all warriors, most celebrated of heroes, cannot regret the path he chose, sacrificing long life for glory? "Do not you make light of death, illustrious Odysseus," Achilles replies. "I would rather work the soil as a serf to some landless impoverished peasant than be king of all these lifeless dead."

And so in the end it was all for nothing. After all the young blood that drenched the dust around Troy, all the women left widowed and the parents left grieving, after the deaths of Patroclus, Hector and even Achilles himself—after all that, the great hero is condemned to the dark and empty realm of death like everyone else. Homer saw the futility of seeking glory through bloodshed. Perhaps Alexander should have taken heed.

SOCRATES, who taught Plato, who taught Aristotle, who taught Alexander, also closely observed the vainglory of his times. He was convinced by the words of Diotima, the wise woman who was his "instructor in the arts of love": these great deeds of the heroes, she said, are the acts of men whose "souls are pregnant" with the need to leave some symbolic descendant to live after them. But women can be "pregnant in the body . . . giving them the blessedness and immortality which they desire in the future." In other words, men fight battles or write books only because they can't have babies. Which brings us neatly to the second half of the Legacy Narrative.

9

❧

THE IMMORTAL SEED

Genes, Gaia and the Things in Between

THERE is no doubt that Alexander III of Macedon was a remarkable man. But there is also no doubt that he would not have come to be known as Alexander *the Great* were it not for an equally remarkable woman: his mother.

We know Olympias only from snippets—mostly disapproving asides from male historians more concerned with chronicling the deeds of her great son. But the picture that emerges is of a woman who makes Alexander seem almost pale by comparison: a priestess and sorceress, power-monger and murderess. Even her warrior-king husband, Philip, was said to be scared of her after he found her sleeping with a giant snake—surely, he concluded, a visiting god. It was Olympias who taught Alexander to believe in his heroic destiny, then cleared the way for him to fulfill it.

The ancient sources claim that Philip II of Macedon fell instantly for the young princess from the neighboring state of Molossia while they were both being initiated into a mystery cult. But romantic as that may sound, King Philip was generous with his affections: he already had three wives when he married Olympias, and he subsequently took a further three more. As a consequence the young queen had to struggle continually to maintain her status in the royal household, and first and foremost, this meant producing a son.

Luckily for her, in 356 bce, a year after their marriage, she gave birth to Alexander. But with Philip's many other wives just as determined to produce the next king, the contest to secure her legacy did not end there. Around the same time as Alexander was born, another queen also gave birth to a son, named Arrhidaeus.

As he was a rival to Alexander's prospects of attaining the throne, Olympias had good reason to wish Arrhidaeus ill. But according to the historian Plutarch, she did much more than merely wish: through her knowledge of the arts of *pharmaka*—drugs, potions and spells—she ensured Arrhidaeus grew to be both mentally and physically retarded. Alexander, on the other hand, flourished in both his martial and academic training. And as he grew in ability, so Olympias also nurtured his ambitions: she encouraged him to aspire to the heroism of their forebear Achilles and even planted the idea that it was no mere king who was his father but one of the gods rumored to frequent her bed.

Alexander's obvious talents made it easy for Philip to see him as his heir, and at the age of sixteen he was trusted with running the kingdom while the king was away on campaign; a year later, father and son were leading the Macedonian army together. Olympias's hopes seemed on the verge of being fulfilled. But perhaps Philip came to think Alexander's rise a little too rapid and his ambitions a little too grand, or perhaps he was simply struck by another young beauty; either way, in his midforties, the king took his seventh wife—Cleopatra, the niece of one of his senior generals—and set about producing more heirs.

The possibility of further competition for inheritance of the throne clearly unnerved Olympias and her precocious son. At the very drunken wedding ceremony, these tensions exploded: the uncle of the bride suggested it was about time some *legitimate* heirs were produced; Alexander threw a cup at him and demanded an explanation. The king and bridegroom rose to rebuke his son but fell drunkenly to the floor, at which point Alexander said mockingly, "See the man who prepares to cross from Europe into Asia; he cannot cross from one seat to another."

Olympias and Alexander then fled the country. But Philip clearly regretted the rift with his brilliant son and a reconciliation was made, which included a royal wedding: Olympias and Philip's daughter married Olympias's brother, now king of Molossia. It proved to be Philip's last act: as he led the procession he was stabbed to death by one of his own bodyguards. The assassin fled but was caught and killed by a group of Alexander's friends. The army proclaimed Alexander king.

Unsurprisingly, many ancient historians believed Olympias had a hand in the king's murder and wanted to do away with him while Alexander was the unrivaled heir. There was no love lost between her and Philip—at least not since the snake incident. And she was entirely capable of using murder to achieve her goals: with Philip out of the way, she set about eliminating her and Alexander's rivals, starting with Philip's newest wife—the cause of the recent spat—who by now had a baby. According to some accounts, Olympias had mother and baby burned alive, whereas others suggest Olympias killed the baby herself before having the young queen hanged.

Throughout Alexander's long campaign, mother and son remained in close contact. She sought to look after his interests at home while advising him on who could be trusted and who not. When seriously wounded after one battle, Alexander expressed the wish to see his mother made into a goddess—perhaps so they would one day be reunited on Mount Olympus, home of the gods. When the conqueror finally died in 323 bce in faraway Babylon, it must for Olympias have been calamitous, inconceivable—for a decade it had seemed that her son really was the invincible hero. But however devastated she must have been, she was quick to find a new object for her ambitions: her grandson, born to Alexander's Persian wife, Roxana.

In the chaos that followed the conqueror's death, both this baby son, Alexander IV, and Alexander the Great's retarded half brother, Arrhidaeus—the one Olympias was earlier accused of working her magic on—were made king, while various generals also set about forming rival dynasties. The Macedonian forces were split, and a showdown became unavoidable. In 317 bce, Olympias led an army against the forces behind Arrhidaeus—fronted by another formidable woman, Arrhidaeus's wife, a self-styled warrior queen. But at the sight of Olympias, mother of the great Alexander, dressed in the full regalia of a high priestess of Dionysus, the opposing army defected en masse. She was victorious once more. Poor Arrhidaeus was stabbed to death and his wife hanged. Alexander IV became (albeit, as it turned out, rather briefly) sole king of Macedon, with Olympias as his regent. No doubt she was keen to tell him that the blood of Achilles flowed in his veins too, but more to the point, so did hers.

CHIPS OFF THE OLD BLOCK

"OUR death is not an end if we can live on in our children," wrote Albert Einstein, "for they are us; our bodies are only wilted leaves on the tree of life." In writing this to console the widow of a friend, Einstein captured the essence of biological immortality, the second part of the Legacy Narrative. It is the belief that we live on in our offspring, that we and they are connected in a profound way that makes us in some crucial sense the same being. So when these individual bodies have withered and died, still we might flourish in the verdancy of the next generation.

In a way, the pursuit of biological legacy takes us back to the very beginning of our journey: alongside the raw fight for survival, it is the most instinctive means by which we attempt to fling ourselves into an endless future. Across the world, billions of creatures are at it right now—wooing and seducing, laying eggs and spurting semen, birthing and weaning, building nests and herding harems. As Aristotle wrote almost two and a half thousand years ago, "For any living thing . . . the most natural act is the production of another like itself, an animal producing an animal, a plant a plant, in order that, as far as its nature allows, it may partake of the eternal."

But to allow you to partake of the eternal this claim to biological immortality must prove itself to be something more than just a metaphor. It is one thing to believe that a part of you lives on in your children, another that this part is enough to secure your survival. Only if *you* survive through your children is biological legacy a path to living forever. But a strong case can be made for exactly that, though it will take us far beyond your connection to your own offspring—as proud as you might be of the few buds springing directly from your own little twig on the tree of life, much more important is your connection back to the whole, root and branch.

We saw in chapter 8 that for the Legacy Narrative to have any plausibility we have to look at the self in a wholly new way. The other three narratives—Staying Alive, Resurrection and Soul—promise that the person, whether in body or mind, will live on in something like a recognizable form. But it is clear that nothing like Alexander's body or mind survived in the ordinary sense through his cultural legacy—so we looked at the bundle theory, which suggested that you are not a single coherent self but a collection of memories, ideas and so on that could live on even if dispersed. Similarly, it is clear that neither Olympias's body nor her mind survived in the ordinary sense in the form of her son or grandson. But the supporter of the biological Legacy Narrative would say that this ordinary sense is wrong; you are not what you think you are.

"CHILDREN are the only form of immortality that we can be sure of," said the writer and actor Peter Ustinov. This is a common thought, perhaps because it is indisputable that *something* of us is passed on to our children—hope of biological immortality is therefore not quite so blind as the wait for the resurrection. The question, however, is whether that something is enough to warrant a claim to eternal life. Nowadays we can state precisely what a parent's biological legacy is: 50 percent of their genes, which then make up 50 percent of their children's genes, combining with an equal amount from the other parent.

Of course, Olympias, like most other parents, passed on more to Alexander than just genes, including, for example, a belief in her and her son's heroic ancestry and divine destiny. But such values and ideas belong to the realm of cultural legacy that we have already examined; our concern in this chapter is with the blood and guts of biology. And biologically speaking, it is the genes that leap from generation to generation, outliving the individual bodies of their carriers. That is why, according to the evolutionary biologist Richard Dawkins, "the genes are the immortals . . . we, the individual survival machines in the world, can expect to live a few more decades. But the genes in the world have an expectation of life that must be measured not in decades but in thousands and millions of years."

But it is of course one thing to say that our genes are immortal, quite another to say that *you and I* are therefore immortal. Indeed, the standard version of the gene's-eye view of life offers little hope for our prospects of living on; rather, it portrays us humans as temporary, short-lived vehicles for the ruthless striving of the genes. The real action, according to this story, started with the evolution of DNA (the stuff that genes are made of) long before our births and will continue long after our deaths. And one thing that genes have learned in their long history is that it is much more efficient to code for organisms that reproduce than to try to build ones that individually last a long time. The wear and tear of life is just too great to risk investing everything in a super-vehicle. Much better to have disposable containers such as human beings, which continually produce fresh new containers. So at first sight, talk of immortal genes does not sound very promising for your survival—at least, not if *you* are one of these disposable containers. But perhaps that is the wrong way of looking at the continuum of life and your role in it.

Genes get a lot of attention, partly because they are regarded as the primary unit of natural selection. But that does not make them the primary unit of life; that privilege goes to the cell. Cells are microscopic yet hugely sophisticated self-contained bundles of biological activity. Curled up in the nucleus of each cell are its genes, acting something like the cell's construction manual and route map in one. Cells are, if you like, genes' way of getting around in the world.

You are a collective of around one hundred trillion cells, each of which contains a separate, complete copy of your genes (except either your eggs or sperm, which only contain 50 percent). Usually when we look at life, we tend to focus on other big multicellular beings such as fellow humans, dogs, grass and carrots. But the vast majority of organisms on earth are simply one single cell, and until recently (in evolutionary terms) *all* life on earth consisted of such single cells roaming free, going it alone. At various points in the history of evolution, these individual cells have decided to combine their resources and gang together. Plants, animals and other multicellular beings are the product of this communal living. On one level, you appear to be an organism in your own right; but on another, you are simply a colony of cells, each controlled by its little ball of genes.

A few further facts help to make this clear. Some of your cells, such as certain white blood cells, live largely autonomous lives roaming around your bloodstream waiting for a signal to attack their prey, such as unwelcome microbes. Such cells are an essential part of your immune system. Yet very similar cells can be found in any pond, where we call them amoebas and consider them to be independent organisms. As the evolutionary biologist Lynn Margulis put it, "humans are integrated colonies of ameboid beings."

Our cells are now too specialized to live outside of the collective that we call a human being, but that is not true of all animals. Some sponges (which are animals, albeit rather simple ones) can be pushed through a sieve and their cells will continue to live independently, eventually searching each other out and reassembling. In the case of such a sponge, the question of what the real agent is in all this—the genes, or the cell they control, or the multicellular collective—seems a matter of perspective. And the same is true of you.

It might seem obvious that a human is something over and above a lump of individual cells. But if this seems obvious when looking at a fully grown human being, it is much less obvious when looking at a newly conceived one. The fact is, you were quite literally once a single cell: you started out as the fusion of an egg cell produced by your mother and a (much smaller) sperm cell from your father. This cell then divided into two, and the two resulting cells then divided again, and so on and so on to produce the trillions of cells that make up your body. As it grew, this clump of cells slowly acquired new abilities as a collective, over and above what an individual cell could do alone—such as the capacities to do math and make music. This clump can also produce further cells—eggs or sperm—that are capable of fusing with another cell to produce a whole new clump carrying 50 percent of the first clump's genes.

Therefore from the point of view of your genes, traveling the world in their little cells, the chain of life looks unbroken from generation to generation. There are no abrupt starts and stops such as we see at the level of the multicellular human. When a cell replicates, it first replicates its genetic code, then fully divides itself, ensuring both halves get a complete set of genes. Although we call the resulting cells "daughters," each is really a direct continuation of the original. Nothing in this process *dies* or disappears or is lost;

there is no corpse. One living thing has become two, and it lives on in a quite literal, physical way in both the successors.

The original single cell from which your body started is therefore still very much alive and present in all the trillions of cells that have resulted from the first splitting; not only do they have an identical set of genes, but they have arisen from an unbroken series of divisions. But that first cell was of course a fusion of offshoots from the great clumps of cells that were your mother and father. And they each started out as one cell, each of which was itself a fusion of offshoots from your grandparents. Even Alexander the Great began his career as a single cell, and that arose from the fusion of an egg cell that was once a literal part of Olympias and a sperm cell that was once a part of Philip. He, like all of us, was a literal, physical continuation of his parents. As Erasmus Darwin, grandfather of the more famous Charles and an important scientist in his own right, wrote in 1796, "the offspring is termed a new animal; but it is, in truth, a branch or elongation of the parent."

From this perspective the history of life does not look like a series of discrete organisms that live and die but rather an unbroken chain of splitting and fusing cells, driven by busily replicating genes. The chain widens as a fertilized egg divides to produce something of human form, then narrows when that large cluster of cells itself produces a single egg or sperm, which in turn will produce the next link. You live on in your children because you are not really the distinct individual that you think you are; you are just a widening of a chain of life that is billions of years old and has no end in sight. Talk of you as a particular person with a date of birth and one day a date of death is therefore just a convenient shorthand. To quote Lynn Margulis once again, "From an everyday, uncontentious perspective 'you' began in your mother's womb some nine months before whatever your age is. From a deeper, evolutionary perspective, however, 'you' began with life's daring genesis—its succession, more than 4,000 million years ago, from the witch's brew of the early Earth."

FAMILY CONSCIOUSNESS

ALTHOUGH we moderns know more about the underlying mechanics of heredity than any other people in history, we might nonetheless also be the least able to empathize with the biological Legacy Narrative. The reason is that we have such a highly developed sense of ourselves as individuals, as we saw in chapter 6. Anthropologists believe that people in most other cultures in history and around the world regarded themselves much less strongly as individuals and identified instead with their family, clan or tribe. The influential French ethnologist Lucien Lévy-Bruhl wrote a hundred years ago that in traditional societies "the individual is apprehended only by virtue of his being an element of the group of which he is part, which alone is the true unit."

Take, for example, this epitaph from a member of that proud Roman dynasty the Scipios, every aspect of which relates the individual to the broader biological unit: "By my conduct I added to the virtues of my family; I begat offspring and sought to equal the deeds of my father. I maintained the glory of my ancestors, so that they rejoice that I was their offspring; my honors have ennobled my stock." Before the arrival of Greek philosophy and Hebrew religion, ancient Roman culture was based on a form of ancestor worship, with each family having its own cult. Every family member was defined by his or her relationship— biological, social and ethical—to ancestors and offspring.

The Austrian sociologist Franz Borkenau described this as the "Jewish strategy" (in contrast to the "Hellenic strategy" of pursuing undying glory, which we examined in chapter 8). We saw in chapter 4 that individual immortality in the form of resurrection developed only relatively late in the history of Judaism; prior to this we find instead emphasis upon the survival of the tribe of Israel as a collective. As the theologian John Hick put it, initially the Hebrew religion was focused "fully upon God's covenant with the nation, as an organism that continued through the centuries while successive generations lived and died."

This is a worldview that would also be instantly recognizable to people from China, Japan, Korea and many parts of Africa. The biological Legacy Narrative has been influential throughout history not only in the obvious sense that we have children, but also as a powerful ideology that has defined the contours of many people's lives. In all cases, along with contributing to the well-being of both the dead and the living, such ancestor veneration strongly reinforces the identity of all family members as part of something greater than each individual, something that extends back into the distant past and will survive long after their own deaths. It offers a strong sense of collective immortality, in which the particular person recognizes that he or she is a part of an ancient and continuing whole. For people in such societies the conclusion that we are a mere link in a chain of life would not have come as a surprise at all, but rather reflected a deep, lived reality.

THERE is therefore a way of seeing life that makes it look much more like an unbroken continuity than a series of lives and deaths, and many people have identified profoundly with this view. But there is a stumbling block to taking the claims of biological immortality literally: consciousness.

What is it that we want when we want to live on, whether until tomorrow, next year or next millennium? Following our discussions of the Resurrection and Soul Narratives, I would suggest that what we most want is the continuation of our consciousness. Or put another way, if someone tells me that I will still be alive in the summer next year, then I should reasonably be able to look forward to feeling the summer sun on my face and seeing my children playing in the garden. We might want lots of other things too, like the preservation of certain character traits or memories, but at the root of it all is the continuity of the same consciousness. Of course, I might lose this consciousness before death—for example, if I entered a permanent vegetative state. But that is exactly why I would consider such a thing to be *just as bad* as actually dying.

This is a problem for the biological Legacy Narrative. It may be true that an individual human is just a phase in a small part of the undying web of life. It may be true that it is therefore a mistake to think that "I" am really born and really die, as "I" am actually part of a broader continuum. But this "phase" that is me gives every impression of having a distinct, individual consciousness, and when the phase is over, that consciousness disappears. Even if we decide we no longer want to call the end of that phase "death," we still might think that, like being in a permanent vegetative state, the loss of my distinct, individual consciousness makes it just as bad as death. I might live on in the great web of life, but if not consciously, then that claim to immortality rings a little hollow.

As I write this, I can hear one of my young daughters playing in the room next door. As much as I love her and empathize with her struggles and successes, I do not literally see the world through her eyes. I am in this room, she in the next, and the door between us is closed. When I die, this will not change. My consciousness will not leap into her—or at least, nothing about the way we understand consciousness to work suggests this will be so. Even if there is a way of looking at the world that implies a profound continuity between us, we remain separate conscious beings. And that does not bode well for my bid to live forever.

But perhaps we simply need to shift perspectives again. We have zoomed in to the micro level to examine the nature of the continuity between parent and child; now it is time to zoom out—to a super-macro level, where a whole new degree of connectedness becomes apparent. And perhaps even a whole new consciousness.

THE BIGGER PICTURE

THE image of the chain in which you are a link fails to capture the real extent to which you are part of a much wider story. If you have siblings, then they are also offshoots of your parents' cells, just like you are. On average, you will share as much genetic material with them as you do with your own children or with each individual parent. Your cellular connections do not just reach backward and forward in the generations, but also sideways. There is not a single thread, but rather a web, continually forking and rejoining.

There is nothing abstract about this web: it is both a biological reality and a reality in the lives of many people. It manifests itself in the idea of the clan, the tribe and the nation. Despite consisting of hundreds of thousands or even many millions of people, most nations have some myth of common ancestry, and their members see themselves as alike—in contrast to all "foreigners." One of the prophets of German nationalism, Johann Gottlieb Fichte, wrote that for the good German, immortality lay in "the hope of eternal continuance of the people without admixture of, or corruption by, any alien element." The nation is, in Fichte's words, the "eternal thing to which he entrusts the eternity of himself."

Within each tribe or nation, the sense of commonality can be a hugely positive force, leading to strong mutual support mechanisms, both formal and informal. Indeed, it was in Germany, not long after Fichte's death, that the first welfare state was created. If you feel closely connected to another person, you will be more likely to help them out in hard times, whether directly or through paying taxes that pay for their social benefits. A narrative of collective immortality makes this impulse even stronger, encouraging people to sacrifice even their lives for the sake of the greater whole. The psychiatrist and historian Robert Jay Lifton has documented this effect in the countries that experienced communist revolutions in the twentieth century. In China, for example, communist ideology built on a long tradition of ancestor worship to refocus identity from one's own family to the broader community of the national proletariat.

But of course there is also a darker side to this narrative. Family and community might sound like innocent values, but they are intimately linked with the struggle to preserve *our* legacy at the expense of others. Indeed, raising one's own group to the status of "chosen" or somehow superior to others is a sure way of strengthening that group's myth of immortality—whether that group is an aristocratic family or a billion-strong nation. An ancient impulse, this destructive ideology reached its apotheosis in the twentieth century, when 170 million people died in war, the defining motif of which was chauvinistic nationalism—as the sociologist Zygmunt Bauman put it, "seldom . . . expressed so frankly as in the Nazi project of the world made fit for the immortality of the healthiest and most virile of races."

Now we can measure the genetic differences between peoples of different nations and see just how minuscule—or indeed nonexistent—they are. In evolutionary terms, it is not long ago that all humans had a common ancestor—a mere two hundred thousand years. A more positive ideology based on the biological Legacy Narrative would encompass the whole human race as our immortality vehicle. And indeed there are idealists, such as Einstein and Linus Pauling, who advocated just this.

But why stop at humans? Not so long ago (about six million years) we had a common ancestor with chimpanzees, with whom we share about 95 percent of our genes (estimates vary depending on the method of calculation). Before that (about six hundred million years ago), we had a common ancestor with all animals—even now, we share some 44 percent of our genes with fruit flies. And before that, we shared common ancestors with fungi (with whom we have about a quarter of our genes in common), plants (about a fifth) and many single-celled organisms such as bacteria. A few simple creatures that started replicating a very long time ago have covered the earth with a tissue of life—the biosphere—all of which is profoundly interconnected. The question is, can any of these super-macro perspectives of nation, species or biosphere provide a plausible immortality vehicle—one that might even solve the problem of consciousness?

A clue can be found in ants. Those who study these social insects have long known that individual organisms working in extremely close cooperation can produce what seems to be a whole new entity—a superorganism. Colonies of ants can do things far beyond the capacity—and almost certainly the understanding—of any single ant, such as build complex nests with carefully regulated internal temperature and humidity, or farm fungus and herd aphids. In many ways, individual ants make up the greater whole that is a colony in the same way that your cells make up a human being. And contrary to what otherwise seems a universal imperative to survive and reproduce, most ants are quite content to sacrifice themselves for the greater good: as long as the colony lives on, they do not seem at all worried about their individual immortality.

Some thinkers have suggested that human communities are similar. This was a popular idea in the nineteenth century, advocated by writers like the philosopher and scientist Herbert Spencer, coiner of the phrase "survival of the fittest," and it is now being taken seriously once again. People in modern cities long ago lost the ability to survive independently—we are utterly reliant on a complex higher-level system for clean water, food, clothing, shelter, medicine, security and energy. Like the specialized cells of our bodies, which have given up their independence for the greater strength and security offered by life as part of a macro-organism, we have each given up our independence to be part of strong and secure superorganisms.

Just as a human has abilities that no individual cell has, and an ant colony has abilities that no individual ant has, our societies have abilities that none of us as individuals has. No one understands every aspect of how a modern city works—which would require knowing everything about hospitals, transport logistics, nuclear energy production and so on. Yet somehow these things *do* work, and with a kind of coordination that regulates and sustains huge communities. The system therefore manifests an intelligence and ability exceeding that of any of its individual members. In the words of the biologist Alison Jolly, "Homo sapiens is slowly evolving into something akin to a superorganism, a highly-structured global society in which the lives of everyone on the planet will become so interdependent that they may grow and develop with a common purpose."

So both your city and the entire global society can make claims to being real, living entities—wholes of which you are a part and that will (probably) outlive any individual member. But it is an even more macro perspective that is currently receiving the most attention, that of the biggest superorganism of them all: the planet Earth, otherwise known as Gaia.

The Gaia hypothesis is the claim that our entire planet is an integrated system that regulates itself in a way that is conducive to life. This system does not only consist of all living things but includes other aspects of the planet, such as the atmosphere, oceans, rocks and ice caps. First put forward by the English scientist James Lovelock in the 1970s and named after the Greek goddess of the earth, supporters of the Gaia hypothesis argue that this entire system is directly comparable to what we ordinarily consider a single organism, such as you or me.

Lynn Margulis is one such advocate. She writes, "Atmospheric, astronomical, and oceanographic evidence attest that life manifests itself on a planetary scale. The steadiness of mean planetary temperature of the past three thousand million years, the 700-million-year maintenance of earth's reactive atmosphere between high-oxygen levels of combustibility and low-oxygen levels of asphyxiation, and the apparently continuous removal of hazardous salts from oceans—all these point to mammal-like purposefulness in the organization of life as a whole . . . Life on Earth—fauna, flora, and microbiota—is a single, gas-entrenched, ocean-connected planetary system, the largest organic being in the solar system."

From this super-macro perspective, the human quest for personal immortality looks increasingly like a kind of mix-up. Individual humans are merely temporary forms taken by the single, shifting web of life on earth. To suggest one should live forever is like trying to preserve the shape of a particular dune in the shifting sands of a desert. If humans are not really separate things, then their births and deaths are also not real, but simply one way of seeing the rhythms of life. Margulis thinks so: "Death is illusory in quite a real sense," she writes. "As sheer persistence of biochemistry, 'we' have never died during the passage of three thousand million years. Mountains and seas and even supercontinents have come and gone, but we have persisted."

GLOBAL CONSCIOUSNESS AND YOU

MANY find this a reassuring view. It is, in a way, the flip side to the cultural Legacy Narrative that required you to assert your uniqueness, to rise above the masses and prove your specialness. The biological Legacy Narrative, in contrast, dissolves you into a greater whole; it releases you from the struggle to become someone special, emphasizing instead the natural connectedness and continuity of being. Ernest Becker described these two contrary impulses as "the need to expand oneself as an individual heroic personality" versus "the need to surrender oneself in full to the rest of nature, to become a part of it by laying down one's whole existence to some higher meaning."

Religions play upon both these impulses. We have seen how the belief in an immortal soul and a personal God encourage an individual's sense of heroic self-worth. Equally, other traditions—including within the same religions—offer opportunities for submerging oneself in a greater whole. "Islam," for example, means "submission" and requires the believer to submit to the unimaginable greatness that is Allah. The idea of dissolving the self into a greater whole is also crucial to the Buddhist idea of nirvana and fundamental to some strands of Hinduism and to Taoism. Indeed, recognizing yourself to be part of a deeper reality is for many the first step on the spiritual path. The Taoists say that the only difference between the immortals and the rest of us is that the former have recognized their unity with the underlying eternal reality, whereas we poor mortals still believe in individual death.

But, for all its attractions, this super-macro version of the biological immortality narrative faces two major challenges. The first is the consciousness problem that we met above when looking at our genetic legacy. The second is the end of the world—a prospect that looks set to stop even Gaia's aspirations to eternity.

GLOBAL CONSCIOUSNESS AND YOU

WE saw above that if biological legacy is to deliver meaningful survival, then it must deliver some kind of continuity of consciousness. But I know that my consciousness does not continue in my children. Can the biosphere step in to help?

There is much about consciousness that we do not yet understand. But as we saw in chapter 7, we do know that *your* consciousness as a human being emerges from the massively complex interactions of billions of individual brain cells—even if we don't know exactly how. Now we have just seen that ant colonies, human societies and even the entire earth function much like organisms. These entities all seem to sense and respond to their environment in ways that transcend the actions of any of their component parts. In humans, such purposeful behavior and consciousness go hand in hand. The possibility therefore suggests itself that the seemingly purposeful behavior in entities like cities or Gaia is also accompanied by a kind of consciousness, produced by the interaction of the countless humans and other organisms. In other words, Earth, as an interconnected system comparable in complexity to a brain, might literally have a mind of her own.

We don't know. Worse, we don't even know how we could know, as no one has yet invented a conscious-o-meter to measure whether cities, anthills or bacterial communities have minds of their own. There is increasing awareness among scientists that the kind of complex interconnectivity that produces consciousness in the brain can be found in other systems, from biospheres even down to microbial communities. This gives some measure of plausibility to ideas of global or cosmic consciousness that have long been popular with philosophers and mystics. The question for the biological immortalist, then, is this: Do we have reason to think that when we die, our consciousness somehow lives on in that of a higher entity, whether society, Gaia or the cosmos?

It does not look promising. Although there is much we do not understand, the idea that your consciousness can survive the death of your body certainly does not sit very well with what we *do* understand—that, as we saw in chapter 7, your individual mind seems dependent upon the functioning of your brain.

The argument from neuroscience against the existence of the soul was this: If a soul enables your memory or sight or beliefs or emotions to continue after the destruction of your whole brain and body on death, why does it not enable the continuation of these faculties after the failure of merely *parts* of your brain when you are alive? This argument applies equally well to the claim that your individual consciousness survives at some other level of being: If the various aspects of your consciousness can reside in Gaia after your death, then why before death do we lose aspects of our consciousness—or lose consciousness completely—when just parts of our brain shut down?

Why isn't the cosmic consciousness kicking in to fill in the gap when our brain is shut down by general anesthetic, for example?

Of course, believers can find answers to these questions, but only with additional ad hoc and unprovable hypotheses. There is nothing about the way consciousness seems to work that would support the idea that it can transfer from one entity to another. In fact, to the extent that consciousness seems to arise as an emergent property from a complex physical system—and therefore to be dependent on that system—it seems difficult to even make sense of the idea that it is a thing that might be transferred. If consciousness is something my brain *does*, then talk of it being transferred makes as much sense as talk of my digestion being transferred or my idiosyncratic gait.

In the believer-versus-skeptic bout, this argument is a strong enough blow to award victory to the skeptic on points. Positive scientific evidence is lacking for other levels of consciousness, and our best understanding of consciousness does not support the idea of its being transferred. But the argument is not a knockout: the believer could reply that there *is* some evidence that people can tap into the consciousness of entities, such as Gaia, of which we are a part. This is the anecdotal report of mystics who, for thousands of years, have claimed to attain new levels of consciousness in which they become one with all other living things, or even with the cosmos itself.

Such claims are ancient and widespread. And they can even respond to the criticism that one's own individual consciousness could not survive as part of this greater entity: that is the point, they say. Freedom from the petty concerns, troublesome memories and shallow desires of individual life is for many Buddhists, Hindus and Taoists the highest aim. This is the extinguishing of the self—the literal meaning of "nirvana." If the individual consciousness has been left behind in the process of identifying with the higher consciousness, then the goal of transcendence has been achieved.

And if you are wondering why *you* have not experienced higher-level awareness, the yogi's answer is straightforward: You haven't learned how. Years of training are required to master one's own consciousness, and this is exactly what practices such as Buddhism have spent millennia doing.

The problem with these reports is that we cannot distinguish whether the mystics have really experienced another level of consciousness or whether they simply interpret certain unusual individual states of consciousness that way. Nor can we find an answer through taking all such mystical experiences at face value, as many simply contradict each other (e.g., some people experience the presence of a personal God, some an impersonal cosmos; some the persistence of the individual, some the extinguishing of the self). We could therefore only begin to see these experiences as useful evidence if we had a theoretical framework of consciousness in which they (or some of them) would make sense. Currently, such a framework is lacking, and indeed our best framework points strongly to these states being distinctive *individual* experiences, even if they *feel* pretty cosmic. There might be all sorts of reasons why such states of consciousness are worth striving for, but they are unlikely to be intimations of immortality.

THE END *REALLY IS* NIGH

NONETHELESS, it might at the very least be reassuring that *some* consciousness will continue after you and I are gone, or that we are parts of greater wholes who will outlive any individual humans. We all yearn to be part of a greater drama, and life on earth is certainly that. But immortality is supposed to be forever; humanity, Gaia, and even the universe seem, however, to be fleeting things.

In the longevity stakes, the planet Earth is doing well at some 4.5 billion years old, and life has been around for much of that time. There have been at least five major extinctions in which half of existing species were wiped out, such as the one that finished the dinosaurs, but life has always endured, despite bombardment from asteroids, volcanic eruptions and major changes to earth's atmosphere and climate. No doubt many more cataclysms will come this planet's way, some of them perhaps man-made, but life, with or without humans, should pull through.

There are, however, some cosmic shocks that nothing could survive: a close encounter with a black hole, for example, or getting in the way of a massive gamma-ray burst from a nearby exploding star. And even if earth is lucky enough to avoid these, in about five billion years our sun will have grown so large that it will burn away all life—at least as we know it. More worrying still, the sun could suck in and engulf the entire planet. But even if not, after another few billion years, the sun will shrivel and grow cold and it will be lights-out in our solar system for good. Not even Gaia will be around forever.

Some Gaia supporters, however, believe that, like all organisms, earth will reproduce, and we humans, with our aspirations to travel into space and colonize new planets, are the means—we are Gaia's spores. This is an imaginative response to the challenge of a doomed earth, and perhaps, if we have not already destroyed ourselves by then, we will one day have the technology to start anew in different solar systems or faraway galaxies.

But it seems that we cannot keep running forever: the majority of cosmologists believe that the entire universe will one day end. They disagree on how; current theories include a Big Freeze (wherein energy spreads out until the universe is effectively empty with a temperature so close to absolute zero that nothing can happen anymore), a Big Rip (all matter eventually being torn apart into fundamental particles) or a Big Crunch (the universe collapsing in on itself). Whichever of these theories proves to be closest to the truth, it does not look good for our prospects of being at home in the cosmos forever.

Fortunately, all these scenarios are a very long way away. And they may all be wrong. For now, all we can say is that the universe, life, and certainly human science are still young. Perhaps one day we—or some far more evolved successor—will be able to seed new universes that are fit for life. Indeed, perhaps we are already in one, seeded by some earlier civilization.

RISE AND FALL

THE Legacy Narrative in both its forms is a hugely productive force. The impulse to produce something of us that will live on beyond the individual body drives us to heroic deeds and high art, and to care for our families, tribes, nations or all of life. And of course each one of us *is* the product of two people's attempt to create something that will live on after their own bodies have failed.

But we have also seen that it can quickly turn into a darker force too. Olympias, for example, in her desire to secure the position of her grandson, Alexander IV, was happy to continue the killing practiced on such a grand scale by the little boy's great father. When she established herself as regent in Macedon, she tore into the heart of the country's elite, torturing, imprisoning and killing those who she believed opposed her. But in doing so she turned the people against her, and when the son of one of Alexander's generals raised another army, he found it easy to win support among the Macedonian nobility. Olympias was quickly defeated, tried and condemned to death.

For all her failings and transgressions, ancient reports are in agreement that Olympias faced her death with courage and composure. One report says that she went out to meet her executioners so boldly that they could not bring themselves to do their duty and others had to be sent for, another that she was in the end stoned by the relatives of those whom she had herself killed. Perhaps she believed that she had already done enough to pave the way for her grandson to one day take the throne for himself alone. But it was not to be: once the new regime was well entrenched, the boy-king Alexander IV was quietly done away with. After all the bloodshed across three continents, Olympias's dynasty was finished.

Nowadays we know that the genetic difference between Olympias's direct descendants and any other Macedonian—indeed any other human being—would be minuscule. If the biological immortality narrative has any plausibility at all, then it is not in promoting your own offspring at the expense of others, but rather in identifying as broadly as possible with the wider community—whether of humanity or even of all living things. But as with the cultural half of the Legacy Narrative, this plausibility is limited: there are many benefits to identifying widely with our fellow creatures, but eternal life is not one of them.

Which means all four fundamental immortality narratives are illusions. None of them will enable us to live forever. Yet we have seen that they serve both to fuel human progress and to protect us from a crippling fear of death. The question therefore becomes whether we can live without them. I believe we can, and as my witness I call a king whose epic adventure was recorded at the very beginnings of civilization: Gilgamesh.

CONCLUSION

10

❧

HE WHO SAW THE DEEP

Wisdom and Mortality

A MAN walked into a bar. He looked haggard, tired, like he had been sleeping rough, his face raw from the wind and the sun. A hunter, perhaps, thought the barmaid—one of the rugged types who were among the few to make it out to this remote inn. But then something in his manner told her he was—or had been—more than just a woodsman. Either way, he looked like he badly needed a drink.

"What's up, stranger?" she asked, handing him a beer. He took a sip, then looked up and told his story.

"I was a king," he said. She raised her eyebrows. "And the strongest in my land. But I was an idiot, full of myself, bullying my people and beating my chest. So the gods created a wild man who would be my match. Enkidu, he was called. He came into my city and challenged me—we wrestled until the foundations shook, until we both knew the match was too even and neither of us could win. Then we embraced and became the best of friends. Together we slew Humbaba, the ogre who guarded the Forest of Cedar, and killed the lions in the mountain passes."

Still polishing earthenware cups, the barmaid asked, "Well, if you are a king, then why do you wander the wild? If you are the one who killed Humbaba, why do you now have sunken cheeks and wear a hunter's garb?"

"Why? I'll tell you. Because Enkidu and I slew the Bull of Heaven, sent by Ishtar to lay waste to the land, and that, for the gods, was too much. They decreed that one of us must die. Enkidu went down with a fever; twelve days he lay sick; then on the twelfth he passed into the land from which none return.

"My friend! Like a panther, he was. I loved him so much; together we went through every danger. For a week, I wept over his body and would not allow it to be taken, hoping he might rise again, until a maggot dropped from his nostril and I knew Death had taken him.

"But that is not the worst of it—it was then that I saw: I too would one day be like him. If Death can claim Enkidu, strongest of the strong, then why not also a king? One day, I too will fall, never to rise again. It is too much to bear! I can look any man in the face, but not Death! And so, since I buried my friend, I have wandered the wilds, living on the flesh of beasts. I seek the one who survived the flood, Utnapishtim, the one they say is immortal, that I might learn his secret. Tell me, where can I find him?"

"Then you must be Gilgamesh," replied the barmaid. "But don't you see, immortality is not for the likes of us.

"The life that you seek you never will find:
when the gods created mankind,
death they dispensed to mankind,
life they kept for themselves.

But you, Gilgamesh, let your belly be full,
enjoy yourself always by day and by night!
Make merry each day,
dance and play day and night!

Let your clothes be clean,
let your head be washed, may you bathe in water!
Gaze on the child who holds your hand,
let your wife enjoy your repeated embrace!"

Gilgamesh looked the barmaid in the eye. "Just tell me where I can find Utnapishtim."

"You must pay the boatman to take you across the Waters of Death," she replied. And with that, he paid up and left.

It was 2700 bce and civilization was young when Gilgamesh left the tavern at the end of the world and persuaded the mysterious boatman to take him to Utnapishtim. He had wandered far from his kingdom of Uruk in the fertile lands between the Tigris and Euphrates Rivers, close to Babylon and modern-day Baghdad. According to the records of the Sumerian people who lived in this region, Gilgamesh was a historical figure—though one whose deeds had become legend.

Across the Waters of Death, the wandering king found the only immortal, Utnapishtim. The old man explained that he and his wife alone had been permitted to live forever—this was their reward for having built the ark and saved life on earth from the Deluge. This great flood had been sent to destroy a humanity that was overrunning the land; in order to prevent them from once again reaching such numbers, the gods then decreed that all subsequent humans were to be mortal.

The wise old man then challenged Gilgamesh: if he wanted to defeat Death so much, first he should show that he could defeat its little brother: Sleep. He had only to go without slumber for seven nights. Of course Gilgamesh, exhausted from his travels, failed. "See the fellow who so desired life!" said Utnapishtim mockingly. "Sleep like a fog already breathes over him!"

Echoing the advice of the barmaid, Utnapishtim told Gilgamesh to clean himself up, go home and start acting like a proper king. Then, in a last aside, he revealed to him the existence of an underwater plant that could turn back aging. Immediately, the hero dived into the ocean and plucked the magic herb, determined to bring it back to Uruk. This turned out, however, only to be the final taunt at his aspirations—on his journey home, when the hero was bathing, a snake stole the plant and bore it off, shedding its skin as it went. Weeping, Gilgamesh finally accepted that eternal life would never be his.

TO DWELL IN DARKNESS

WHICH is the position in which we too find ourselves. We have now examined all four immortality narratives and seen that none of them has a credible chance of delivering on its promise. Despite their ancient histories, millions of followers and enormous influence in shaping human civilization, the four paths all fall far short of the summit. Eternal life will never be ours.

This leaves us in something of a fix. We saw at the very beginning of this book that we all have the instinct to perpetuate ourselves indefinitely into the future—the will to immortality. And we saw that the flip side of this is an inborn fear of death. The four paths serve to reassure us that the will to immortality will be satisfied, and so the fear is assuaged. For thousands of years and across the globe they have served as lullabies to soothe our existential angst. What does it mean for us if they are all illusions? Must we, like Gilgamesh, wander the desert weeping?

Many have thought so. St. Paul, who did so much to encourage hope in the hereafter, was one: "If *in this life only* we have hope in Christ, we of all men are most miserable," he wrote (1 Corinthians 15:19, emphasis added). Plenty of scholars, priests and poets since have agreed that a finite life cannot be a good life; so illustrious a philosopher as Immanuel Kant argued that neither happiness nor ethics was possible without an unending hereafter. The prospect of death's finality makes all our projects seem futile and fills us with dread.

To create such a wonderful creature as a human being only to permit him or her to turn to dust seems indeed an extraordinary waste, a cruel, cosmic joke at our expense. As Alfred, Lord Tennyson, put it, "If immortality be not true, then no God but a mocking fiend created us." (Rather petulantly adding, "If there is no immortality, I shall hurl myself into the sea!") More recently, the psychologists behind Terror Management Theory suggested that without our comforting illusions, we will become "twitching blobs of biological protoplasm completely perfused with anxiety."

The Mortality Paradox only worsens the situation, as we saw in chapter 1. The truth of the first part, that we must die like all other living things, goes unmitigated, while the second part, that we cannot imagine our own nonexistence, plays terrible tricks on us. We have seen that this intuition can serve as a scaffold on which immortality narratives can be built, with their promises of a happy afterlife among friends and angels. But if we have dismissed the immortality narratives, then we are deprived of such positive pictures—yet this does not make it any the easier to grasp the prospect of not being. And so we fill the imaginative void with nightmares. In the absence of a positive image of eternity, we cannot help but imagine death to be endless gloom, an eternal exile in the abyss—the House of Darkness feared by the ancients.

We can see this fear of the emptiness of eternity reflected in the efforts many have taken to ensure they would not be alone. The First Emperor of China had not only terra-cotta soldiers, bureaucrats and musicians buried with him, but also real live concubines and many others. He had no intention of stepping unaccompanied into the void. Most of us, however, must face death without such an entourage. This prospect—of nonbeing, of nothingness—becomes defined in our minds only by the utter absence of all that we know in life.

Like Gilgamesh, we are therefore left without comfort: afraid that any moment might be our last; knowing that our drive to live on, our very essence, will——*must*——be thwarted; certain that life is a failure waiting to happen. And when that failure comes, then all will be lost; we will be plunged into eons of lonely oblivion and, as Gilgamesh's companion Enkidu puts it, "see no light, but dwell in darkness." To live and die without the promise of immortality seems a terrible fate.

AND that is only from the individual's point of view; from the perspective of civilization it gets worse still. We have seen repeatedly that civilization itself has been driven onward by our quest to triumph over death, indeed that the founding raison d'être of many civilizations is the promise of immortality. We saw that science and the ideology of progress emerged from the pursuit of indefinitely increasing lifespans, that religions thrive through their assurance of an afterlife, that most cultural products are our attempts to replicate ourselves in the symbolic realm and that having children reflects a biological urge to perpetuate ourselves into the future. We have seen that these are all misguided as attempts to secure the immortality of the individual——but what kind of a society is possible without them?

A much-impoverished one according to some scholars. Recall the words of the psychologist William McDougall writing on the decline of the belief in a soul that it was "highly probable that the passing away of this belief would be calamitous for our civilisation." He went on: "For every vigorous nation seems to have possessed this belief, and the loss of it has accompanied the decay of national vigour in many instances." The Cambridge philosopher C. D. Broad, himself skeptical about belief in a hereafter, went so far as to recommend that measures be taken to prevent such a loss of vigor: "It is quite possible," he wrote, "that the doctrine of human immortality (whether it be in fact true or false) is one of these socially valuable 'myths' which the State ought to remove from the arena of public discussion."

But "the State" has not so acted, and we are free to worry ourselves with our doubts and questions. Having worried ourselves to the point that none of the immortality narratives seems satisfactory, will we continue to work, worship and create—knowing that these activities will not after all deliver us from death? Can there be progress, justice and culture if we know that all our efforts will end in dust? Or should we for the sake of both our sanity and our civilization forget all our hard-won insights and attempt to recloak ourselves in the illusion of life everlasting?

This final chapter is dedicated to answering these questions. It is my belief that we do not need to despair, that it is possible to lead a decent and satisfying life in the face of finitude. Indeed, it might even be easier: immortality would have downsides at which we have so far only barely hinted. We will look at some of these and at a broader tradition of thought that offers an alternative to the four immortality narratives—a *fifth* narrative that we can also find weaving its influence throughout the ages. This alternative also attempts to grapple with the will to immortality and the Mortality Paradox, yet without promising to deliver eternal life. And though ancient, it fits well with the findings of modern science. We might call it—for reasons that will soon become clear—the *Wisdom Narrative*.

UNCIVILIZED

IN drawing the conclusions from the previous chapters we have so far mostly focused on the benefits of the immortality narratives, that which we stand to lose if these belief systems are rejected. But the effects of these narratives are far from purely positive: the struggle up the Mount of the Immortals has been as much one of bloodshed, atrocity and injustice as of growth and innovation. As

Zygmunt Bauman wrote, "All too often . . . the audacious dream of killing death turns into the practice of killing people."

We saw this only too clearly with Alexander the Great and his snake-worshipping, dagger-wielding mother, Olympias. Their pursuit of legacy, in one case cultural, in the other biological, left hundreds of thousands of ruined lives in its wake. We might find civilization inconceivable without the artist's pursuit of posterity, but it is worth remembering that many attempts at fame or glory are much less benign. Equally, we would not want to do without a mother's love for her child, but the biological immortality narrative also frequently transmutes into racism, nationalism and xenophobia: expelling or killing the Other becomes a way of preserving one's own purity and demonstrating that one's own kind stands above death. Thus Ernest Becker argued that our "urge to deny mortality and achieve a heroic self-image are the root causes of human evil."

So whereas many civilizations have arisen as means to immortal ends, just as many have met their downfall as a consequence of these narratives—those who stood in the way of Alexander, for example. Wars between cultures with differing immortality narratives are seen not just as matters of life and death but as matters of *eternal* life and death. Such wars therefore all become, in the words of the American philosopher Sam Keen, "holy wars" in which eternity is at stake. If you have given your life to furthering the revolution of the proletariat, then the victory of capitalism will destroy your part in posterity; if you wish to dedicate your life to Allah, the advance of secularism threatens to prevent you from finding your place in paradise. So we fight for the truth of our particular myth, and there are as many losers as winners.

But the negative effects of the immortality narratives are not only confined to conflict *between* civilizations—they are just as manifest *within* each society. We saw in chapter 7 that these narratives play an important role in many ethical systems—providing everlasting sticks and carrots as punishment or reward for one's peccadilloes on earth. But the flip side of these ethical systems is a rigid conservatism capable of condoning the most outrageous injustice. The clearest examples are the caste systems of South Asia, which are supported by a belief in reincarnation that teaches that if someone is born to a lowly station then it is only because they deserved it through bad deeds in a previous life.

Many commentators have recognized the correlation between a focus on an eternal afterlife and a willingness to unquestioningly accept injustice and deprivation in this world. This is no doubt why medieval European rulers found Christianity so useful—it taught their exploited subjects to avert their eyes from the horror of their daily lives and dream instead of a future paradise. This is what Nietzsche called the "slave morality," as it causes the downtrodden to accept their miserable lot and fantasize about revenge and gratification in an imaginary world to come. It is frequently noted that the great social-reform movements of the last centuries—emancipation of slaves, equality between sexes and races, social welfare and so on—arose only when the preoccupation with the next world began to lose its grip on Western society. Justice and happiness need not be sought now if an eternity of righteous pleasure is to come.

This focus on the next world can therefore exact a terrible price from those in this world: think only of the holy warriors who go to die in the expectation of a reward in paradise, whether as once with sword in hand or as now with explosives around their waist. If this life here on earth is regarded merely as a series of tests for a place in another life, then it is necessarily devalued: with eyes fixed firmly on future bliss, the immortalist fails to grasp the value of being *now*.

Finally, it is worth noting that most immortality narratives foster a profound selfishness. Such doctrines teach you to obsess about the infinite survival of your own individual personality; all actions are then measured by whether they make your personal survival more or less likely or your expected eternity more or less pleasurable. Outwardly admirable actions—such as giving to the poor—are performed for the sake of your soul. Even where this contributes to a more stable society, it does nothing to cultivate real virtues such as empathy or compassion for others but focuses all attention purely on the implications of an action for *you*.

Such a system teaches us to maintain the self-absorption of the infant motivated only by reward or punishment from its parent. What then passes as spirituality—with all the positive, elevated connotations of that word—often amounts largely to someone being so entirely obsessed with the state of their own immortal soul that they withdraw from society to cultivate its eternal prospects.

So when we recognize that the four immortality narratives have contributed to making our civilizations what they are, we must equally recognize that this includes these civilizations' profound flaws—their belligerence, their xenophobia, their injustice and the self-centeredness of their citizens. These are the downsides of the immortality narratives as they are, but there is more to add to the charge sheet—that is, what might happen if their promises were fulfilled and we really were to achieve personal immortality. For there is good reason to think that the effects on both sanity and civilization would be catastrophic.

THE LONG DARK TEA-TIME OF THE SOUL

I N chapter 2 we recalled the novelist Susan Ertz's observation that "millions long for immortality who don't know what to do with themselves on a rainy Sunday afternoon." Clearly there is something particularly sobering about the prospect of an eternity of Sunday afternoons; it is a prospect that can burst the bubble of all but the most ardent immortalist. Douglas Adams, in his five-part "trilogy" *The Hitchhiker's Guide to the Galaxy*, described a man who stumbled across immortality: "To begin with, it was fun . . . But in the end, it was the Sunday afternoons he couldn't cope with, and that terrible listlessness which starts to set in at about 2:55, when you know that you've had all the baths you can usefully have that day, that however hard you stare at any given paragraph in the papers you will never actually read it . . . and that as you stare at the clock the hands will move relentlessly on to four o'clock, and you will enter the long dark tea-time of the soul."

We noted in chapter 3 that achieving immortality on earth could lead to problems like overpopulation and our destruction at the hands of the very technologies designed to make us live forever, and we saw subsequently that it is anyway extremely unlikely to happen. But suspending disbelief for a moment, I want here to focus on the psychological effects of eternity—on the long dark tea-time of the soul. There are as I see it two sets of problems: on the one hand, the boredom and apathy that would result from having done and seen everything there is to do—that is, from having already lived a very long time—and on the other hand, the paralysis that would result from having an infinite future in which to do any further things. Both these problems, the backward looking and the forward looking, threaten to suck the meaning out of life and leave one wishing for a terminal deadline.

WE should not deny that life as we know it on earth for many people ends too soon. Most of us could write a list of things we would do with a little extra time—or even with a lot of extra time. But, as we have noted before, infinity is not simply extra time, it is endless time. We might love travel and dearly wish to live long enough to visit the thousand most beautiful or interesting places on earth, but we might be less inspired subsequently to visit the thousand slightly less beautiful and interesting places. Or the thousand after that. In the great scheme of infinity, it would not be long before we were left only with the thousand dullest places on the planet, at which point we might find our motivation seriously flagging.

Of course, there are some pleasures we enjoy more than once.

A good meal or conversation with friends or taking part in a favorite sport or hearing a favorite piece of music——these things seem at least as good the second, third or hundredth time. But a man who eats caviar every day will grow sick of it eventually, and we will one day——even if a million years hence——tire of all our friends' jokes. After we have enjoyed them long enough, all luxuries become commonplace and dull. Given endless repetition, whatever activities we pursue we would eventually feel like Sisyphus, the ancient Greek king condemned by the gods to spend eternity pushing a boulder up a hill only for it continually to roll back down.

It is easy to see why many immortality narratives promise some kind of radical transformation——either of us or our surroundings, or both. We might enjoy our lives now——but the prospect not just of more of the same but of *infinitely* more of the same is a chastening one, as the philosophically inclined Argentinean writer Jorge Luis Borges captured in his 1949 story "The Immortal." It tells of a soldier of ancient Rome who seeks a river "which cleanses men of death." After a long and terrible journey, he finds a land of "troglodytes" who live in shallow pits, naked, withered and subsisting on snake meat. They are indifferent and apathetic: one stood up so rarely that a bird had nested on his chest.

These troglodytes, it turns out, are the immortals. One of them——who happens to be the legendary poet Homer——explains to the Roman why they live as they do. They had realized that, given infinite time, all men would become great and all pathetic; they would each perform every goodness and every perversity. "Homer composed the *Odyssey*; if we postulate an infinite period of time, with infinite circumstances and changes, the impossible thing is not to compose the *Odyssey*, at least once."

Borges's hypothesis is that, given an infinite amount of time, any event with a finite probability would happen. You would inevitably one day be a TV chef, at another time prime minister of Belgium and at some point a stripper in a go-go bar. And possibly all these things many times over. And as all things would happen to all of us, there would be nothing to distinguish us one from another: "No one is anyone, one single immortal man is all men," Borges writes. After we had many times been both victim and perpetrator, monarch and subject, we would cease to regard anything as better or worse than anything else; meaning would collapse. Faced with infinity, life would become a joke——and we would already know the punch line.

The most ardent immortal might see a way around these problems: our memories are not perfect, they could argue; perhaps, by the time we have seen all the interesting places there are to see and tried all the delicious dishes or studied all the subjects under the sun we will have forgotten what the first most interesting place was like, or how caviar tastes, or the finer points of quantum physics, and so will be able to begin the whole journey once again. In other words, with the proper pacing of our pleasures——whether over months or millennia——we could ensure they always seemed fresh.

Perhaps this is so; there is nothing logically incoherent in the idea of a temporal wheel of happiness, involving continuous discovering, forgetting and rediscovering. But such an elaborate cycle of delightful experiences is unlikely to be the reality for billions of immortals on an overcrowded planet, should we tomorrow find the elixir of life. Nor is it the vision of the afterlife promised by most religions (recall the book of Revelation's description of heaven as a place whose inhabitants "are before the throne of God, and worship him day and night"). In the end, the problem of boredom might be one of personality: there might be those whose natural joie de vivre carries them through eternity, while the rest of us grow weary of the world and——most of all——ourselves.

BUT even more troubling for the immortal than the problem of having so much time behind them is how much time they would still have ahead of them. The constraint of finite time shapes our every decision. It is what drives us to get out of bed in the morning, to finish studying and get into the world, to earn money for a decent retirement. The dread that, on our deathbed, we might look back on a wasted life propels us to realize our dreams. The clock that steals a second of our lives with every tick reminds us that the time to act is now. In other words: death is the source of all our deadlines.

What happens if we find an elixir and this deadline disappears? For a start, those who leave everything to the last minute would be in trouble—as there would never be one. Procrastination could be taken to a whole new level. If it looked to be a rainy millennium, you could spend the thousand years in bed. If your time were infinite, it would no longer make sense to talk of it being wasted: life as we know it may be too short to watch daytime TV, but eternity wouldn't be.

The deep problem is this: the value of a thing is related to its scarcity—people conscious of their mortality value their time and aim to spend it wisely because they know their days are numbered. But if our days were not numbered, this incentive would disappear: given infinity, time would lose its worth. And once time is worthless, it becomes impossible to make rational decisions about how to spend it. The consequences of this for an individual would be bad enough; for a civilization of such ditherers it would be disastrous.

If this speculation about infinite time sounds a little abstract, we can look at the experience of those who suddenly realize their time is very finite. People who narrowly escape death frequently experience a realization of the shortness of life and at the same time a newfound joy in its preciousness. The psychiatrist Irvin D. Yalom, who works with the terminally ill, has noted that even those diagnosed with diseases such as cancer experience an "enhanced sense of living . . . a vivid appreciation of the elemental facts of life . . . and deeper communication with loved ones." So evidence suggests that life is already so long that we fail to appreciate it—more time, or indeed infinite time, could only exacerbate this.

Many philosophers have argued that only death makes our deeds count. It gives urgency to our choices and makes the outcomes matter. It is by choosing to sacrifice some of our precious, limited time—or even our lives—in the service of others that we demonstrate virtue. These skeptics point to the stories of the Greek gods as a case study: freed from the bonds of mortality, they are fickle and frivolous. They are spectators on a world in which only the mortals can demonstrate heroism or decency.

The existentialists say we are defined by the choices we make, such as whether to collaborate with the invaders or risk our lives fighting for *la résistance*. But these choices are only meaningful because life is short. If I have a mere seventy years before me, it is a crucial question whether I spend them in a decadent jamboree or building hospitals for the poor, but with infinite time I can—and if Borges is right, will—do all these things many times over. Our choices become meaningless, and there is nothing left to define us as moral beings.

What is particularly interesting about this problem—the problem of an infinite future—is that it does not affect all immortality narratives equally. If, for example, one of Linus Pauling's successors formulates a medical elixir that could stave off aging indefinitely, they would not thereby make us immune to death in all its forms. So-called medical immortals could always hope to live to the next year or decade or century, yet the Reaper's scythe would still be hovering. Given all the things that could go wrong, from a piano falling on their head to the heat death of the universe, the medical immortals would not therefore be faced with a truly infinite future. They might have a challenging time planning their lives, not knowing if those lives would last fifty years or fifty thousand, but it would not be impossible.

The situation of what we might call a "true immortal" who cannot die would be quite different. As we saw in chapter 6, such a person really would be confronted with billions and billions of years—and that just for starters—then billions and billions more, extending into an unending future. This would be the lot of all of us if we have (or more properly *are*) immortal and indestructible souls, as Plato and plenty since have argued. For a person with such a soul, nonexistence is not an option, and the aimlessness of unceasing eons beckons.

TOGETHER, these two problems suggest it would be disastrous for a civilization if its members really were to achieve personal immortality. In Borges's story, the immortals begin by building their dream city, but as tedium and aimlessness set in, they make their city ever more absurd, until it is a nonsensical labyrinth of dead ends and staircases leading nowhere. Finally they abandon it altogether to live like troglodytes in the desert. This is a fitting allegory: in a society where time has no value and everything worth doing has been done, there remains only ever-more-pointless and destructive play. If civilization exists to aid our perpetuation into the future, then if that perpetuation were guaranteed, civilization would be redundant. A meaningful life and a productive society require limitations that define them. We need finitude.

THE WISDOM NARRATIVE

"MANY people find that their belief in immortality is strongest when they think least about it," wrote the American philosopher J. B. Pratt in 1920. After one thinks about these beliefs a great deal, it is clear why. Our predicament now is this: we yearn to live forever, but if we did it would be awful. We need finitude to give life value, yet that finitude comes packaged with the fear of death. Civilization exists to give us immortality, but if it ever succeeded it would fall apart. Given these contradictions, the immortality narratives seem to have found the right solution: promise eternity but don't deliver.

But once you have seen their many flaws, it is difficult again to find solace in their assurances. We of course are not the first to find ourselves in this position: for as long as there has been civilization, there have been doubters, those who have seen through the dominant narrative of their day and remained unpersuaded by the alternatives. And among those doubters were those not willing to accept that living without the illusion of immortality meant living with the constant fear of death. They therefore looked deeper into the human condition, to attack the very roots of the fear of death and the will to immortality. We owe the origins of the Wisdom Narrative to such rebellious and profound thinkers—thinkers like Shiduri, the barmaid at the end of the world.

When Gilgamesh met the barmaid he was gripped by existential angst. "I am afraid of death," he lamented, "so I wander the wild." The death of his friend Enkidu had made his own mortality real to him—which is of course just the realization that forms the first part of the Mortality Paradox. This realization constitutes *knowledge*—of the reality of death—but not yet wisdom. Just as we have seen many times in our study, Gilgamesh reacted to this knowledge by pursuing the immortality narratives—indeed, to varying degrees all four, though by the time he reached the inn at the end of the world his focus was on the most primal: Staying Alive. As we have seen, he failed in his quest—but the story does not quite end there.

Having exhausted the four paths and accepted his mortality, Gilgamesh returned to take his proper place as king. In the poem's brief climax, he marvels at the beauty and strength of his city—its walls, temples and date groves. According to Sumerian legend, he then went on to bring many decades of peace and prosperity to his people. He was hailed as the one who looked into "the deep" and "saw what was secret." This "secret" was revealed by the barmaid: that the immortality narratives were nonsense—eternal life the gods kept for themselves, and we should therefore learn to value what life we have: "enjoy yourself always by night and by day." This was "of everything the sum of wisdom."

Wisdom, therefore, meant finding a way to accept and live with mortality. This was not the only narrative to be found in Sumerian-Babylonian culture—other texts, for example, have lively portrayals of the afterlife, some even with Gilgamesh as its ruler. But it was a persistent one, diligently copied out by generations of scribes for two and a half thousand years (until the arrival of Alexander the Great absorbed this region into the Greco-Roman world). And it was an influential one: a tradition of what has come to be known as "wisdom literature" spread throughout the Near East and Mediterranean. One example of this literature is still read by millions of people around the world, for it is in the heart of the Hebrew Bible and Christian Old Testament.

Of course, as we have seen, the Bible contains powerful *im*mortality narratives, including the Resurrection Narrative that emerges toward the end of the Old Testament and dominates the New Testament, and the hints at a Soul Narrative that have subsequently come to be so influential in the Christian tradition. But the Bible has many threads with many authors—and some of them sympathized instead with the barmaid's seditious alternative. These authors wrote those books of the Bible that explicitly concern themselves with the meaning of wisdom. They are usually grouped together in the middle of the Old Testament, even though possibly written at very different times, and include at least Job, Psalms, Proverbs, Ecclesiastes and the Song of Songs. In places, the parallels between these works and the message— even the wording—of the Gilgamesh epic are astonishing.

Ecclesiastes, for example, begins with a fine expression of the recognition of the fact of death: "For the fate of humans and the fate of animals is the same; as one dies, so dies the other" (3:19). The author goes on to make clear that neither glorious afterlife nor legacy awaits: "The dead know nothing; they have no more reward, and even the memory of them is lost" (9:5). And what conclusion does the author draw for what we mortals should then do? "Go thy way, eat thy bread with joy, and drink thy wine with a merry heart . . . Let thy garments be always white; and let thy head lack no ointment. Live joyfully with the wife whom thou lovest all the days of the life of thy vanity" (9:7–9). This is the barmaid's speech almost verbatim.

Psalm 90 puts the central message even more pithily: after acknowledging that our fate is to "turn back to dust," the psalmist urges, "So teach us to number our days"—that is, to realize they are limited and so appreciate their worth—"that we may get a heart of wisdom." Such writing came in different forms with different points of emphasis, but throughout, as the historian of religion Alan Segal succinctly put it, "wisdom and mortality are unconditionally wed."

Nowhere did the Wisdom Narrative come to eclipse all immortality narratives. But throughout this region, the cradle of civilization, its presence can be found—even in Egypt, with its fabulously sophisticated immortality system interweaving all four narratives. One text found inscribed in the tomb of a King Intef of Thebes dating back to around 2000 bce asks: What has become of those who built the great pyramids? The walls of their tombs are now crumbling, and "none returns from there to tell their conditions, to tell of their state, to reassure us . . . [So] follow your heart and happiness! Make your things on earth!"

IN these early civilizations, this alternative narrative never got beyond exhortations along the "make merry while you can" lines. This is the kernel of the narrative but by no means its full extent. As usual, it took the arrival of the Greeks to turn insight and intuition into rigorous philosophy. "Philosophy" of course means "love of wisdom," and Greek philosophy followed in the wisdom-literature tradition of its Mediterranean neighbors by concerning itself primarily with the question of how to live—and in particular, how to live given the fact of death. Some philosophers, like

Plato, developed immortality narratives. But others followed the barmaid—such as the Epicureans and the Stoics, two schools that developed in the third century bce. Despite their differences, both of these schools taught that the fear of death could be conquered without resorting to illusions of everlasting life.

When Greek philosophers took these ideas to Rome they found favor with an urban elite increasingly rejecting the family-based traditional religion, with its vague notions of biological legacy and a shadowy afterlife. A strong Wisdom Narrative subsequently thrived in Rome's crowded marketplace of ideas, with Stoicism becoming something like the empire's unofficial philosophy. Its heights were reached in the second century ce in the work of the emperor Marcus Aurelius, a thoughtful philosopher and committed Stoic.

But two centuries later, the Wisdom Narrative—temporarily—all but disappeared from view, as it was eclipsed by the powerful Resurrection Narrative promoted by the early Christians. Of course, it continued to be carried in those Hebrew wisdom books that the Christians kept in what they called their Old Testament. But Christianity's main selling point as it swept to prominence across the Roman Empire in the fourth century ce was its promise of an imminent and tangible paradise to come.

With the revival of classical learning and the loosening of Christianity's cultural grip during the Renaissance came the reemergence of the Wisdom Narrative tradition in Europe, with representatives such as the French essayist Michel de Montaigne. "All the wisdom and argument in the world eventually come down to one conclusion," he wrote in 1580, "which is to teach us not to be afraid of dying." At the same time, similar threads can also be found in other cultures, including Hinduism and especially Buddhism. Now in our much more secular and open age, these ideas are once again being explored as an alternative to the illusions of the immortality narratives.

There is therefore a long tradition of those who have challenged the grip of the will to immortality and sought ways of tackling the fear of death that do not have us wandering the desert on a fool's quest. In what remains, I will use the thinking of the Near Eastern wisdom literature and the philosophers of Greece and Rome to show that this alternative can help us to maintain both our sanity and our civilization even in the face of an existence that must end.

DEATH IS NOTHING TO US

THE immortality narratives take the problem of mortality at face value: death thwarts our will to live on; death itself is therefore the problem; so the solution is to deny death. Followers of the wisdom approach cannot do this: they have seen that immortality is the illusion; death is the reality. In order to succeed, they must therefore reach deeper—to undermine the causes that drive us to develop these comforting illusions in the first place.

The first step to undermining the will to immortality is to realize that genuinely unending life would most likely be a terrible curse—we looked at the reasons for this in previous pages. But although this might make us less keen to live forever, it is unlikely to persuade us that it is fine to be dead instead. The second step therefore tackles exactly this—and in this section we will explore the argument that the fear of actually being dead is nonsensical. The third and final step is to cultivate virtues that undermine those aspects of our nature that lead to both the will to persist forever and the corresponding existential angst.

Gilgamesh said to the barmaid that he was scared to look upon the face of Death. But later, having reached Utnapishtim, the wise man told him, "No one at all sees Death." It is a mysterious comment, given that the old immortal had just explained how everyone (barring him and the gods) must die. One would think that we would *all* see Death. But Utnapishtim was right.

We have seen that the second part of the Mortality Paradox, the inability to imagine our own nonexistence, leads us to see death as a kind of eternal darkness. Gilgamesh was terrified of exile in this "House of Dust . . . whose residents are deprived of light." But he was wrong to see death this way—and this seems to be what Utnap- ishtim was telling him. We do not "see" or experience death; death is the end of all experience. Once we have rejected the immortality narratives, then we all know that this is the case—yet the impossibil- ity of imagining it makes it very hard to accept. Predictably, it was a Greek philosopher who came along to spell it out for us: Epicurus.

"Death is nothing to us," he wrote around 300 bce: "For all good and evil lies in sensation and death is the end of all sensation." We cannot conceive of such a state, but we must try to understand and internalize it—only then can we live free of fear, he believed. Such fear, though natural, is irrational: "While we are, death is not; when death is come, we are not. Death is thus of no concern either to the living or to the dead. For it is not with the living, and the dead do not exist."

Though much quoted, this idea is also often misunderstood. Many modern philosophers take it to mean we should be utterly indifferent to dying. But this is not Epicurus's main concern. We might be anxious about the process of dying, fearing it might be painful (though many who have near-death experiences describe it as quite pleasant), and we might wish to prolong the pleasures of life, and so in that sense see death as unwelcome. Epicurus's main point, however, is that we should not fear the state of *being dead*. He was addressing the anxiety that Shakespeare described when he wrote, "The weariest and most loathed worldly life / That age, ache, penury and imprisonment / Can lay on nature is a paradise / To what we fear of death."

In seeing this, Epicurus was perhaps the first person in history to have overcome the lure of the second part of the Mortality Para- dox, the trap of a self-consciousness that cannot see outside of itself. Until then, people could not help but see death as an eternity of semiconscious being, as conjured by ideas of Sheol, Hades or the House of Darkness. Epicurus showed us how we might finally close the gates to the underworld.

His argument is exactly what the natural sciences also teach: that we are *essentially* living things. From this follows the explosive conclusion that neither you nor I can ever literally *be* dead. Living things cannot be dead things. To talk of someone "being dead" is just a shorthand for saying they have ceased to exist. Ludwig Wittgenstein, the philosophical giant of the last century, summed up what this means for us as conscious, experiencing creatures: "Death is not an event in life," he wrote. "We do not live to experience death." He concluded from this that in this sense "life has no end." That is, we can never be aware of it having an end—we can never know anything but life.

We might compare ourselves to an ocean wave: when it breaks on the shore, its short life is over, but it does not then enter some new state of being "a dead wave" or "an ex-wave." Rather, the parts that made it up are dissipated and absorbed back into the sea. Similarly with us: when the self-regulating, organized complexity of a human organism fails, then that person reaches a full stop; they have not entered into a new state of death. They have ceased, and their constituent elements slowly lose their human shape and are subsumed once more into the whole.

The teachings that try to reassure us that death is just a transition—like shedding an old set of clothes for a new one, as the Bhagavad Gita says—are playing on our intuitive fear of death as a step into the abyss. But they could not be more wrong: a transition is exactly what death is not, whether into the abyss or anywhere else. It is an ending—and that, when properly understood, is exactly why we should *not* be afraid. This is something those Roman stoics understood who had inscribed on their tombstones "*Non fui, fui, non sum, non curo*" ("I was not; I was; I am not; I do not care").

"I'm not afraid of death," said Woody Allen. "I just don't want to be there when it happens." He can rest assured: he won't be. As Utnapishtim said, "No one at all sees Death"; when he reaches out for us, we are already gone. We therefore cannot miss, regret or suffer from that which is outside the bounds of our life. We do not linger like uninvited guests at our own funeral, nor are we plunged into the lonely void. We stop. The conscious experiences we have had *are* the totality of our lives; death, like birth, is just a term that defines the bounds of those experiences, like the frame of a painting that serves to delineate and accentuate the image within.

THE second step along the path of wisdom is therefore this realization that we can never *be* dead, that fearing being dead is therefore a nonsense. Combining this with the first step—realizing the problems of immortality—we can now conclude that neither is living forever so good nor death so bad as our intuitions would have us believe. Still, powerful instincts are at work that distort our perceptions of mortality and the way we use what time we have. The third step of the Wisdom Narrative is to cultivate virtues that hold these instincts in check.

THE THREE VIRTUES

WE noted in chapter 1 that we of all creatures have certain highly developed cognitive capacities, of which three in particular influence our view of life and death: a refined consciousness of self, an ability to conceive of an indefinite future, and the capacity to imagine possible threatening scenarios. These three faculties allow us to picture all the endless ways in which our cherished selves could be done grievous harm—which, as we noted, has considerable evolutionary advantages, as we can then plan to avoid such harms.

But these three capacities also come at a high price. They lead directly to the Mortality Paradox—awareness of our mortality and an inability to conceive of ourselves as not existing—and thus to the fear of death. Instead of focusing on death itself, this next step of the Wisdom Narrative attempts to confront the way these three faculties lead us alone of creatures to so obsess about mortality. The aim is not to do away with these faculties, which are of course enormously useful, but rather to maintain them in a proper perspective.

So: awareness of self might be important, but excessive concern with the self only exacerbates the fear of death, or loss of self, and leads one to a life of self-absorption. In order to combat this, we should cultivate selflessness, or identifying with others. Similarly, picturing the future helps us to plan a successful life, but excessive concern with the future causes us to focus on the tribulations that lie ahead of us——and we forget to live now. Therefore we should learn to live more in the present moment. And third, imagining all the things that could threaten our existence might help us to avoid them, but in excess it leads us only to worry about what we might lose rather than appreciate what we have. Therefore we should cultivate gratitude.

In varying ways and to varying extents, I suggest these are the three main themes of wisdom literature from Gilgamesh through the Bible and the Greeks to the present day. It is worth looking at each of these in a little more detail to see how they together add up to a coherent Wisdom Narrative; then we will look at the effect they might have on civilization.

Identifying with Others

Excessive focus on oneself is a powerful cause of the fear of death. Concern for the self has of course evolved to help us perpetuate that self——if our ancestors were not concerned for themselves, they would likely not have lived long enough to reproduce, and we as a consequence would not be here. But in excess, this self-obsession can become morbid and debilitating. Unfortunately, just such excess is encouraged by modern societies.

The social psychologist Roy Baumeister, a leading researcher on ideas of the self, observed that "the increasing use of selfhood as the major value base for legitimizing and justifying human striving is a trend that aggravates the threat of death." In chapter 6, we saw that this obsession with the self grew out of the doctrine of the immortal soul. We in the developed world who have inherited this inflated sense of self but do not believe in the immortality narrative from which it comes are consequently in the worst possible position—we are effectively facing the end of the only thing we hold dear: ourselves. For us moderns, it is all the more difficult but all the more urgent that we actively seek causes and others with which or whom we can identify to help us get over ourselves.

Fortunately, in humans, as in other social animals, our concern for self is balanced by concern for offspring, family or tribe, and in humans in particular, by concern for other interests too, such as justice, science or the local football team. By focusing more on these other interests, the end of the individual self can come to seem a lot less important.

This is an important part of the barmaid's lesson, expressed through her instruction to Gilgamesh: "Gaze on the child who holds your hand, / let your wife enjoy your repeated embrace!" And the poem ends with his returning to Uruk and finding pride and joy in his city. In the Greek tradition, this virtue was most prominent in Stoicism, which considered full engagement with the community and love of all mankind to be a foremost duty. This was partly a product of the cosmopolitan and empathetic outlook that this philosophy encouraged. Using phrases that would be familiar to any Taoist, Marcus Aurelius summed this outlook up so: "Think often of the bond that unites all things in the universe, and their dependence upon one another. All are, as it were, interwoven, and in consequence linked in mutual affection."

The idea of identifying with others and engaging with wider interests sounds somewhat like the Legacy Narrative, and in a sense it is indeed taking what is insightful from that approach while leaving behind its immortalist rhetoric. Neither the barmaid nor the Stoics were suggesting that this engagement would make you live forever; rather, their point was that it would make your own mortality seem less important to you. Bertrand Russell put it well in an essay on growing old (and he grew to be ninety-seven): "The fear of death is somewhat abject and ignoble. The best way to overcome it——so at least it seems to me——is to make your interests gradually wider and more impersonal, until bit by bit the walls of the ego recede, and your life becomes increasingly merged in the universal life."

The success of this approach is borne out by experience. The psychiatrist Irvin D. Yalom concluded after a career working with the terminally ill that connecting to others was the single most important method for ameliorating death anxiety. And psychologist Roy Baumeister recommends a similar antidote to the problem he is quoted above as identifying: "The most effective solution to this threat [of death] is to place one's life in some context that will outlast the self. If one's efforts are devoted to goals and values that project many generations into the future, then death does not undermine them."

Focus on the Present

The virtue of connecting with others will help to put our own selves in proper perspective. This is intimately connected with the next problem: our tendency to fill our hours with thoughts of what might become of us in the future and so fail to appreciate the present. When left to their own devices, our minds busy themselves with plans, plots, worries and idle speculation——much of it about things that might go badly for us. The capacity to think about the future is of course enormously useful, but it can also foster angst and seriously undermine our prospects of happiness. By dwelling on all manner of possible threats, we bring death into life, only then to die without having really lived.

This was the position of Gilgamesh when he met the barmaid:

squandering his life with worry that ahead of him lay only death. Her response—"Make merry each day"—is an attempt to pull him back into the present. For as many sages have known, happiness is only to be found in the present moment, as only the present moment is real. The past is gone, the future mere speculation. If you are happy now, then you are happy always, as there is only now. But equally, if you spend each moment worrying about your future happiness, then happiness will always elude you, and your life will be one of anxiety. And, as we have seen, worrying about death—something we can never experience—is the most foolish worry of all.

The French historian Pierre Hadot described the goal of Epicureanism and Stoicism as "to allow people to free themselves from the past and the future, so that they could live within the present." This would be instantly recognizable to followers of many other religious and philosophical traditions. In Buddhism, for example, it is known as "mindfulness" and is one of the key steps on the path to enlightenment. Buddhists cultivate this virtue through the ancient practice of meditation, which anyone can take up—and which is now also recommended by Western science.

Clinical psychologists have adopted Buddhist mindfulness techniques in order to treat stress, anxiety and depression. Like the practice of gratitude, learning to live more in the moment is proven to bring many benefits. The Hungarian-American psychologist Mihaly Csikszentmihalyi, who first documented the phenomenon of being "in the flow," was perhaps the first to demonstrate this, proving an association between focusing full attention on a task in the present moment and the experience of "pleasure, happiness, satisfaction and enjoyment." A 2010 Harvard study reinforced this, gathering a great deal of evidence to show that people all around the world make themselves unhappy by continually imagining possible future scenarios, many of them anxiety inducing, and that those who are happiest spend the most time wholly in the moment.

This thought is sometimes expressed as living each day as if it would be your last. Indeed an awareness that this day might be your last (and who knows, it might be—one day surely will be) does help to focus the mind on the present. But it could of course also lead to abandoning anything that might contribute to longer-term projects. And that you might regret: after all, this day also might *not* be your last. We must find a way of appreciating the present while acknowledging that the stream of moments might extend some way yet. This is a balance. We could put it like this: live so you will have no regrets if you die tomorrow but also no regrets if you don't. The first part might prompt you to quit the job you hate, but the second should stop you from punching your boss on the way out.

Gratitude

Third, the wisdom literature addresses our natural tendency to focus on the dark side of life. True enough, we have a powerful drive to live on, and true enough, it will be thwarted. That is our curse. But let us look at the flip side of those facts. This urge is part of our evolutionary inheritance, without which our ancestors would not have survived or undergone the trials of childbirth—in other words, without which we would not be here. That an unbroken chain of many millions of ancestors over billions of years all managed to do their bit to bring us into existence, that is our blessing. And it is an extraordinary one, involving more strokes of luck and cosmic coincidences than are possibly countable.

We can barely begin to measure the good fortune that led to the development first of life, then of animals, of mammals, of humans, of your family, and, finally, of you. Complex life—and in particular the life of any individual—is remarkable. Astonishing. Wondrous. And it would not have happened without the cycle of birth and death. If our fishy ancestors some few hundred million years ago had attained immortality instead of making way for the next generation, we would never have come to be. A long, long history of death has made possible the incredible fact that you are alive now.

Added to that, the very faculties that make you aware of death also enable you to love, experience the sublime, appreciate art, connect with other people and with nature, to build and create and understand. Modern science has if anything taught us that these facts—of life and mind—are even more extraordinary than our ancestors might have thought. And what these facts suggest is that before we rue our plight of a short life overshadowed by death, we should be grateful—very, very grateful—that we have a shot at life at all, and with a brain capable of appreciating and creating so much wonder.

This is part of what the barmaid was trying to tell Gilgamesh: appreciate what you have. The Bible too, like almost every other religious tradition, contains enjoinders to be thankful. With the Epicureans and the Stoics, gratitude became part of a systematic philosophy. The Greek Epicurean Philodemus, for example, wrote, "Receive each additional moment of time in a manner appropriate to its value; as if one were having an incredible stroke of luck"—something that should be even easier now we know that each moment of life really *is* an incredible stroke of luck. Instead of being resentful that it will end, we should be grateful for every minute of it. Then when your time comes, in the words of Marcus Aurelius, "go to your rest with a good grace, as an olive falls in its season, with a blessing for the earth that bore it and a thanksgiving to the tree that gave it life."

We have evolved to focus on what we stand to lose—ultimately on the threat of death—causing us to live in fear instead of reveling in the extraordinary good fortune of being. Overcoming such an instinct is not easy: it takes continual work, lest we drift back to the evolved norm. Religions from Christianity to Buddhism have developed practices that help people internalize a grateful attitude, such as daily prayers of thanks. Modern positive psychologists advocate various secular equivalents, such as keeping a daily journal of things for which one might be grateful.

Tacky as this might sound to some, the effects can be extraordinary. Robert Emmons, a leading researcher into the effects of gratitude, after surveying the evidence concluded that "gratitude is positively related to such critical outcomes as life satisfaction, vitality, happiness, self-esteem, optimism, hope, empathy, and the willingness to provide emotional and tangible support for other people, whereas being ungrateful is related to anxiety, depression, envy, materialism, and loneliness." It is no coincidence that gratitude is one of the common themes throughout the world's wisdom literature and a powerful antidote to the fear of death. As the Greek Stoic Epictetus put it, "He is a wise man who does not grieve for the things which he has not, but rejoices for those which he has."

"WISDOM GIVETH LIFE" (Ecclesiastes 7:12)

THE difference between those who swallow 250 dietary supplements per day and the rest of us is not that they will live forever and we will not. No: we will all die, even the transhumanists. The difference is that they tell themselves a story about achieving "longevity escape velocity," which helps them to alleviate their existential angst. They are therefore following a long tradition of elixir seekers, resurrectionists, reincarnationists and others who have attempted to deny the fact of death.

Most of this book has been concerned with exploring how these immortality narratives have shaped civilization—for good and ill—and whether they have any plausibility. The conclusion is that whatever plausibility they have, it is not enough: they are all fatally (if you excuse the pun) flawed. But more than that, we have seen that by taking the fear of death at face value, all four immortality narratives exacerbate the very attitudes that underpin that fear. By encouraging people to obsess about their own health, or the state of their own soul, or their particular legacy, they encourage the very self-centered, future-oriented and negative view that caused the fear in the first place.

The fact is, we have not evolved to be carefree and joyful; we have evolved to strive to perpetuate ourselves—at the expense of everything else, including our happiness. The immortality narratives only fuel this striving and its underlying causes. Although these narratives might sometimes succeed in assuaging our existential angst, they are not otherwise a recipe for contentment. The Wisdom Narrative is different: instead of dismissing existential anxiety by denying death, it attacks the underlying attitudes that make us think we ought to be afraid of death in the first place. By doing so, it aims to cultivate an appreciation of this life and this world, as it is, right now.

This is not easy: as we have seen, the attitudes and virtues we need run contrary to powerful impulses. They must therefore be actively developed. This is something the ancient philosophers knew: the Stoic teacher Epictetus, for example, believed that any doctrine that was merely theoretical was pseudo-philosophy—the real thing had to be practiced daily. Stoics therefore followed daily exercises to train themselves in wisdom—an approach to life that will be familiar to many religious practitioners. Even the Dalai Lama will tell you that compassion for all living things does not always come easily.

I am not claiming that all people would be happier if they gave up their immortality narratives. No doubt some people are muddling along just fine with, for example, their reassuring belief in an immortal soul. But I am claiming that giving up these narratives need not lead to nihilism and despair—that, contrary to Tennyson, we need not hurl ourselves into the sea. The Wisdom Narrative is a powerful alternative to these beliefs, one that balances a positive love of life with managing the fear of that life's end. And by focusing our attention on the here and now and on the world outside of the self, it might also help to make the one life we have a better, richer, more meaningful one.

But will civilization grind to a halt if the masses stop their ceaseless pursuit of eternity? We have seen many times in this study how the pursuit of immortality has motivated almost every aspect of our cultural development. Nonetheless, this need not mean that if we accept mortality we will all be back living in caves. For a start, there is nothing in the Wisdom Narrative that undermines the value of a long and secure life: we still have a reason to build strong houses and take our medicine, even to pursue a cure for cancer. And we will still have reason to partake in those civilized activities that bring us joy, whether making music, playing football or tending roses. Some of these pursuits might have developed as means to perpetuate ourselves into the future, but that does not mean we can't enjoy them knowing they won't. If we have evolved to take pleasure in having children, then we should continue to do so—and relieved of the illusion that they are our immortality vehicle, we (and they) might even enjoy it all the more.

We would also have reason to practice those activities that give meaning to life, such as caring for others or furthering knowledge. Even spirituality: although most religions have a strong immortality narrative, they mostly also have other elements that fit in the wisdom tradition. We have seen that this is the case with those religions that consider the Old Testament or Hebrew Bible to be scripture, and it is also the case with Taoism, Buddhism, Hinduism and most forms of New Age and alternative spirituality. But the virtues of gratitude, mindfulness and empathy with others are also all compatible with naturalism—that is, a worldview that rejects the supernatural—and can bring what we might consider a spiritual dimension to this philosophy.

There are ways in which a civilization that rejects the immortality narratives might even be better than those we know. We have seen that a focus on this world rather than the next has unleashed hugely positive social reform—those who know this life is their only shot are less likely to tolerate injustice and oppression. Perhaps some people would work less hard to create a name or fortune or other legacy that might outlive them—but this is as often done through destructive means as constructive, so it too might be no bad thing. And it is easy to see how the cultivation of empathy could lead to progress: the world would probably be a better place if we in developed countries worried a bit less about whether we will live to one hundred and a bit more about whether children born in the poorest countries will live to see their first birthday.

A civilization of those who face up to their mortality is therefore one worth striving for. Indeed, combining this with the rest of the Wisdom Narrative, we could even boldly claim that awareness of mortality offers the best of all possible situations: knowing that life will have an end puts a limit on our time and so makes it valuable. The fact of mortality imparts to our existence an urgency and allows us to give it shape and meaning—we have reason to get up in the morning and engage with the world while we can; we have reason to make this the best of all worlds, because we know there is no other. Yet that which sets the limit—death—is not something we can ever suffer from or in any way experience. As essentially living things, we cannot even literally be dead. All we can ever know is life, and by accepting that it is finite, we can also know to treasure it.

Our lives are bounded by beginning and end yet composed of moments that can reach out far beyond ourselves, touching other people and places in countless ways. In this sense, they are like a book, which is self-contained within its covers yet able to encompass distant landscapes, exotic figures and long-gone times. The book's characters know no horizons; they, like we, can only know the moments that make up their lives, even when the book is closed. They are therefore untroubled by reaching the last page. And so it should be with us.

Acknowledgments

THE idea for this book goes back to the graduate work I did at Cambridge in the 1990s. I would first like to thank my then PhD supervisor, Eric Olson, who more than anyone has attempted to teach me the business of philosophy and who has continued to advise and encourage me since, including on this work.

I completed the book in Berlin while on a long secondment from the British Diplomatic Service; my thanks to those in the Foreign and Commonwealth Office who allowed this to happen, and to all my friends there who have given support and encouragement.

I am also grateful to my agents, Matthias Landwehr, Frank Jakobs, Zoë Pagnamenta and Robert Kirby, for their faith in this project and their highly professional work in ensuring it found an audience. And I am particularly grateful to my editor at Crown, Rick Horgan, whose suggestions have made this a bigger and better book than it would otherwise have been.

I would also like to thank those people who have read or advised on the manuscript and whose comments have helped give some polish to what was at first very rough: Sten Inge Jørgensen, Stefan Klein and the other members of the Berlin Lunar Society; Polina Aronson, Annette Barnes, Elly Truitt and Toby Rouse.

There are two people without whom this book would be barely imaginable, whose influence reaches from the first word to the last. First, I am very grateful to Samuel Tracey, with whom I have been discussing these questions for nearly two decades and yet who remains an endless source of fresh ideas and good humor.

And most of all, I would like to thank my wife, Friederike von Tiesenhausen. I and this work have benefited beyond measure from her insightful suggestions and exceptional editing, and even more from her boundless love, patience and support. It is to her that this book is dedicated.

Notes and Further Reading

IN this section are references for all works that I have cited, plus others that may be useful for a reader wishing to find out more. Many, many other works have influenced me in the course of my research, both directly for this book and earlier; my thanks to their authors and apologies that they remain here unmentioned.

CHAPTER 1: A BEAUTIFUL WOMAN HAS COME

The best popular introduction to Nefertiti is Joyce Tyldesley's *Nefertiti: Egypt's Sun Queen* (Penguin, 2005). There are numerous good accounts of Akhenaten's life and times. Nicholas Reeves's *Akhenaten: Egypt's False Prophet* (Thames and Hudson, 2001) is well illustrated and readable, if unflattering. There are also many entertaining fictional accounts of both Nefertiti's and Akhenaten's lives, including one by Naguib Mahfouz, winner of the Nobel Prize in Literature (*Akhenaten: Dweller in Truth*, Bantam Doubleday, 2000).

Death and the Afterlife in Ancient Egypt by John H. Taylor (British Museum Press, 2001) is a comprehensive guide to all things mummy related. The Akhenaten expert Barry Kemp's *How to Read the "Egyptian Book of the Dead"* (Granta, 2007) is an excellent short guide to Egyptian beliefs about the afterlife, while the *Egyptian Book of the Dead* itself is available in many translations. The fascinating idea that Akhenaten was linked to the biblical Moses is made by Sigmund Freud in *Moses and Monotheism* (Vintage, 1939) and is discussed by the great Egyptologist Jan Assmann in *Moses the Egyptian: The Memory of Egypt in Western Monotheism* (Harvard University Press, 1997).

The schema of the four immortality narratives is my own. Alternative categorizations can be found in Paul Edwards's introduction to his extremely useful edited collection *Immortality* (Prometheus Books, 1997); in Corliss Lamont's equally excellent monograph *The Illusion of Immortality* (Continuum, 1935), which I will cite frequently in this study; and in the work of Robert Jay Lifton, such as for example *Living and Dying*, written with Eric Olson (Praeger, 1974).

The Zygmunt Bauman quotes are from his fascinating book *Mortality, Immortality, and Other Life Strategies* (Polity, 1992), which I will be citing often. The two quotes by Robert Jay Lifton are from *The Future of Immortality and Other Essays for a Nuclear Age* (Basic Books, 1987).

The Richard Dawkins quote is from *The Selfish Gene* (Oxford University Press, 1976). The Raymond D. Gastil quote is from his article "Immortality Revisited" in *Futures Research Quarterly* 9, no. 3 (1993). An example of the work of Antonio Damasio connecting emotions to the aim of survival is his book *Descartes' Error* (Grosset Putnam, 1994). The James Chisholm quote is from *Death, Hope and Sex: Steps to an Evolutionary Ecology of Mind and Morality* (Cambridge University Press, 1999). Arthur Schopenhauer's theory of the will to live can be found in his monumental work *The World as Will and Representation* (available in various editions, first published 1818). The Dutch philosopher Baruch Spinoza also expressed the thought that the essence of life was to indefinitely "persist in its own being" in 1676 (in his magnum opus *Ethics*).

When quoting the Bible, I have variously used both *The New Revised Standard Version (Anglicized Edition)* (1995) and the *Authorised King James Version with Apocrypha* (as published by Oxford University Press, 1997).

Martin Heidegger's thoughts on "being-toward-death" can be found in *Being and Time* (English edition: Blackwell, 1962). The Jorge Luis Borges quote is from his short story "The Immortal," first published in his collection *The Aleph* in 1949 (available in translation in a Penguin Modern Classics edition). Michel de Montaigne's thoughts on death are taken from his essay "To Philosophize Is to Learn How to Die" (first published 1580, available from Penguin Books, translated by M. A. Screech).

Freud's comments on the impossibility of imagining nonexistence are from his essay "Thoughts for the Times on War and Death" (1915, available for example in the collection *Civilization, Society and Religion*, Penguin, 1991). The Edward Young quote is from his poem "Night Thoughts" (1742–1745). Jessie Bering reports his research into the cognitive mechanisms underpinning belief in immortality in his book *The God Instinct: The Psychology of Souls, Destiny and the Meaning of Life* (Nicholas Brealey, 2010).

The quote by the Spanish-American philosopher George Santayana is from *Reason in Religion* (first published 1905, reissued by Bibliobazaar in 2009 and available online). Also see the chapter "Death" in the philosopher Thomas Nagel's *The View from Nowhere* (Oxford University Press, 1986) for a discussion of the distinction between first-person and third-person perspectives on one's own death.

Freud's disciple Otto Rank did the most to develop the idea that this could be important in understanding human culture, in particular in *Psychology and the Soul* (first published in German in 1930, available in English from Johns Hopkins University Press, 1998). It was Rank's work that subsequently inspired the anthropologist

Ernest Becker to write his Pulitzer Prize—winning book *The Denial of Death* (Free Press, 1973) and his book *Escape from Evil* (Free Press, 1975), which portray civilization as a series of "immortality projects." Becker in turn inspired Sheldon Solomon, Jeff Greenberg and Tom Pyszczynski in their research on the impact of mortality awareness on other beliefs—see for example their paper "Tales from the Crypt: On the Role of Death in Life" (first published in *Zygon* 33, no. 1 [March 1998], and available online), from which the quotes are taken.

The quote by Bryan Appleyard is from his entertaining account of the modern quest for medical immortality, *How to Live Forever or Die Trying* (Simon and Schuster, 2007).

CHAPTER 2: MAGIC BARRIERS

There are a couple of introductory biographies of the First Emperor available, of which the best is Jonathan Clements's *The First Emperor of China* (Sutton Publishing, 2006). But such biographies largely only retell, with a bit of extra context, the stories told by the only substantial historical source on the emperor's life: the "historical records" of the Chinese court historian Sima Qian, written in the second century BCE. Those parts of the records that concern the First Emperor have been collected and published in a fine Oxford Classics edition translated by Raymond Dawson and titled *The First Emperor: Selections from the Historical Records* (Oxford University Press, 2007). The beautiful 2002 film *Hero*, directed by Zhang Yimou, is a stylized retelling of the assassination attempts on the First Emperor.

The Borges quote on the Great Wall and the book burning is from his short essay "The Wall and the Books," first published in 1961 in the collection *Antología Personal* (this translation by Gaither Stewart and available online).

The Arthur C. Clarke quote is from *Profiles of the Future* (Phoenix, 1961).

The ancient Egyptian elixir recipe referred to is from the Edwin Smith Papyrus, held by the New York Academy of Medicine. The modern research into the use of the Chinese medicinal herb astragalus was reported in the *New Scientist* on November 13, 2008 (" 'Elixir of Youth' Drug Could Fight HIV and Ageing" by Linda Geddes).

The Gerald Gruman quote is from his excellent 1965 study, *A History of Ideas About the Prolongation of Life* (reissued by the International Longevity Center), from which I have also taken the quote by Roger Bacon on alchemy (originally from part 6 of his *Opus Majus*, translated by Robert Belle Burke, Russell & Russell, 1928). Gruman's book takes the reader up to 1800; David Boyd Haycock's *Mortal Coil: A Short History of Living Longer* (Yale University Press, 2008) picks up the life-extension story in the eighteenth century and takes it up to the modern day. It is from here that I have taken the details and quote relating to the Steinach operation.

The set of yogurt commercials mentioned is the prize-winning "In Soviet Georgia" campaign from Dannon yogurt, which ran from 1973 to 1978.

There are numerous introductions to Taoism (also spelled "Daoism") available. A particularly charming one is *Taoism: The Quest for Immortality* by John Blofeld (Unwin, 1979), though it is a little old-fashioned. There are also many Taoist texts on immortality available in English translation, such as *The Jade Emperor's Mind Seal Classic: The Taoist Guide to Health, Longevity, and Immortality*, compiled by Stuart Alve Olson (Inner Traditions, 2003). The *Tao Te Ching* by Lao Tzu is also widely available in translation.

The Japanese fairy tale about Xu Fu and Sentaro is usually known as "The Story of the Man Who Did Not Wish to Die" and can be found in numerous collections, including for example *Japanese Fairy Tales* by Yei Theodora Ozaki (1908). Another entertaining, if old-

fashioned, source of Chinese and Japanese folklore is Donald Mac-
Kenzie's *China and Japan: Myths and Legends* (Senate, 1923), which
includes many of the tales of elixirs and immortal islands.

   The Susan Ertz quote is from her novel *Anger in the Sky* (Harper
and Broso, 1943). Karel Čapek's 1922 play *The Makropulos Affair*
can be found in English in the collection *Toward the Radical Center:
A Karel Capek Reader* (Catbird Press, 1990). Thought-provoking
discussions of the desirability of immortality can be found in two
short introductory books on the philosophy of death: *Death* by
Geoffrey Scarre (Acumen, 2007) and *Death* by Todd May (Acumen, 2009), and the slightly more technical *The Philosophy of Death*
by Steven Luper (Cambridge University Press, 2009).

CHAPTER 3: THE VITAMIN CURE

There are various biographies of Linus Pauling available: *Linus
Pauling: A Life in Science and Politics* by Ted Goertzel and Ben
Goertzel (Basic Books, 1995) is interesting for the fact that one of
the authors—the cognitive scientist Ben Goertzel—has gone on
to be a leading prophet of our immortalist future. Thomas Hager's
Force of Nature: The Life of Linus Pauling (Simon and Schuster, 1995)
is more comprehensive while remaining accessible. But the interested reader might just as well turn to the writings of Pauling himself: his *How to Live Longer and Feel Better* (Avon Books, 1986), for
example, is still widely available and a good introduction to his
views on the importance of vitamins, whereas *Linus Pauling in His
Own Words: Selections from His Writings, Speeches and Interviews* (edited
by Barbara Marinacci, Touchstone, 1995) includes extracts on science, politics and medicine.

   The ancient Egyptian medical papyrus referred to is the Ebers
Papyrus at the University of Leipzig, Germany. The Linus Pauling
quote on life as a relationship between molecules is from the above-
mentioned biography by Thomas Hager. The quote by Nicolas de

Condorcet is from his classic treatise on the idea of progress: *Outlines of an Historical View of the Progress of the Human Mind* (available in various editions and online, 1795). Ivan Illich's pathbreaking account of the spread of "medicalization" can be found in his book *Medical Nemesis: The Expropriation of Health* (Pelican Books, 1975). The Zygmunt Bauman quotes are from his aforementioned *Mortality, Immortality, and Other Life Strategies.*

The seekers of medical immortality are well represented by the gerontologist Aubrey de Grey, whose book *Ending Aging: The Rejuvenation Breakthroughs That Could Reverse Human Aging in Our Lifetime* (St. Martin's Griffin, 2008, written with his assistant Michael Rae) details his Engineering Approach to defeating aging. Another enthusiastic and readable immortalist is Ray Kurzweil, as reflected in his many books and articles on the subject, most notably *Fantastic Voyage: Living Long Enough to Live Forever* (with Terry Grossman, Rodale, 2004), *Transcend: Nine Steps to Living Well Forever* (also with Terry Grossman, Rodale, 2009) and *The Singularity Is Near: When Humans Transcend Biology* (Viking, 2005).

The Immortality Institute, an organization dedicated to promoting radical life extension, has also published a collection of articles on the science and philosophy of the immortalists (including by Kurzweil and de Grey) called *The Scientific Conquest of Death: Essays on Infinite Lifespans* (Libros en Red, 2004). At the time this book went to print, this collection was also available to download for free from imminst.org/book.

A philosophical defense of radical life extension is offered by the work of John Harris, for example in *Enhancing Evolution: The Ethical Case for Making People Better* (Princeton University Press, 2007), whereas those altogether opposed to such attempts are well represented by Francis Fukuyama in his book *Our Posthuman Future: Consequences of the Biotechnology Revolution* (Profile Books, 2002).

Bryan Appleyard's aforementioned *How to Live Forever or Die Trying* and Jonathan Weiner's *Long for This World: The Strange Science of*

Immortality (HarperCollins, 2010) both give good (somewhat skeptical) layman's accounts of the modern life-extension movement's aims and leading personalities.

The demographer who calculated that curing cancer would add only three years to our lives was S. Jay Olshansky, and the pessimistic view of the possibility of radical life extension can be found in his book (with Bruce A. Carnes) *The Quest for Immortality: Science at the Frontiers of Aging* (W. W. Norton, 2001). An excellent overview of the science of life, death, aging and immortality can be found in *The Living End* by the gerontologist Guy Brown (Palgrave Macmillan, 2007).

The figures cited for the average life expectancy of medical immortals calculated by Professor Steven N. Austad are taken from personal correspondence with the author. His book *Why We Age* (John Wiley & Sons, 1997) is a very good introduction to the aging process—including why it is unlikely we will ever be able to fully defeat it.

The former British astronomer royal and president of the Royal Society, Martin Rees, has written a terrifying account of the many ways in which our species might be doomed: *Our Final Century: Will the Human Race Survive the Twenty-first Century?* (Heinemann, 2003).

CHAPTER 4: ST. PAUL AND THE CANNIBALS

There are many thousands of studies on the life and works of St. Paul available. Two nice little introductions are Edward Stourton's *In the Footsteps of St. Paul* (Hodder & Stoughton, 2004) and E. P. Sanders's *Paul: A Very Short Introduction* (Oxford University Press, 2001). Two extremely useful scholarly introductions are *The Writings of St. Paul: A Norton Critical Edition*, edited by Wayne A. Meeks and John T. Fitzgerald (W. W. Norton, 2007) and *The Cambridge Companion to St. Paul*, edited by James D. G. Dunn (Cambridge

University Press, 2003). Paul's Judaism and its implications for his theology are explored in *Paul and Rabbinic Judaism* by W. D. Davies (SPCK Publishing, 1948) and more recently by Alan F. Segal in *Paul the Convert: The Apostolate and Apostasy of Saul the Pharisee* (Yale University Press, 1990), and his influence on Christianity is debated accessibly in A. N. Wilson's *Paul: The Mind of the Apostle* (W. W. Norton, 1998) and *What Saint Paul Really Said* by Tom Wright (Lion Hudson, 2003).

The Martin Luther quote is taken from Corliss Lamont's aforementioned *The Illusion of Immortality*. The Karen Armstrong quote is from *A Short History of Myth* (Cannongate, 2005). A good introduction to the nature of ritual, including the aspects I mention, is *Ritual: Perspectives and Dimensions* by Catherine Bell (Oxford University Press, 1997). A magnificent account of the development of afterlife beliefs in the ancient world can be found in Alan F. Segal's *Life After Death: A History of the Afterlife in Western Religion* (Doubleday Religion, 2004). An overview of the state of scholarly thinking on the "dying and rising gods" can be found in *The Riddle of Resurrection: "Dying and Rising Gods" in the Ancient Near East* by Tryggve N. D. Mettinger (Almqvist & Wiksell, 2001).

The Sigmund Freud quote is from *The Future of an Illusion* (Penguin, 1927). Sir James Frazer's *The Golden Bough: A Study in Magic and Religion* was first published in 1890 and is available in various editions.

Oscar Cullmann's comparison of the deaths of Socrates and Jesus and subsequent insightful discussion can be found in his *Immortality of the Soul or Resurrection of the Dead?* (The Epworth Press, 1958). The *Catholic Encyclopedia* (original version from 1914) is available in various editions and online. Nerina Rustomji's analysis of the Islamic afterlife is published as *The Garden and the Fire: Heaven and Hell in Islamic Culture* (Columbia University Press, 2009). The quote from Jon Levenson is from *Resurrection and the Restoration of Israel: The Ultimate Victory of the God of Life* (Yale University Press, 2006).

Diarmaid MacCulloch's discussion of the resurrection is taken from his monumental work *A History of Christianity* (Allen Lane, 2009). The report of a Roman persecution of Christians in Gaul is taken from a letter from the church of Lyons to the church of Vienne, as described by the Dutch historian of religion Jan N. Bremmer in his thought-provoking collection of essays *The Rise and Fall of the Afterlife* (Routledge, 2002). A very interesting account of the idea of resurrection in the early Church is Caroline W. Bynum's *The Resurrection of the Body in Western Christianity: 200–1336* (Columbia University Press, 1995). The estimate that we replace 98 percent of our atoms every year is from *What Is Life?* by Lynn Margulis and Dorion Sagan (University of California Press, 1995).

The area of philosophy that asks what kind of thing humans or persons are (e.g., a body or a soul) and whether they can survive bodily death is "personal identity theory." A good introduction to the technical discussion is Harold Noonan's *Personal Identity* (Routledge, 2003), whereas an excellent, less technical exploration is Julian Baggini's *The Ego Trick: What Does It Mean to Be You?* (Granta, 2011). Essays particularly concerned with personal identity and the afterlife can be found in Paul Edwards's aforementioned collection *Immortality*. This latter book contains the important paper "The Possibility of Resurrection" by Peter van Inwagen (first published in the *International Journal for the Philosophy of Religion* 9 [1978] 114–21), from which I take the problem of resurrecting both the child and adult versions of the same person.

CHAPTER 5: FRANKENSTEIN REDUX

Mary Shelley first published *Frankenstein* in 1818, then a revised version in 1831. Most modern editions use the 1831 text (which is the one I quote), but good ones, such as that from Penguin Classics, also list the revisions so that it is possible to see how the text evolved. Mary Shelley's account of the story's inspiration is in her introduction to the revised edition. The other Mary Shelley stories referred to—"Roger Dodsworth: The Reanimated Englishman" and "The Mortal Immortal"—can both be found for free online. Mary Shelley's diary entry on losing her first baby is taken from *Mary Shelley: Her Life, Her Fiction, Her Monsters* by Anne K. Mellor (Routledge, 1988), a seminal analysis that skillfully summarizes the feminist critique of scientific discourse found in *Frankenstein*.

The account of Giovanni Aldini's galvanic experiments can be found in Richard Holmes's *The Age of Wonder* (Harper, 2008), a fascinating introduction to the science and personalities of the Romantic period. It is also retold in the aforementioned *Mortal Coil: A Short History of Living Longer* by David Boyd Haycock. The quotes from Descartes and Bacon are both taken from Gerald Gruman's aforementioned *A History of Ideas About the Prolongation of Life*.

The Zygmunt Bauman quote is of course from *Mortality, Immortality, and Other Life Strategies*, mentioned above, which has a good account of the drive to mastery as the essence of modernity. The quote from Braden R. Allenby and Daniel Sarewitz is from their book *The Techno-Human Condition* (MIT Press, 2011). The thesis that the Enlightenment offered a secular version of Christian apocalyptic thinking was first advanced by Carl L. Becker in *The Heavenly City of the Eighteenth Century Philosophers* (Yale University Press, 1933). It was subsequently developed by the historian David F. Noble in his book *The Religion of Technology* (Penguin, 1997) and brilliantly explored by John Gray in his books *Black Mass: Apocalyptic Religion and the Death of Utopia* (Penguin, 2007) and *The Immortalization Commission: Science and the Strange Quest to Cheat Death* (Allen Lane, 2011).

The story of New England folktales is taken from Stuart Alve Olson's *The Jade Emperor's Mind Seal Classic* (Inner Traditions, 2003). Those wishing to find out more about cryonics or mind-uploading should best search the Internet. The cryonics institution Alcor Life Extension Foundation at press time has a useful online library of information on the science and philosophy of cryopreserving human

beings (www.alcor.org). The book considered to have launched the
cryonics movement is Robert C. W. Ettinger's *The Prospect of Immortality* (Doubleday, 1964). One leading exponent of mind-uploading is
the roboticist and futurist Hans Moravec, for example, in *Mind Children: The Future of Robot and Human Intelligence* (Harvard University
Press, 1988). Ian Pearson's prediction of mind-uploading by 2050 is
taken from an interview with the *Observer* newspaper, May 22, 2005.
Frank Tipler expounds his extraordinary thesis in *The Physics of Christianity* (Doubleday, 2007) and *The Physics of Immortality: Modern Cosmology, God and the Resurrection of the Dead* (Doubleday, 1994).

The arguments *against* the view that we can survive through
reproduction of our psychology (and therefore could survive such
things as mind-uploading) have a long history. In recent times, they
were stated clearly by Bernard Williams in his book *Problems of the
Self* (Cambridge University Press, 1973). But a hugely influential
defense of this view was recently given by Derek Parfit in *Reasons and
Persons* (Oxford University Press, 1984), after which the view
flourished. But it is now giving ground once again, largely in the
face of arguments from the philosophical position known as "ani-
malism," the seminal text of which is Eric Olson's *The Human Animal* (Oxford University Press, 1997). The philosopher who
suggested that God snatches our bodies in order to keep them safely
for the resurrection is Peter van Inwagen, in his paper "The Possibility of Resurrection," referred to above.

CHAPTER 6: BEATRICE'S SMILE

All the quotes in the first section are from Dante's *Vita Nuova*
("New Life," first published in 1295 and available in many editions
and online), his early collection of poetry and prose mostly dedicated to his infatuation with Beatrice. Dante's *Divine Comedy* is also
available in many editions; I have mostly relied on the 1993 Oxford
World's Classics edition with translation by Charles H. Sisson.

Augustine's views on the role of the female body in heaven are taken from Colleen McDannell and Bernhard Lang's excellent *Heaven: A History* (Yale Nota Bene, 1988). Good accounts of how Christianity adopted Plato's view of the soul can be found in Alan Segal's aforementioned *Life After Death: A History of the Afterlife in Western Religion* and in Raymond Martin and John Barresi's *The Rise and Fall of Soul and Self* (Columbia University Press, 2006). From the latter comes the quote about the idea of the soul shaping the mind-set of Western civilization.

The Ernest Becker quote on Christianity is again from *The Denial of Death*. Louis Dumont's account of Christianity's role in the development of individualism is from his essay "The Christian Beginnings of Modern Individualism," which can be found in the book *The Category of the Person: Anthropology, Philosophy, History* (Cambridge University Press, 1985), edited by Michael Carrithers, Steven Collins and Steven Lukes.

I have borrowed Boccaccio's tale of Dante's charred beard from Lisa Miller's *Heaven: Our Enduring Fascination with the Afterlife* (Harper, 2010). The quotation from the judgment against Galileo is taken from *The Galileo Affair: A Documentary History*, edited and translated by Maurice A. Finocchiaro (University of California Press, 1989). The C. S. Lewis image of us moderns staring out into the void is from his *The Discarded Image: An Introduction to Medieval and Renaissance Literature* (Cambridge University Press, 1964). The views of Joseph Ratzinger (Pope Benedict XVI) on heaven can be found in his book *Eschatology: Death and Eternal Life* (The Catholic University of America Press, 2007).

More details on the Islamic view of the afterlife can be found in the aforementioned *The Garden and the Fire: Heaven and Hell in Islamic Culture* by Nerina Rustomji. The female companions in paradise are mentioned in the Qur'an, for example sura 55, verses 46–78, though the idea that there are seventy-two is not, but belongs to one of many traditions of commentary.

Élie Reclus's story of Eskimo heaven comes from his book *Primitive Folk* (1885, reprinted by Kessinger Publishing, 2006) and is also cited by Corliss Lamont in the aforementioned *The Illusion of Immortality*. An account of the impact of the American Civil War on ideas of heaven can be found in Rebecca Price Janney's *Who Goes There? A Cultural History of Heaven and Hell* (Moody Publishers, 2009). The pastor James L. Garlow's view of heaven is in his book with Keith Wall, *Heaven and the Afterlife* (Bethany House Publishers, 2009). The modern guide to the afterlife cited is Bryan McAnally's *Life After Death & Heaven and Hell* (Guidepost Books, 2009).

The quote from theologian Paul Tillich is from *The Eternal Now* (Prentice Hall, 1963).

CHAPTER 7: THE LOST SOUL

The Dalai Lama tells his own story in the fascinating *Freedom in Exile: The Autobiography of the Dalai Lama of Tibet* (Abacus, 1998). Numerous other biographies also recount the story of his discovery, with varying details. There are many introductions to Buddhist and Hindu thought available; those by Klaus Klostermaier are good. I have mostly relied on W. J. Johnson's translation of the Bhagavad Gita (Oxford World's Classics, 1994). The Dalai Lama's view on the nature of the spiritual something that survives bodily death is taken from the fascinating account of his 1989 conversations with neuroscientists *Consciousness at the Crossroads: Conversations with the Dalai Lama on Brain Science and Buddhism* (Snow Lion Publications, 1999).

The forty-two sins of ancient Egypt can be found in the Papyrus of Ani, one of the so-called Books of the Dead, and is available in various editions. The William McDougall quote is taken from his *Modern Materialism and Emergent Evolution* (Methuen, 1934) and is also cited by Corliss Lamont in his aforementioned *The Illusion of Immortality*. An important modern example of arguing that there must be immortality as there would otherwise be no justice is found in the philosopher Mark Johnston's book *Surviving Death* (Princeton University Press, 2010). Modern Western philosophy has engaged little with the belief in reincarnation; Paul Edwards's *Reincarnation: A Critical Examination* (Prometheus Books, 1996) is a significant exception.

The percentages of those in the United States and United Kingdom who believe in ghosts are from a 2009 Harris Poll and a 2007 Ipsos Mori poll, respectively. Recent research on the cognitive mechanisms responsible for our seeing ghosts can be found in the aforementioned *The God Instinct: The Psychology of Souls, Destiny and the Meaning of Life* (Nicholas Brealey, 2010) by Jessie Bering, from which the later quote on the evidence of science is also taken. The reference to clergyman Joseph Glanvill is taken from Shane McCorristine's *Spectres of the Self: Thinking About Ghosts and Ghost-Seeing in England, 1750–1920* (Cambridge University Press, 2010). Deepak Chopra's view on ghosts can be found in his *Life After Death* (Rider, 2008) and James L. Garlow's in his aforementioned *Heaven and the Afterlife*.

Martin and Barresi's aforementioned *The Rise and Fall of Soul and Self* gives a good account of the origins and development of belief in a soul in the Western tradition. Two perspectives on out-of-body experiences and near-death experiences can be found in Susan Blackmore's *Dying to Live: Near-Death Experiences* (Prometheus, 1993) and Sam Parnia's *What Happens When We Die* (Hay House, 2005). John Gray's aforementioned *The Immortalization Commission* gives a good account of the early days of the Society for Psychical Research.

The Voltaire quote is taken from "The Soul, Identity and Immortality" in Paul Edwards's aforementioned collection *Immortality*. Phineas Gage's story is told, inter alia, in Antonio Damasio's excellent book on the role of the whole brain and body in producing the mind, *Descartes' Error* (Grosset Putnam, 1996), from which also the quote on hunger is taken. Damasio also features in the above-mentioned conversations with the Dalai Lama, *Consciousness at the*

Crossroads. There are many other accessible accounts of the effects of brain damage on the mind available, such as, for example, the work of Oliver Sacks.

The *Catholic Encyclopedia* is available online. The Thomas Jefferson quote is taken from *Encountering Naturalism: A Worldview and Its Uses* by Thomas W. Clark (Center for Naturalism, 2007). The Jesse Bering quote is taken from his aforementioned *The God Instinct*.

Many works discuss the relationship between mind and body, for example Corliss Lamont's book mentioned above; Anthony Flew's *The Logic of Mortality* (Blackwell, 1987); many of the essays in the collection *Immortality*, edited by Paul Edwards (Prometheus, 1997); and Richard Swinburne's *The Evolution of the Soul* (Clarendon Press, 1997). The problem for soul theorists of unconsciousness is an old one and well told in, for example, Eric T. Olson's *What Are We? A Study in Personal Ontology* (Oxford University Press, 2007). The Qur'an quote is from the translation by M. A. S. Abdel Haleem (Oxford University Press, 2004). Duncan MacDougall's weighing of the soul was reported in the *New York Times* on March 11, 1907; accounts are now widely available on the Internet and elsewhere.

CHAPTER 8: LOOK ON MY WORKS, YE MIGHTY

There are many accounts of the life of Alexander the Great available, varying from Robin Lane Fox's eulogizing *Alexander the Great* (Penguin, 1974—the inspiration behind Oliver Stone's biopic of Alexander) to the highly critical *Envy of the Gods: Alexander the Great's Ill-Fated Journey Across Asia* by John Prevas (Da Capo Press, 2004). *Alexander the Great: The Hunt for a New Past* by Paul Cartledge (Macmillan, 2004) is a balanced recent addition.

Various writers have made a distinction similar to that between the biological and cultural forms of the Legacy Narrative. Robert Jay Lifton, for example, talks about the biological (or sometimes "biosocial") mode compared to the cultural mode (see *Living and Dying*, with Jay Olson, Praeger, 1974), and Corliss Lamont distinguishes between the biological and the social and historical forms of immortality (in the aforementioned *The Illusion of Immortality*).

The words of Achilles, Sarpedon and Glaucus are of course all from Homer's *Iliad*. I have mostly relied on the translation by Emile Victor Rieu (Penguin Classics, 1950/2003) but have also drawn on some of the many other translations available, for example, Samuel Butler's (available online). I have also used Rieu's translation of *The Odyssey* (Penguin Classics, 1946/1991).

The Ernest Becker quote about seeking to preserve immortality versus life is from the aforementioned *Escape from Evil*. Ernst Cassirer described humans as the symbolic animal in his 1944 *An Essay on Man*. The Gregory Nagy quote is from his essay "Poetic Visions of Immortality for the Hero" in *Homer's "The Iliad,"* edited by Harold Bloom (Chelsea House, 1987). The Ernest Becker quote about heroism is from the above-mentioned *Denial of Death*. The Leo Braudy quote is from his brilliant *The Frenzy of Renown: Fame and Its History* (Vintage Books, 1997).

The Miguel de Unamuno quotes are from his extraordinary poetic-philosophical meditation on immortality *The Tragic Sense of Life* (in English by Macmillan, 1921). The John Milton quote, originally from his poem "Lycidas," is taken from *Illusions of Immortality: A Psychology of Fame and Celebrity* by David Giles (Macmillan, 2000). The Corliss Lamont quote is of course from *The Illusion of Immortality*. The Morrissey and James Dean quotes are also taken from Giles's *Illusions of Immortality*. Later quotes by Giles are from the same work. The Socrates quote is from Plato's *Symposium*, translated by Benjamin Jowett and available in various editions, including online.

The relevance of the Herostratus syndrome to modern terrorism is explored in depth in *Terrorism for Self-Glorification: The Herostratos Syndrome* by Albert Borowitz (Kent State University

Press, 2005—the alternative spelling of the name is not a typo but the Greek transliteration rather than the more usual Latinized version). Lionel Shriver's magnificent novel *We Need to Talk About Kevin* (Serpent's Tail, 2003) explores, among other themes, the role of celebrity culture in motivating a fictional high school massacre. The Zygmunt Bauman quote is from the aforementioned *Mortality, Immortality, and Other Life Strategies*. The Jean Rostand quote is from *Pensée d'un biologiste* (Stock, 1939).

The James Henry Breasted quote on Akhenaten is taken from Dominic Montserrat's *Akhenaten: History, Fantasy and Ancient Egypt* (Routledge, 2000). The data on blogging is from www.blogpulse.com. The survey of online presence in the United States was conducted by AVG.com in November 2010.

The debate about the plausibility of the bundle theory of the self is an old one, going back at least to David Hume, who proposed it, and his fellow Scot Thomas Reid, who criticized it. The theory and its difficulties are well summarized in Eric Olson's aforementioned book *What Are We?*

Roy Baumeister's views on posterity are from his book *Meanings of Life* (Guilford Press, 1991). The Marcus Aurelius quote is from his *Meditations*, available in many editions.

CHAPTER 9: THE IMMORTAL SEED

Although there are countless books on Alexander the Great available, there is only one book-length treatment of his mother that I am aware of: *Olympias: Mother of Alexander the Great* by Elizabeth Carney (Routledge, 2006).

Einstein's consoling words are from a letter he wrote to the Dutch physicist Heike Kamerlingh Onnes's widow, February 25, 1926. The Aristotle quote is from *De Anima*, book 2, chapter 4, translated by J. A. Smith (available online). The Richard Dawkins quote is from his classic *The Selfish Gene* (Oxford University Press,

1976), which remains a superb introduction to the gene's-eye view of life. A good introduction to cells, genes and their role in humans is *How We Live and Why We Die* by Lewis Wolpert (Faber, 2009).

All quotes by Lynn Margulis are from her excellent book written with Dorion Sagan *What Is Life?* (University of California Press, 1995), from which the Erasmus Darwin quote is also taken.

The Lucien Lévy-Bruhl quote is taken from Godfrey Lienhardt's essay "African Representations of Self," itself to be found in the aforementioned collection *The Category of the Person*, edited by Michael Carrithers, Steven Collins and Steven Lukes, which contains many other examples of a collectivized sense of self in traditional societies. For further anthropological research on the primacy of the biological immortality narrative, see for example the work of Michael Kearl, much of which is available online, including his contributions to the online *Encyclopedia of Death and Dying*. The Scipio epitaph is from *The Roman Mind* by M. L. Clarke (Norton, 1956). Franz Berkenau's account of the Jewish versus the Hellenic strategy is taken from Zygmunt Bauman's aforementioned *Mortality, Immortality, and Other Life Strategies*. John Hick's similar thoughts are from his paper "The Recreation of the Psycho-Physical Person" (republished in Paul Edwards's aforementioned book *Immortality*).

The Fichte quote on German nationalism is also taken from Bauman's *Mortality, Immortality, and Other Life Strategies*, which contains an insightful discussion of biological and group immortality narratives. Robert Jay Lifton's work on revolutionary immortality narratives can be found for example in the aforementioned *Living and Dying*, written with Eric Olson. The estimate of 170 million people dying in war in the twentieth century is taken from David Livingstone Smith's *The Most Dangerous Animal: Human Nature and the Origins of War* (St. Martin's Press, 2007).

Herbert Spencer promoted the idea of a human superorganism in his essay *The Social Organism* (1860, available online). The quote on superorganisms from Alison Jolly is taken from her 1999 article in the *New Scientist* (vol. 2218) "The Fifth Step" and is based on her book *Lucy's Legacy: Sex and Intelligence in Human Evolution* (Harvard University Press, 1999).

More on the Gaia hypothesis can be found in any of the books by its originator, James Lovelock, such as *The Vanishing Face of Gaia: A Final Warning* (Basic Books, 2010). The Ernest Becker quote is once again from *The Denial of Death*. And a fascinating discussion of catastrophic threats to life on earth can be found in Martin Rees's aforementioned *Our Final Century*.

CHAPTER 10: HE WHO SAW THE DEEP

I have used the excellent Penguin Classics (1999) edition of *The Epic of Gilgamesh*, beautifully translated by Andrew George.

The quotes by Tennyson, William McDougall (quoted also in chapter 6) and C. D. Broad are from Corliss Lamont's now oft-mentioned *The Illusion of Immortality*. The Zygmunt Bauman quote is once again from *Mortality, Immortality, and Other Life Strategies*. The Ernest Becker quote is from *Escape from Evil*. The Sam Keen quote is from his foreword to the 1997 edition of Ernest Becker's *The Denial of Death* (Free Press). Friedrich Nietzsche's discussion of Christianity as the "slave morality" can be found in his *On the Genealogy of Morals* (first published 1887).

The Douglas Adams quote is from the third of the five *Hitchhiker* books, *Life, the Universe and Everything* (Pan Books, 1982). Jorge Luis Borges's short story "The Immortal" was first published in his collection *The Aleph* in 1949 (available in translation in a Penguin Modern Classics edition) and can also be found in the Penguin Modern Classics collection of Borges's work *Labyrinths: Selected Stories and Other Writings*. Irvin D. Yalom's experiences of the transformational power of mortality awareness can be found in his books

Existential Psychotherapy (Basic Books, 1980) and *Staring at the Sun: Overcoming the Terror of Death* (Jossey Bass, 2009).

The quote from J. B. Pratt is from his book *The Religious Consciousness* (Macmillan, 1920). The Alan Segal quote is from his aforementioned *Life After Death: A History of the Afterlife in Western Religion*, which contains a fascinating discussion of Near Eastern wisdom literature. The quote from the tomb of King Intef is taken from the aforementioned *Death and the Afterlife in Ancient Egypt* by John H. Taylor. The Michel de Montaigne quote is from his aforementioned essay "To Philosophize Is to Learn How to Die."

Very few of Epicurus's own writings have survived. The quotes on the fear of death are taken from his "Letter to Menoeceus," which, like all his surviving works, is short, well worth reading and found in various editions. I have used the translation by John Gaskin in *The Epicurean Philosophers* (Everyman, 1995). The Shakespeare quote is from *Measure for Measure*. The Wittgenstein quote is from *Tractatus Logico Philosophicus* (Routledge, 1921).

The quote from psychologist Roy Baumeister is from his aforementioned *Meanings of Life*. All quotations and references to Marcus Aurelius are from his *Meditations*, of which many versions are available. I have mostly used the translation by Maxwell Stanifoth (1964), available from Penguin Books. *Meditations* is certainly the best surviving insight into Stoic thought. The Bertrand Russell quote is taken from his essay "How to Grow Old" in *Portraits from Memory and Other Essays* (George Allen, 1956). Irvin D. Yalom's conclusions on managing death anxiety are in the above-mentioned *Staring at the Sun*.

Pierre Hadot's thoughts on the lessons of Epicureanism and Stoicism are from *Philosophy as a Way of Life: Spiritual Exercises from Socrates to Foucault* (translated by Michael Chase, Blackwell, 1995). The Mihaly Csikszentmihalyi quote is from "The Flow Experience and Its Significance for Human Pyschology" in the book *Optimal Experience: Psychological Studies of Flow in Consciousness* (edited by

Mihaly Csikszentmihalyi and Isabella Selega Csikszentmihalyi, Cambridge University Press, 1988). The Harvard happiness study is reported in the journal *Science* ("A Wandering Mind Is an Unhappy Mind" by Matthew A. Killingsworth and Daniel T. Gilbert 330, no. 6006 ([November 12, 2010], p. 932). Appreciating the present moment is also the core teaching of the bestselling *The Power of Now* by Eckhart Tolle (Hodder, 1999), which draws on many of these wisdom traditions.

The quote by Philodemus is taken from Hadot's *Philosophy as a Way of Life,* which contains fascinating discussions of the ancient Greek philosophers' approach to gratitude and the present moment. Professor Robert Emmons's conclusions on the power of gratitude are taken from his book *Thanks! How the New Science of Gratitude Can Make You Happier* (Houghton Mifflin, 2007), from which I have also taken the Epictetus quote.

INDEX

à l'immortalité, 210

Abrahamic religions, 101, 102, 150, 151, 191, 221

accidental death, 74–75

Achilles (Greek hero), 6, 151, 203, 206–11, 223–26

Adams, Douglas, 262–63

afterlife:
  Christian, 160–63
  injustice and eternal, 261
  Islamic, 163–64

aging:
  ancient cures for, 42
  and disease, 36, 68, 78
  secret of, 70
  super-long-lived persons, 43, 71
  transhumanists and conquering, 64

Akhenaten, 10–13, 28, 214–16

alchemy, 44–46, 117

Aldini, Giovanni, 115, 126

Alexander IV, 230, 249–50

Alexander the Great, 201–30, 260, 270

Allen, Woody, 205, 207, 275–76

Allenby, Braden R., 119

ancestor worship, 236, 240

ancestors, common, 240–41

anthropocentric heaven, 161, 162–65, 168

Appleyard, Bryan, 24

Aquinas, St. Thomas, 148, 156, 187

Aristotle, 185, 203, 225, 226, 231

Armstrong, Karen, 90

Arrhidaeus, 228, 230

atman (Hindu soul), 174, 176

atoms, 106, 108, 129

Augustine, St., 147, 150, 160, 166, 168

Austad, Steven, 74

avatars, 5, 123–24, 134

Bacon, Francis, 118, 120

Bacon, Roger, 45

bacteria, 241

barbarism, 36

Barresi, John, 148

Bauman, Zygmunt, 20, 26, 62, 119, 213, 240, 260

Baumeister, Roy, 224, 277–78, 279

Becker, Ernest, 22, 149, 151, 154, 207, 209, 243, 260

"being-toward-death," 17

Benedict XVI, Pope, 148, 158, 161, 166

Bering, Jesse, 19, 24, 191

Bhagavad Gita, 175, 275

Bible, 18, 19, 270–71
  Acts, book of, 87, 110
  Corinthians, 96, 97, 256
  Ecclesiastes, book of, 19, 270–71
  Genesis, book of, 18
  the Gospels, 92, 94, 95, 98, 100
  heaven in the, 160, 265
  New Testament, 95, 97, 103
  Old Testament, 43, 96, 99, 104, 110
  and Resurrection Narrative, 85, 86, 94–100, 109–11
  Thessalonians, 99

biological immortality, 205, 230–31, 236–38, 240–43, 244

biology, 14, 55, 56

biosphere, 76, 241

Boccaccio, Giovanni, 155

book burning, 36
Borchardt, Ludwig, 1–2, 10, 27–28
Borges, Jorge Luis, 17–18, 36, 264–65, 267, 268
Borkenau, Franz, 236
Boyle, Robert, 46
brain, human, 16
　brain injuries, 185–86
　neuroscience, 187–92
　relationship between mind and, 185–87, 188, 189–92
　See also mind
Braudy, Leo, 209
Breasted, James Henry, 214
Broad, C. D., 258–59
Bruno, Giordano, 157
Buddha (Siddhartha Gautama), 173–74
Buddhism, 5, 152, 272
　brain science and, 191–92
　consciousness in, 244, 246, 247
　mindfulness techniques, 280
　reincarnation and, 169–77, 194, 196, 197
bundle theory of the self, 219–22, 224
Bush, George W., 76
Byron, Lord George Gordon, 114, 115

Caesar, Julius, 216
Calment, Jeanne, 71
cancer, 55–56, 61, 68–69, 77, 266
Cancer and Vitamin C (Pauling), 55
cannibalism, resurrection and, 105–6, 129
"capacity for awareness," 177
Čapek, Karel, 50
Cassirer, Ernst, 208
caste system, 175, 261
Catholic Encyclopedia, 101, 189, 190
Catholicism, 111, 148, 156, 185
celebrities, 205, 210–11, 217, 220
celestial spheres, 156, 167
cells, biological, 233–35

Chaucer, Geoffrey, 209
children:
　and beliefs about the mind, 19
　as biological legacy, 6, 230–32, 258
chimpanzees, 17, 159, 240
China, ancient:
　alchemists of, 44–45
　ancestor worship, 240
　creation myths, 41
　early Chinese culture, 40
　Great Wall, 35, 36
　terracotta army, 52–53, 257
　traditional medicine in, 42, 45
　See also First Emperor (of China)
Chisholm, James, 15
Chopra, Deepak, 181
Christianity:
　icons in, 221
　longer-lived Patriarchs, 43
　Plato's theories and, 146, 147–48
　resurrection in, 5, 95, 97–100, 101, 104–5, 110, 146
　and ritualistic behavior, 91, 92
　Romans conversion to, 7, 146–47, 152
　soul in, 5, 146–53
　and usefulness to early rulers, 261
civilization:
　barbarism and, 36
　conflicts between civilizations, 260
　creation of Chinese, 31–32, 34, 35–36
　and cultural worldviews about death, 22–23
　defined, 35
　elixir of life as pinnacle of, 40–41, 42
　founding myths of, 41–42
　progress and success of, 58
　and promise of immortality, 258
Clarke, Arthur C., 39
cognitive psychology, and death scenario, 19, 24

Cold War, 73, 75
communism, 72, 143, 239–40
communities, human, 241–42
computational resurrection, 123, 134
Condorcet, Nicolas de, 60
consciousness:
    and biological immortality, 237–38
    and death scenario, 19
    global, 243–47
    soul and, 182, 184, 192–96
Copernicus, Nicolaus, 156–57, 158
copies, identical, in resurrection,
    133–34
cosmic justice, 177–81
cosmic punishments, 179
cosmic significance, 149, 151, 154,
    158, 179, 209
cosmology, 156–57
creation, Frankenstein's act of,
    126–27, 128
creation myths, 41–42
Crick, Francis, 72
cryonics, 5, 120, 121–22, 129
cryopreservation, 121
Csikszentmihalyi, Mihaly, 280
Cullmann, Oscar, 98
cultural immortality, 205, 211, 213,
    243
cultural reproduction, 216, 218
cultural space, 6
cyborgs, 66, 124
cyclical time, 92, 94

Dalai Lama, 169–71, 172–73, 177,
    182, 191–92, 196, 284
Damasio, Antonio, 15, 188
damnatio memoriae, 9, 212
Dante Alighieri, 137, 141–42,
    154–56, 157, 159, 164, 166,
    167–68, 209
Darwin, Charles, 158–59
Darwin, Erasmus, 235
Dawkins, Richard, 14, 232

Day of Judgment, 102, 105, 108, 135
de Grey, Aubrey, 64
Dean, James, 211
death:
    and accumulation of wealth, 78
    boundary from life to, 103
    elixir of life myths and, 40–41
    and finite time, 265–66, 267
    mortality and, 16–21
    process of dying, 274
    and Resurrection Narrative,
        85–111
    scientific mastery of nature and,
        116–19
    as a solvable problem, 61
    Terror Management Theory,
        22–23, 24, 34–35
    Wisdom Narrative and, 273–76
    worldviews and fear of, 21–22
death-avoidance to-do lists, 63
deities, 11, 41, 93–94, 203–4, 216
dementia, 67, 68
Demeter (goddess), 93
Descartes, René, 60, 118
DigiGod, 125, 134
digital immortality, 5, 124, 134,
    137
digital reproduction, 218
digital revolution, 216–17
Diotima, 211–12, 226
disease:
    aging and, 36, 68, 78
    debilitating diseases, 67, 68–69
    infectious diseases, 61
    scientific advances and diagnosing,
        59
Divine Comedy (Dante), 160, 209
DNA, 72, 232
dreams and visions, soul in, 144
drugs:
    antibiotics, 61
    in out-of-body experiences, 183
dualism, 189

Dumont, Louis, 152, 153, 154
duplication, resurrection and, 107–8, 128–36
dying and rising gods, 93–94

Earth, planet, longevity of, 247–48
Eastern religions:
  and reincarnation, 171–77
  traditions of, 165, 166
Egypt, ancient:
  Akhenaten, 10–13, 28, 214–16
  Alexander in, 203–4
  and belief in two souls, 144
  concepts of time, 92–93
  founding myth of, 41
  immortality system, 7–13
  medical papyruses, 59
  mummification process, 8–9, 12, 41, 93, 104
  Nefertiti, 1–2, 8, 9–13, 26–28, 214, 215, 216
  and Otherworld, 9, 12, 177–78
Einstein, Albert, 71, 230, 240
elixir of life, 42–46, 57, 58, 80, 117
  Chinese myths on, 37–40, 41
  ingredients, 53
  living forever, 46–51
  as pinnacle of civilization, 40–41, 42
Elizabeth I (England), 216
Emmons, Robert, 283
end of the universe, 248–49
End Times, 95, 99, 110, 116, 146, 147
energy, converting humans into, 134–35
Engineering Approach to immortality, 59–64, 65, 66–67, 71, 74, 118, 130
Enlightenment, the, 58, 60, 190
Eos (goddess), 67
Epictetus, 283, 284
Epicureanism, 280, 282
Epicurus, 274–75

Ertz, Susan, 48–49, 262
eternal life, 2–3
  elixir legend and, 46–51
  eternal second life, 10
  legends on pursuit of, 40
  psychological effects of eternity, 263–65
  theologians views on, 166
ethical behavior, living forever and, 178–79, 262
evolution, 14–15, 158–59, 232–33, 235
existential risks, 78
extinction, 22, 24, 34

fame:
  and immortality, 6, 7, 201–26
  and notoriety, 212–14
family:
  ancestor worship, 236, 240
  identification with, 236
Fichte, Johann Gottlieb, 239
First Emperor (of China), 39–40, 41, 43
  creation of China, 31–37
  death of, 51, 53
  and elixir of life search, 36–39, 42, 44
  and prolonging life, 34–36
  tomb of, 51–53, 257
first longevity revolution, 61, 67, 76, 114
flow, the, 280
focusing on the present, virtue of, 279–81
Four Noble Truths, Buddha's, 174
France:
  life expectancy in, 60–61
  longest-lived person, 71
Frankenstein; or, the Modern Prometheus (M. Shelley), 115–16, 117, 119, 126–27, 137
Franklin, Rosalind, 72

Frazer, Sir James, 93
freezing bodies, 5, 120–21
Freud, Sigmund, 12, 18, 22, 25, 43, 91
futurologists, 122, 123

Gagarin, Yuri, 157
Gage, Phineas, 185–86
Gaia, 6, 242–43, 245, 248
Galileo, Galilei, 156–57
Galvani, Luigi, 115
galvanism, 115, 126
Garlow, James L., 162, 181
Gastil, Raymond D., 15
genes, 69–70, 232–34
genetic engineering, 64–65, 79
genetics, 64, 65, 240–41
German nationalism, 239
ghosts:
    belief in, 180–81, 182, 183
    ghost stories, 114–16
Giles, David, 216, 220, 222, 223
Gilgamesh, 42, 250, 253–56, 258,
    269–70, 273–74, 278, 279–80,
    282
Glanvill, Joseph, 181
global population, 76–78
gods, resurrection and worship of
    ancient. *See* deities.
Godwin, William, 119
Goethe, Johann Wolfgang von, 19
Golden Bough, The (Frazer), 93
gratitude, virtue of, 280, 281–83
gravestones, digital, 218
Greeks, ancient:
    alchemy and its origins from, 45
    and belief in soul, 97, 98, 181–82
    culture of fame and immortality, 7
    Egyptian culture and, 7
    Greek gods and mortality, 267
    Greek heroes, 202–9
    mystery cults of, 91, 93, 100,
        144–45
    philosophy, 271–72

resurrection and, 97, 98, 99, 137
    Tithonus legend, 67, 71
Greenberg, Jeff, 22
Gruman, Gerald, 43

Hadot, Pierre, 280
hallucinations, 181
heart disease, 61, 68–69
heaven, 98, 151, 154–58, 160–67, 265
Hegel, G. W. F., 24
Heidegger, Martin, 17
Hellenic strategy, of undying glory, 236
Hemingway, Ernest, 220
herbs, 42, 45
Hercules (demigod), 202, 203
hero worship, 213
Herodotus, 8–9
heroism, 209
heroes, Greek, 202–4, 205–9
Herostratus syndrome, 212–14
Hick, John, 236–37
hieroglyphs, 11, 13, 46
Hinduism, 5, 152, 191, 272
    consciousness in, 244, 246
    reincarnation and, 172, 174–76,
        177, 197
*Hitchhiker's Guide to the Galaxy,
    The* (Adams), 262–63
Holy Grail, 46
holy wars, 260
Homer, 146, 203, 206, 207, 225–
    26, 264
Horemheb, 8, 10, 12
Horus (god), 11
House of Fame (Chaucer), 209
Huang Di (Yellow Emperor), 40, 41,
    43, 58

identifying with others, virtue of,
    277–79
Iliad, The (Homer), 203, 206, 225
Illich, Ivan, 62
image-making techniques, 216, 221

"Immortal, The" (Borges), 264–65,
     268
immortality narratives, four, 2–7, 256
   contradictions of, 268–69
   contributions of, 261–62
   Legacy Narrative, 6, 9–10, 26,
      205–26
   negative effects of, 260–61
   Resurrection Narrative, 4–5, 8,
      26, 82, 85–111, 135, 137, 142,
      146, 148, 181
   Soul Narrative, 5–6, 9, 26, 144–68
   Staying Alive Narrative, 4, 8, 15–16,
      43, 52, 57, 62, 63, 88–89, 135
India, ancient, 175, 182–83
individualism, 152, 153, 154
infinite time, 263–66, 267
Isis (goddess), 11, 41
Islam, 7, 244
   alchemy and origins from, 45
   and belief in soul, 193
   Islamic afterlife, 163–64
   religious conversions to, 151
   and resurrection, 5, 101

Japan, ancient, elixir legend and,
      38–39, 40, 46–51
Jefferson, Thomas, 190
Jesus of Nazareth, 85, 86, 87, 94–
      96, 99, 102–4, 105, 110–11,
      152, 162, 165, 182
Jewish strategy, of undying glory,
      236–37
Jolly, Alison, 242
Judaism:
   and belief in resurrection, 5, 82,
      86, 94–95, 96–97, 101, 110
   longer-lived patriarchs, 43

ka, Egyptian (life force), 9, 26, 60
Kaku, Michio, 134
Kant, Immanuel, 180, 256–57
karma, 175, 176, 177, 179, 192

Keen, Sam, 260
Kennedy, Jacqueline, 73
Kurzweil, Ray, 70

Lamont, Corliss, 210
Lefebvre, Gustave, 27
Legacy Narrative, 6, 9–10, 26,
      205–26, 249–50
   biological immortality, 205,
      230–32, 236–38, 240–43, 244
   cultural immortality, 205, 211,
      213, 243
Levenson, Jon, 102
Lévy-Bruhl, Lucien, 236
Lewis, C. S., 157
liberation, 176, 197
life:
   boundary from life to death, 103
   and existence of the soul, 182–83
   traditional belief systems of, 60
life expectancy, 59
   debilitating diseases and, 68–69
   doubled, 61, 67
   genetics and increase in, 65
   increase in developed countries,
      60–61, 64, 68
   longevity revolutions and, 61, 67–68
lifespans:
   calculations of, 67–68
   of medical immortals, 74–75
   unlimited/extended, 43, 60
Lifton, Robert Jay, 13, 24–25, 239–40
linear time, 92–94
living long enough to live forever, 64
long dark tea-time of the soul, 263
long-lived persons, 43, 71
longevity escape velocity, 64, 120
longevity revolutions, 61, 67, 68
Lovelock, James, 242
Luther, Martin, 89, 152–53

McCarthy, Joseph, 72
MacCulloch, Diarmaid, 103

MacDougall, Duncan, 194
McDougall, William, 178, 258
Maimonides, Moses, 101
"making a name for oneself," 215
Makropulos Affair, The (Capek), 50
Marcus Aurelius, 224, 272, 278, 282
Margulis, Lynn, 234, 235, 242–43
Martin, Raymond, 148
Marx, Groucho, 218
medical immortality, 63
   average lifespan, 74–75
   genetic engineering and, 79
   global population and, 76–78
medical mortals, 267
"medicalization of daily life," 62
medicine:
   herbs and ancient, 42
   hygiene and, 114
   and nutrition, 57
memorial sites, social networking,
   217–18
microbes, 61
Milton, John, 210
mind:
   bodily death and the, 19, 191
   existence of the soul and the,
   184–85
   mind-uploading, 5, 120, 122–24,
   129–30, 134
   nanobots for mind expansion, 65–66
   relationship between brain and,
   185–87, 188, 189–91
moksha (liberation), 176
monotheism, 5, 11, 12
Montaigne, Michel de, 18, 272
Morrissey (singer), 210–11
"Mortal Immortal, The" (M. Shelley), 137
Mortality Paradox, 16–21, 23–24,
   88, 276
   in conquest of nature, 118
   inability to imagine death in, 175,
   181, 223, 273–74

reality of death in, 22, 23, 33–34,
   62, 150, 174, 257, 269
   resurrection and, 118, 136
   soul and, 148–50, 191
   and those in positions of power,
   33–34
Moses, 12, 85, 109, 110
Mount of the Immortals, 3, 26, 34,
   58, 204, 259
multiple souls, 9, 144
mummies, 8–9, 12, 41, 93, 104,
   121
mystery cults, 91, 93, 100, 144–45
mysticism, 165, 166
myths:
   Chinese elixir of life, 37–40
   creation, 41–42
   founding myths of civilization, 41

Nagy, Gregory, 209
nanobots, 65–66, 79
nanomedicine, 64
nanotechnology, 65, 79
nationalism, 240
natural selection, 14–15, 69, 158–
   59, 233
nature:
   scientific mastery of, 116–19
   symbolic world and, 208
Nature (journal), 80
Nefertiti, 1–2, 8, 9–13, 26–28, 214,
   215, 216
neuroimaging, 187
neuroscience, 187–92, 245
New Scientist (magazine), 42
Newton, Sir Isaac, 46
Nicene Creed, 101
Nietzsche, Friedrich, 261
nirvana, 174, 176, 197, 244, 246
Nobel Prize, 43, 54, 55, 56,
   72–73
nuclear weapons, 71–73
nutrition, 55–56, 57

Odysseus, 151
Odyssey, The (Homer), 225–26,
264
Olympias, 202–3, 227–30, 231,
232, 249–50, 260
Omega Point, 125
Osiris (god), 11, 12, 41, 93
out-of-body experiences (OBEs),
183–84
overpopulation, 76–78
"Ozymandias" (P. B. Shelley), 224–25

paradise, 146, 160–65
paranormal phenomena, 183
Paul, St., Apostle, 85–88, 94, 95–
100, 102, 107, 109–10, 146, 256
Pauling, Ava Helen, 55–56, 57, 73,
80
Pauling, Herman, 56
Pauling, Linus, 59–60, 70, 240,
267
arms race and technology, 71–73,
75, 78, 79
vitamin cure pursuit, 55–57, 71,
80–81
Pearson, Ian, 123
Peng Zu, 43
Pharisees, 94, 96, 101, 104
Philip II of Macedon, 202, 204,
227–28, 229
Philodemus, 282
Picasso, Pablo, 220
Plato, 98, 145, 146, 147–48, 149,
196, 226, 268, 271–72
Plutarch, 228
poisons, 47, 53
political views, death and, 21–22
Portinari, Beatrice, 141–42, 155,
167–68
portraiture, 216
posterity, pursuit of, 214–18, 223
posthuman immortals, 63
Pratt, J. B., 268

progress:
resurrection and, 100
scientific advances and, 59, 60, 62
success of civilization and, 58
Pyszczynski, Tom, 22

quicksilver sea, 51
Qur'an, 101, 193

Rabbinic Judaism, 101
Rank, Otto, 154
Ratzinger, Joseph. *See* Benedict XVI
reanimation, 113–37
Reassembly View of resurrection,
105–8, 117, 129, 130–31
Reclus, Élie, 160–61
Reformation, 152
reincarnation, 169–98, 261
religion:
death and religious views, 21, 22,
24
Eastern religions, 165, 166
and life belief systems, 60
out-of-body experiences and religious beliefs, 183
religious conversions, 151
rituals and, 89–92
Replication View of resurrection,
130, 131, 133, 135
reproduction of the self, 14, 216
Resurrection Narrative, 4–5, 8, 26,
82, 85–111, 135, 137, 142, 146,
148, 181
Cannibal Problem in, 105–6, 129
computational resurrection, 123,
134
Copying Case, 133–34
digital immortality and resurrection, 124, 134, 137
dream of resurrection, 136
Duplicate Case, 131–33, 134
Duplication Problem in, 107–8,
128–36

identity of resurrected person,
128–36
physical resurrection, 101–2, 146
Reassembly View of resurrection,
105–8, 117, 129, 130–31
Replication View of resurrection,
130, 131, 133, 135
scientific mastery of nature and
resurrection, 116–19
soul and resurrection, 142–43
Transformation Problem in, 106–7,
129
Resurrection/Soul Narrative, 147–48
rituals, 89–92, 144
robots, 123, 124
"Roger Dodsworth: The Reanimated
Englishman" (M. Shelley), 120
Rome, ancient:
ancestor worship, 236
conversion to Christianity, 7,
146–47, 152
Egyptian culture and, 7, 9
mystery cults in, 91, 93
Paul in Roman custody, 110
persecution of Christians, 104–6,
110
resurrection and, 99
Rostand, Jean, 214
Russell, Bertrand, 279
Rustomji, Nerina, 101

Sadducees, 162
Santayana, George, 20
Sarewitz, Daniel, 119
Schopenhauer, Arthur, 15
science:
alchemy and, 45, 46
elixir industry and, 42–43
vs. immortality, 55–81
scientific approach to death, 59, 60,
70–71
scientific mastery of nature and
death, 116–19

scientific search for the soul, 159,
172, 181–89
science fiction, 79, 134–35
scientific method, 46, 60, 117
Second Coming, 146
"second death," 10
second longevity revolution, 68
Segal, Alan, 271
selfhood, 277–78
senescence, 64
Sentaro, elixir of life quest, 46–51
sex hormones, 70
Shakespeare, William, 34, 274
Shelley, Mary, 113–18, 120, 126–
28, 137
Shelley, Percy Bysshe, 114, 115, 116,
119, 224–25
Sima Qian, 44–45
single-cell and multicellular organisms, 159
slave morality, 261
social networking, 217
social-reform movements, 261
Society for Psychical Research,
183
Socrates, 98, 182, 184, 211, 226
Solomon, Sheldon, 22
sorcery and science, 42–43
Soul Narrative, 5–6, 9, 26, 144–
68, 197–98
and belief in ghosts, 180–81, 182,
183
belief in soul, 5, 23, 97, 98, 137,
143, 144–45, 148, 181–84
consciousness and, 192–96
matter and, 189–92
reincarnation and, 171–77
science and, 172, 181–89, 245
weight of soul, 194
Spencer, Herbert, 241
spirit, 190
Spiritualist Movement, 161
Star Trek (TV series), 134, 135

Staying Alive Narrative, 4, 8, 15–16, 34–35, 43, 52, 57, 88–89, 135
  Engineering Approach to, 65, 66–67
  scientific and modern version of, 58, 62, 63, 118
Steinach, Eugen, 43
Steinach operation, 43
stem cells, 64, 65
Stoicism, 272, 278, 280, 282, 284
Stone, Irwin, 57
"Strategies for Engineered Negligible Senescence" (de Grey), 64
string theory, 157–58
stroke, life expectancy and, 68–69
super-long-lived persons, 43, 71
superintelligence, 66, 79, 120, 124–25
supermen, 66
superorganism, 6, 242
superstition, 46, 52
survival:
  daily, 74
  and reproduction, 14–15
suspended animation, 120, 135
symbols/symbolic immortality, 207–9, 210, 214, 215, 222–23

Taoism, 4, 45, 65, 244, 246, 278
techno-utopians, 121, 123, 125, 134
telepathy, 66
Ten Commandments, 178
Tennyson, Alfred, Lord, 257, 284
Terror Management Theory, 22–23, 24, 34–35, 257
terrorism, 75–76
theocentric heaven, 160–62, 165–66, 168
three virtues, 276–83
Tillich, Paul, 166
time:
  afterlife without, 166–67
  infinite, 263–66

linear and cyclical, 92–94
Tipler, Frank, 125
Tithonus problem, 67, 71, 77
toxins, 70
transcendence, 165, 246
transformation:
  alchemy and, 45
  resurrection and, 106–7, 129
transhumanists, 63–66, 67, 68, 70, 77–78, 130
transitivity of identity, 131
Trojan war, 203, 206
true immortals, 267–68

Unamuno, Miguel de, 209–10, 215
Ustinov, Peter, 231

vaccines, 61, 79
vasectomy, 43
Virgil, 155
vitamins, 55–57, 71, 80–81
Voltaire, 185

Watson, James, 72
wealth, longevity and, 78
will to live, 15–16
wisdom literature, 270–72, 277
Wisdom Narrative, 259, 268–73, 284–86
Wittgenstein, Ludwig, 275
World Health Organization, 59

Xu Fu, elixir of life quest, 37–39, 40, 46–49, 58

Yalom, Irvin D., 266, 279
Yeats, W. B., 17, 43
Yellow Emperor's Inner Canon, The, 45
yogurt, 43
Young, Edward, 18

Zeus (god), 67, 202, 203

ABOUT THE AUTHOR

Dr. Stephen Cave is a Senior Research Fellow at the University of Cambridge and a director of the Leverhulme Centre for the Future of Intelligence. He has also served as a British diplomat, and written widely on philosophical and scientific issues, including for *The Atlantic* and the *New York Times*.